HOOKED UP FOR MURDER

In that idyllic setting, the body looked so wrong, so out of place, as it lay stretched out only feet from the neatly trimmed hedges that formed the gateway into the nearby home's front walkway.

The body was not very far from the house, only fifteen feet or so. There was only a few feet of front yard, the sidewalk, the strip of grass between the sidewalk and the curb, and then the street.

Police could tell that death had not been instantaneous. There was evidence that the victim had tried to crawl along the edge of the street after he'd been shot, but he hadn't gotten very far.

The victim—a tall and muscular young white male—had been beaten, then shot five times. His wallet was gone—but there was $12 in loose bills in his pockets. Several .22-caliber shell casings were found nearby.

Police blocked off the road. It had begun to rain, and they covered the body with a tarp right away. After talking with Feldman, police estimated that three minutes had elapsed between the shooting and the 911 call, so the time of death was set at 6:38 A.M.

HOOKED UP
FOR MURDER

Robert Mladinich and
Michael Benson

PINNACLE BOOKS
Kensington Publishing Corp.

http://www.kensingtonbooks.com

Some names have been changed to protect the privacy of individuals connected to this story.

PINNACLE BOOKS are published by

Kensington Publishing Corp.
850 Third Avenue
New York, NY 10022

Copyright © 2007 by Robert Mladinich and Michael Benson

All Kensington Titles, Imprints, and Distributed Lines are available at special quantity discounts for bulk purchases for sales promotions, premiums, fund-raising, and educational or institutional use. Special book excerpts or customized printings can also be created to fit specific needs. For details, write or phone the office of the Kensington special sales manager: Kensington Publishing Corp., 850 Third Avenue, New York, NY 10022, attn: Special Sales Department, Phone: 1-800-221-2647.

Pinnacle and the P logo Reg. U.S. Pat. & TM Off.

ISBN-13: 978-0-7860-1865-9
ISBN-10: 0-7860-1865-8

First Printing: July 2007
10 9 8 7 6 5 4 3 2 1

Printed in the United States of America

To Mark Treu, who really knew how to light a fire.

ACKNOWLEDGMENTS

The writing of this book would not have been possible without the assistance of many people. Although I will respect the privacy of those who requested anonymity, I hope that they realize how grateful I am. To the others, I would like to thank them here:

Nancy and Michael Fisher for being so open and honest, even as they talked about the heartbreaking loss of their son. After speaking with them, as well as their surviving son, Michael, at their home, it was easy to understand how Mark Fisher turned out so well.

Michael Fisher for being so open and honest while talking about the loss of his younger brother, with whom he expected to grow old.

Assistant District Attorneys Josh Hanshaft and Patricia M. McNeill, of the Brooklyn District Attorney's Office, for their cooperation, as well as for their resourcefulness and commitment to their profession.

Michael Vecchione, the head of the Rackets Bureau of the Brooklyn District Attorney's Office, and Investigator Tommy Dades, of the same office, for their invaluable logistical support. Having worked alongside Tommy when we were both NYPD detectives, I can say without equivocation that he is one of the most dogged investigators I have ever met.

Doreen Federicci (pseudonym) for her forthrightness

when discussing her son. She conceded that he was no angel but still had an unyielding belief in his innocence and would never stop fighting for his freedom.

John Giuca, who although not allowed to participate in the book by his appeals attorney, granted permission to others to speak on his behalf.

Jennifer Baker, James Petrillo and Scott Powers for proving that true loyalty and friendship can never be broken, even by vast geographic distances.

Defense attorneys Jonathan Fink and Sam Gregory for their honesty and integrity when discussing the merits, as well as the challenges, of their cases.

My mother, Margot, Uncle Jules and good friends Robert Ecksel and Arthur Perry, the latter of whom is a retired NYPD detective. All accompanied me on various assignments for this book and provided more incentive and support than they could imagine.

Giles Anderson, my literary agent, and Jake Elwell, coauthor Michael Benson's literary agent, for their unwavering support throughout this whole process.

Photographer Nathan A. Versace for his complete photographic coverage of Ditmas Park and its relevant locations.

Gary Goldstein, the editor at Kensington Publishing Corp., a veteran of the legendary House of Ideas, who believed in this project from its inception.

—Robert Mladinich, October 2006

AUTHORS' NOTE

Like many suburban kids, Mark Fisher was intrigued by the mysteries of the city. For a kid used to the airy greenness of the suburbs, New York City's gritty scarred-brick urbanscape—so often used as a noir backdrop for adventure and romance movies—had a mythological quality.

Like the tragic hero of an F. Scott Fitzgerald novel, Fisher, a college student and star athlete with a shining future, went on his first "no parents, no teachers, just a bunch of friends looking to drink beer" urban adventure. It was Columbus Day weekend, Saturday night, October 11, 2003.

A coeducational group, which included one of Fisher's football teammates, piled in a car, left their picturesque suburban habitat and headed into the dream.

While barhopping, Mark Fisher—not unexpectedly—met a girl. However, it did register when Mark focused on that woman exclusively for the rest of the time they were in the bar.

Then he'd gone off with her, leaving his friends behind. He was supposed to be in the cab right behind them, but he'd decided he'd rather be with the girl than with them. And so, a little too drunk and without the group he'd started with, Mark Fisher was pulled deeper into the night, to a house party south of Prospect Park in Brooklyn.

At the party Mark was given a pill by the host and told it was a prescription painkiller. The medical examiner later identified it as Ecstasy. He'd entered a dangerous world that night, a world where young people played for keeps.

That morning, near dawn, shots were heard and Fisher was found dead—beaten, shot, robbed and dumped on the street. What followed unfolded like an episode of *Law & Order*.

The investigation into his brutal murder was slowed by a wall of silence from the young people at the party, the last to see Fisher alive. Some of the kids had pretty good connections. Witnesses were tight-lipped and lawyered up.

Through use of a special task force and a grand jury, eyewitnesses were played against one another, and law enforcement tore down that wall. The killers were brought to justice.

Although this is a true story, many names will be changed to protect the privacy of the innocent. Pseudonyms will be noted upon their first usage.

When possible, the spoken words have been quoted verbatim. However, when that was not possible, conversations have been reconstructed as closely as possible to reality based on the recollections of those that spoke and heard those words. In places, there has been slight editing of spoken words, but only to improve readability. The denotations and connotations of the words remain unaltered.

CHAPTER 1

Predawn Gunshots

It was a Sunday-morning tradition for Edward Feldman (pseudonym); he'd get up bright and early, maybe even before the sun came up, and read the online *New York Times* edition.

And that was what Feldman was doing on this Sunday morning, October 12, 2003. All was quiet in the den of his Colonial home in the Ditmas Park section of Brooklyn.

At 6:40 A.M., Feldman's quiet, early-morn solitude was abruptly ruined by a series of loud explosions. Five of them. Very loud. Three of them in a row, a pause, then two more. They sounded like they were coming from right outside his window. Scary close to him. Perhaps on his front lawn.

By the time the explosions had stopped, Feldman recognized them as gunfire. Feldman half-expected to hear his window crashing inward. He ducked under his desk. His window remained intact.

Outside now, there was quiet, but Feldman didn't trust

the silence. He stayed under the desk for some time before taking action. When he did move, he moved quickly, staying low, crossing the room and picking up the phone to call 911. He gave his address and told the operator he had heard shots.

Even after hanging up, Feldman was too frightened to go to the window and peek outside. Only after police arrived, did he look out. He could see that there was a body lying still on a driveway near the sidewalk a few houses away from him.

The police told him to come outside. He went out to look at the body. He looked close enough to determine that he didn't recognize the victim.

There were other neighbors who were curious enough to come out and take a look. No pedestrians. Not before seven in the morning on a Sunday.

After concluding the victim was a stranger, Feldman went back inside.

Police at the Seventieth Precinct in Brooklyn, the Seven-Oh, responded to Feldman's call and arrived in less than two minutes. Police Officer Dillon Stewart was first on the scene. Two calls had been received. Feldman's was the first. At the scene police found a body wrapped in a yellow blanket and dumped near the curb of a tree-lined street. It was a distinctive blanket, with a picture of a large, wild cat on it.

The body was in front of the stately Victorian home, one in a row of stately Victorian homes, a few doors down from the neighbor who called 911. The body was where the sidewalk and driveway crossed, in front of a home on Argyle Road.

The house was beige, with brown trim. It had a traditional brick stoop with pillared overhang, plus an extension at the right front, and a bay window that bulged into the yard. High hedges on the left, and a lower set on the right, provided the homeowners with privacy.

In that idyllic setting, the body looked so wrong, so out of place, as it lay stretched out only feet from the neatly trimmed hedges that formed the gateway into the nearby home's front walkway.

The body was not very far from the house, only fifteen feet or so. There was only a few feet of front yard, the sidewalk, the strip of grass between the sidewalk and the curb, and then the street.

Police could tell that death had not been instantaneous. There was evidence that the victim had tried to crawl along the edge of the street after he'd been shot, but he hadn't gotten very far.

The victim—a tall and muscular young white male—had been beaten, then shot five times. His wallet was gone—but there was $12 in loose bills in his pockets. Several .22-caliber shell casings were found nearby.

Police blocked off the road. It had begun to rain, and they covered the body with a tarp right away. After talking with Feldman, police estimated that three minutes had elapsed between the shooting and the 911 call, so the time of death was set at 6:38 A.M.

Orange cones were placed around the body. Of course, the police on the scene weren't going to let a pedestrian get anywhere close to the body, but the cones were another visual signal that the area was off-limits.

There had been a second 911 call. Police found the lady who had called in the second report and asked her a few questions. She was also a neighbor from the block, but she wasn't very helpful. As one might expect, she said that she had been sleeping and was awoken by five gunshots.

Her description of the loud report's cadence differed

from that of the other earwitness, Feldman. The man had said that he heard three shots, a pause, then two more. The female earwitness said that there was one shot, a pause, and four shots in rapid succession. Both witnesses agreed that there had been a pause in the shooting sequence, and that there had been a total of five shots.

Upon hearing the shots, the female earwitness said, she had jumped out of bed and had looked out the window.

"What did you see?" police asked.

"I couldn't see anything," she replied.

Detective James Gaynor was assigned the homicide case and reported to the Argyle Road crime scene at 8:00 A.M. The area around the body remained cordoned off to keep anyone from contaminating it.

Only authorized personnel would be allowed near the body. A couple of curious civilians came right up to the tape to see what was going on, but no one made an attempt to get closer than they were supposed to.

The street had been blockaded at Beverley Road, so there would be no curiosity-seekers in motor vehicles cruising by the crime scene while the police tried to do their work.

Lifting the tarp, Gaynor saw a body, apparently dead, bleeding from the mouth. The victim was wearing a green shirt, tannish brown pants and work boots.

Upon more careful inspection, the detective saw that there were abrasions on his forehead, on the bridge of his nose, on his chin, his right cheek, and there was an abrasion on the back of his right hand.

The guy hadn't just been shot. He'd been in a scuffle. In addition to the abrasions, which also indicated that he'd been in a fight, there were buttons torn off his shirt. He'd also been robbed by what was apparently an impatient thief. The rear pants pocket had torn.

Crime scene detectives removed the victim's shirt, allowing Gaynor to observe five gunshot wounds between the shoulder and the waistline. The deceased had been struck by five bullets, and two had gone all the way through, causing exit wounds. There were seven holes in the body in all.

The body was designated as a John Doe. The victim had no wallet and had been deemed, for the moment, unidentifiable. There was an ATM receipt found in the pocket. That might turn out to be helpful.

The ATM receipt said that it came from a convenience store on Coney Island Avenue and Beverley Road, only a couple blocks away. Twenty dollars had been withdrawn at 4:23 A.M. A subsequent check of the ATM showed that its clock was an hour off (sixty-two minutes, to be precise), probably not reset during a seasonal time change, and that the money had actually been taken out at approximately 5:25 A.M.

Detective Gaynor observed two .22-caliber shell casings lying on the sidewalk near the body. There was also a yellow blanket with an emblem of a large, wild cat on it. The blanket was basically around the victim's feet.

Detective Joseph Lupo, of the Crime Scene Unit (CSU), arrived on the scene at about 9:00 A.M. It was cool and overcast. Temp was in the 60s. Still drizzling. Both uniformed and nonuniformed police personnel were already at the scene.

Lupo went through the same procedure at every crime scene. When he got to the location, he would speak with the officers at the scene, then the case detectives at the scene.

Then he would do a walk-through of the crime scene to make a mental list of what evidence would need to be collected. He would photograph the scene and prepare sketches.

Lupo noticed immediately that the focal point of the crime scene was a body in a driveway near the sidewalk. Tall. Young. White. Facedown. His face was bloody and he had bullet holes to the right side of his torso.

Underneath the body, between the body and the sidewalk, was a yellow blanket with a picture of a lion or a tiger on it. Looked as if the victim had been wrapped in it, but it had fallen open as the body tumbled to the ground.

The shooting had been cruel. The victim had been shot so that death would not be instantaneous. Shot low to die slow. Three of the wounds were in the right side.

Detective Lupo stepped between the orange cones, removed the tarp from the body and took photos right away. First he took photos of the body as it had been found. Then he lifted the victim's shirt so he could photograph the bullet wounds.

He then prepared what they called a "body sheet," which documented the wounds and the clothing the victim was wearing. That sheet was then sent to the medical examiner's office.

There were not pedestrians. Neighbors peeked out from windows or stood inconspicuously on front porches, but no one had the courage to approach the scene on foot.

The detective looked at a spot near the body, north and a little to the west of the body, where two shell casings had been discharged from a .22-caliber pistol. Lupo placed the casings in an envelope and then clearly labeled the envelope. They would be sent to the police laboratory for analysis.

Lupo spent 2½ hours at the scene, making sure that he'd done a thorough job. His processing of the scene was completed about 11:30 A.M. Unless there was an arrest and a trial, at which he might have to testify, he was done with the case.

Police knew that murders happened in all shapes and sizes, and for all reasons. They knew that killers could be as old as eighty-eight and as young as nine, for both had happened in NYC's five boroughs during 2003.

Police knew that women were twice as likely to kill a current spouse than they were to kill an ex. Men were almost exclusively the killers of their exes.

They knew that the deadliest day of the year was almost always in July when the temperature was just above 90 degrees. Hotter than that and people were too sluggish to kill. Cooler than that and they weren't so angry.

Police knew that the great majority of killings were hot-blooded—friends and loved ones, current and past, killed in an uncontrollable rage. These were understandable. Heartbreaking often, but understandable. People sometimes lost control of themselves. It happened.

But it was the cold-blooded murder that kept homicide investigators awake at night. It was the one where the killer didn't know the victim, or at least didn't care about the victim; the one in which the bodies were disposed of like trash—dumped, law enforcement called it—just like litter. These were the ones that gave police detectives insomnia. This victim had been robbed, killed and thrown out with the trash.

* * *

Law enforcement is not crowded with philosophers, but there are a few, and lawmakers can't fit punishment to crime without weighing philosophical issues. When it came to murder, that disturbing feeling police got over cold-blooded crimes was taken into consideration.

Hot-blooded crimes are often not punished as harshly as their cold-blooded counterparts. Premeditation must be proven for a murder to be considered in the first degree. When it's boiled down to its essence, police and prosecutors must gauge how depraved a murder is in order to know how to punish it.

In thirty-nine states there are provisions for harsher punishments for crimes that are "atrocious," "depraved" and "vile." These terms did not have a legal definition, however, and the interpretation of these words varied greatly from judge to judge.

In order to establish consistent and fair punishments for the worst of crimes, a "depravity scale" has been developed. The father of the scale is Dr. Michael Welner, a forensic psychiatrist at the New York University School of Medicine.

Regarding future use of his scale, Welner has said, "The judge or the jury will still have the burden of saying, 'Here's how I want to call it.' But at least they will be informed."

The scale is based on the results of a questionnaire during which respondents were given descriptions of crimes and asked which they thought most depraved. Welner's scale would allow prosecutors, judges or juries to classify a crime as having low, medium or high depravity.

Shot low to die slow. Put that on your depravity scale. If such a scale had been in effect in Brooklyn at the time of this murder, a "high depravity" conclusion would no doubt have been reached.

* * *

Since the body was missing its wallet, police could not immediately identify it. There was $12 in the pocket, but no identification.

Two shell casings, apparently from a .22 handgun, were found near the body. There were more than two bullet wounds. Metal was missing. Police got a break when a kid from Fairfield University, up in Connecticut, called the precinct and said his friend was missing. He'd last been seen at a party in Brooklyn. His folks lived in New Jersey. The New York Police Department (NYPD) got a photo of the kid from the Fairfield Security Department. Looked like him, so they headed to New Jersey to talk to the kid's parents.

By Sunday evening Michael and Nancy Fisher were beginning to get nervous. They called their son Mark's cell phone but one of his Fairfield classmates answered and reported that he had left it behind the night before. It wasn't like Mark to disappear like this.

At two in the morning on Monday, the doorbell to the Fisher home rang. Mrs. Fisher answered the door. Mr. Fisher was working. When she saw it was a police officer, she became frightened and refused to allow him in.

She sensed that bad news had arrived and she thought she could delay or even prevent the news from being real if only she could keep the messenger outside her home.

Delay, yes. Prevent, no.

Eventually the policeman was allowed in and showed her the photo.

"This your son?"

"Yes," Nancy Fisher replied with a sob.

"I'm afraid I have some bad news, ma'am."

Mark Fisher had been found the previous morning lying on a street in Brooklyn, dead from bullet wounds.

"Mark was murdered," the policeman said.

"No, you're wrong," Nancy Fisher replied.

They had never heard of the Ditmas Park area of Brooklyn before they learned it was the location of Mark's murder. On Tuesday morning Michael and Nancy drove to Brooklyn to visit the neighborhood where he died and to formally identify Mark's body. It would be the first of many trips the couple would make to Ditmas Park over the next few months.

Once police knew who the victim was, they had to figure out how he got there. Mark Fisher had been a long way from both his home and his school when he died. How had he gotten there? The last hours of his life needed to be reconstructed.

CHAPTER 2

Mark

Nineteen-year-old Mark S. Fisher grew up in suburban utopia—Andover, in Byram Township, New Jersey, in a modern home in a scenic wooded valley. The picture-perfect postcard town was only a forty-five-minute drive northwest of New York City, but—with its scores of lakes and autumnal foliage—it might as well have been a million miles away.

Mark was the son of Michael and Nancy Fisher, an attractive, dark-haired couple. The Fishers exuded positive energy. Dad worked as a service engineer, Mom as a realtor.

Nancy Fisher was born and raised in Colombia, and came to the United States when she was seventeen. Although she spoke flawless English, one could still hear an accent. Mom was very high energy, while Dad was more quietly competent and confident, not the kind of guy to toot his own horn.

Both Michael and Nancy were devout Roman Catholics,

and had raised their children the same way. Mark had an older brother, Michael Christopher, twenty-four years old and a graduate of Montclair State College, where he earned a degree in mathematics, and a younger sister, Alexis, who was eighteen.

After stints at Our Savior Preschool, Byram Consolidated School and Byram Intermediate School, Mark attended Lenape Valley Regional High School in Stanhope, New Jersey.

In intermediate school he played Little League baseball and basketball, as well as CYO basketball for St. Michael's, of Netcong.

According to his mom, "He had a passion for both baseball and basketball despite having asthma, allergies and flat feet, which made it difficult for him to run. Mark began pitching in fourth grade and continued to do so throughout his freshman year in high school, also playing on all-star teams throughout each summer. In third grade Mark played Midget League football. He received the Most Valuable Defensive Player Award and played another year, but decided to give up on football. In eighth grade he wanted to give it another try."

He grew to be six-five and a football star. Mark played for the Lenape Valley Arrows High School team and was awarded the Outstanding Offensive Player Award.

A big highlight for Mark came in the final game of his senior season against Sparta, New Jersey, when—after overcoming a broken ankle earlier in the season—he was awarded the Most Valuable Player of the game by the opposing coaches.

Mark loved music and played the guitar and piano. As a lifetime parish member of Our Lady of the Lake Church, he was a volunteer usher. Mark also volunteered his time helping with the Special Olympics and was a regular blood donor.

He was also elected by his teachers to be the king of his senior prom.

Excelling in the classroom, as well as on the athletic field, Mark qualified for the National Honor Society at Lenape High. He was a student council officer.

As a smart and good-looking sports hero, he was used to being not only in control of himself, but the atmosphere around him. Not that life was perfect. For starters, he'd gone to college on a football scholarship, and the school discontinued the football program after his freshman year.

Luckily, the school agreed to stick to its educational commitment to Mark, and he continued to attend school for free, even though there was no longer any football for him to play.

The school was Fairfield University in Fairfield, Connecticut—and even when there was a football team there, and he played a single season of collegiate ball, he had not neglected the books. In fact, he made the Dean's List.

He was athletic. And he was smart. But he wasn't worldly. That was a deficit he was eager to overcome. On October 11, 2003, Fisher made his first-ever unsupervised trip into New York City.

The group, which consisted of one of Mark's Fairfield football teammates and two young women, started out visiting their families. The entire group visited Mark's home in Andover, New Jersey, and met Mark's parents, Michael and Nancy.

The Fishers had lived in the same house in the hills of New Jersey for eighteen years. They had moved there from Clifton when Mark was just a baby.

"It is very safe," Mark's dad later said. "Once you move to Sussex County, you can never get comfortable anywhere else."

Mark's dad was fifty and worked for IBM, night shift at that time. While he was home, Mark made a stop in his old bedroom and took a quick glance at his stuff. Posters of Ken Griffey Jr., his favorite baseball player, and Jimi Hendrix, his favorite musician, were on the blue walls. Everything was in place, including trophies and testimonials to his scholastic and academic achievements while in high school.

When the Fairfield crew left the Fisher house, they visited the parents of another member of the group in Saddle River, New Jersey. They had dinner there and then, with fake IDs hidden deep in pockets and purses, drove into New York City.

After the family tour was through, Mark and his friends hit the bars along the Upper East Side. Fisher couldn't have felt safer. Among the crowd was one of his best friends from school, Chris Peters.

Shit, they'd been through wars together—at least on the gridiron.

Mark and Chris were both football players and had become friends on Day One of freshman year, and they had been close ever since. It was a confident young group. They were going to paint the Big Apple.

The Upper East Side was where Manhattan's skyscraper luxury apartments were located—and they were chock-full of young single women. Those buildings had doormen and sometimes names to go with their addresses, names that conjured up images of wealth and New England blue blood—names like The Newport East and The Dover. There were girls all over the place, and they were fine. The ratio of single gals to guys was like eight to one, or something. It boggled the mind, not to mention the lager-lubricated libido.

Tucked between those huge buildings were touches of old Manhattan, three-story brick or brownstone buildings, with storefronts. And there were bars, many bars. Bars for every occasion. Sports bars, pickup bars, getting-trashed bars, all-of-the-above bars. Some seemed to be catering to the rich singles who were out slumming, like a place called American Trash. Some seemed to be trying to capture the same "my people came over in the *Mayflower*" image being projected by those who named the apartment buildings. Mark Fisher's group didn't want to slum. They picked a place that looked like it had class.

They ended up in a place called Ships' Harbour (pseudonym). The bar was built into the base of a sixteen-story apartment building on the east side of First Avenue, between Seventy-sixth and Seventy-seventh Streets.

The entire main floor of the building was commercial. There was a health-food store called A Matter of Health, a beauty parlor called The Hair Company, a gym that was a member of the New York Sports Club franchise, a Japanese restaurant called Fujiyama, a nail salon and a diner on the corner, which was open twenty-four hours and was perfect for getting late-night breakfast when the drinking was through.

And right in the middle was Ships' Harbour, a long and slender space with the bar on the left. Everything was made of bleached wood, and the taps had large and ornate handles. Over the bar, there were chandeliers with faux candles, actually small electric lights.

Sure the ambience was nice, but that probably was not the reason Mark and his friends stayed. The key factor was that the place served them, which was always a consideration when, like Mark Fisher, you were only nineteen and almost two years away from the legal drinking age.

There had been a bar at that location for years and years, but it had only been under the current name and ownership since St. Patrick's Day, 2002. The decor was

Nantucket harbor, and the desired clientele was young professionals.

There was live acoustic music every evening. It was a great bar for sports, even if it wasn't by definition a sports bar. There were ten TVs, and the bar got DirecTV, so the chances were good that the sporting event one wanted to see was on someplace in the bar, even if that event was soccer from Ireland. They had excellent pub food and buffalo wings.

Fisher and his crew were barely in the place when kismet seemingly kissed the night. He ran into someone he knew: Angel DiGiovanni (pseudonym), from Fairfield. Small world.

"What are you doing here?" Mark Fisher asked, amazed at the coincidence.

"We're here to meet my friend Al; then I don't know what we're doing after that," Angel replied. She wasn't visiting from out of town like him, she explained. She was local. Angel was Brooklyn-born. Raised out on the Island. Garden City—the kind of town that had a fancy grass mall down the center of its main drag.

Angel wasn't alone. She had girlfriends with her, friends from Garden City High School. She introduced Mark Fisher to her friend Meredith "Meri" Flannigan (pseudonym). Both Angel and Meri were pretty blondes. Flannigan also attended a major New England university.

Like Mark, Meri and Angel were in the city because of the long weekend, looking to have some fun. Meri was unattached. Angel was waiting for Al, a college friend of her boyfriend's, who was her friend, too.

Mark Fisher and Meredith Flannigan noticed each other right away. As Mark's football teammate later recalled, "All of a sudden I looked over and Mark was talking to Meri. I just let him be."

One of the Fairfield University girls who was along on

the trip remembered, "Mark and Meri were kind of away from the bar. We just took notice, like, 'Oh, he found somebody.'"

Mark said he was broke. Meri bought him drinks.

It was decided that they should all go get pizza—then go to another bar. Mark and Meri left the bar and stood on the sidewalk outside. Mark must have been amazed at the number of people on the sidewalk and the traffic scooting by, considering the late hour. They didn't call it "the city that never sleeps" for nothing. And so many of the cars were yellow. Taxis. Ha! The total number of taxis he'd seen in his life tripled in about ten seconds.

Across the street was another big building with all kinds of stores carved into its base. There was a huge Duane Reade drugstore, a liquor store, a healthy restaurant called Green Kitchen and a Mail Boxes Etc.

They took a right and crossed Seventy-seventh Street. They went to a pizza parlor on the east side of First Avenue, between Seventy-eighth and Seventy-seventh, a place called Pizza & Pasta.

His friends wanted to move on. Fisher's group was going to another bar called Martell's.

"You coming?" Chris Peters asked.

"Yeah, yeah, yeah," Fisher replied, but he seemed more interested in Meri than in what his friend was saying

"We're getting a cab," Peters said.

"I'll be in the cab right behind you," Fisher said.

As Fisher's friends caught a cab, they last saw him standing on a street corner. They figured he would catch a cab just as he said he would and they would see him at the evening's next stop in a few minutes.

Little did they know that they would never see him again. They were in the new bar for about an hour when they realized that Mark was not going to show up. Smirks all around.

They all assumed that he had found something better to do and didn't worry about him after that. When a guy is six-foot-five, and plays college football, people don't worry about him. They assumed he could take care of himself.

No problem, his friends said. Fisher was clearly getting lucky.

Trouble was, in real life, Fisher was more than a little drunk. What to do? He didn't have enough money for a cab back to Jersey. He could make a call. Shit, he'd lost his cell phone. He would just have to stick with Meri—follow her wherever she went.

Angel and her friends were leaving, too. They were going to a bar called Model T's (pseudonym), a little farther uptown. Meri said no problem. Go on ahead. She would be fine with Mark. Angel and Meri, of course, had each other's cell phone numbers.

When Mark and Meri finished eating their pizza, they left the pizza parlor. Meri got instructions from Angel on how to get to the new bar, eleven blocks up and one over. But, no hurry. Model T's wasn't accepting fake IDs. Some of the kids got in, some didn't. Al and Angel didn't.

There were some friends of Al's there, too—and it was the same deal. The ones who were twenty-one or older were allowed in. Those that weren't had to stay out on the street.

So Mark and Meri walked those twelve blocks, just the two of them, in no hurry, very romantic. When they finally arrived at Model T's they learned that Angel's friend Al had originally been with two friends of his from Brooklyn, but one of them, Tommy, was really twenty-one and had gone into the bar.

Model T's was in the middle of the block on the west

side of Second Avenue, between Eighty-fifth and Eighty-sixth Streets. It was a typical New York City block, a little something for everybody, eclectic and multiethnic. The bar was between a GNC health-food store and a Go Sushi Japanese restaurant. Flanking those stores were a Chinese restaurant and a Cold Stone Creamery ice-cream store. Across the street was a kosher deli, a copy shop and two German *hofbraus* offering frosty steins of richly caloric lager.

When Mark and Meri arrived at Model T's, Al and Angel were standing out front with Al's friend John, who was a few days past his twentieth birthday. His fake identification had not been honored by the keen-eyed guy at the Model T's entrance.

Introductions were made all around. Angel's friend was named Albert "Al" Huggins (pseudonym). Huggins's friend was John Giuca (pronounced Jew-ka). Giuca was a skinny kid with bangs and glasses—and he was angry.

Fisher didn't even know where he was going to sleep that night. He wasn't clear on where the night was headed—he was now with a brand-new crowd—but he knew it would involve Meri Flannigan, and that was cool with him.

Was he even a little concerned? If it had been summertime, a guy could just find a park bench, or something, and snooze, but it was fall and that could get chilly.

Chivalry also no doubt entered his thinking. He wasn't the only one who'd missed the last train and couldn't get home. Angel DiGiovanni and Meri Flannigan had hours to wait for the next train to Long Island, and so—like Mark Fisher—they had no place to go.

What we can't be sure of is if Mark Fisher realized that he wasn't universally beloved by the group of young people he had joined. Fisher was extremely popular with Meri, and Angel at least liked the fact that Meri liked Mark, but the two new guys weren't so amiable.

Albert Huggins, Angel's friend, said the girls could crash at his place in Brooklyn. He had a nice house. (Huggins's mom twice ran for political office. Neither campaign was successful. Mrs. Huggins ran as a Conservative Republican against a popular incumbent in a predominantly Liberal Democrat district, and received only 10 percent of the vote both times. But she made it onto the ballot, and that showed a certain amount of influence, even if it was with the political party that wasn't in charge.)

Albert's invitation came with a hitch, however. Fisher wasn't invited. Flannigan said no thanks. Fisher was a little lost and she didn't want to leave him behind. That was John Giuca's cue to take charge, something he was prone to do anyway.

Giuca was a good-looking kid. He wanted to make a few extra bucks in showbiz. He was a dues-paying member of the Screen Actors Guild (SAG). He'd been in a few things, but only as an extra.

He was in *Spider-Man* and *School of Rock*. A couple of TV shows. He had a videotape of *Spider-Man* and loved showing the scene he was in. He always had to point himself out, in the back of a crowd.

School of Rock was better. He was right up front there for a second, his face almost as big as Joan Cusack's face, and she was the female lead. He got paid for a whole day on that one. They shot that scene at the St. George Theatre in Staten Island, just a couple of blocks from where the ferry lands.

The showbiz stuff was fun, but his dream wasn't to be a movie star. According to his mom, he wanted nothing more than to be a police detective. He wanted to catch bad guys.

That was why he was studying criminal justice in college. He wanted to be a detective, because of the salary they made. But any kind of law enforcement would have been good. He had even pondered becoming a member of the Border Patrol.

Giuca now said they should all go to his house in Brooklyn. His folks were in Florida and he had the place to himself. Everybody was invited. Even Mr. Jock, who looked like he might need a bucket before the night was through.

United by seeming similitude and hasty familiarities, the group moved from the sidewalk to one of those yellow cabs. The backseat smelled of incense. They rode to the Ditmas Park section of Brooklyn.

They got out at a pillared three-story house in an exclusive-looking neighborhood a few blocks south of Prospect Park. Fisher probably registered that it was a nice neighborhood.

The neighborhood could have been in a nice town in New Jersey or Connecticut, with its one-hundred-foot trees on either side of the street, with branches that met those of the tree across the way. When a car drove down the street, it would look like it was emerging through a huge tunnel. Beautiful and green during the daytime, but a little bit spooky at night, it was like a street out of a *Halloween* movie.

When the enclave of luxury called Ditmas Park was built, the street signs were carved into stone and set into brick pillars. The pillars with their carved stone street names still stood at the corners, but the stone had become worn over the hundred years since they had been carved, and were difficult to read, impossible at night, so they'd had to be replaced.

The corner houses in Ditmas Park were the most spectacular, with large wooden porches that showed off carved balustrades. The porches curved to accommodate both the front and side doors. There were no straight lines to be seen. It took a lot of skill to bend wood like that. The builders must have hired ship-builders, skilled craftsmen used to building hulls.

Squint one's eyes and it could have been 1900. In the wee hours of the morning, with a snootful of drink, Giuca's house probably seemed indistinguishable from the others.

If Fisher had been visiting the house in the sunshine while sober, he probably would have noticed that the house showed signs of neglect, even disrepair.

Whereas the other houses on the block were pictures of perfection, manicured, the house Giuca was leading Fisher into was in need of a paint job, and the front stairs were broken.

The bottom step in particular had fallen through, the stone slab cracked in two and collapsed upon a small rubble pile of shattered bricks. Four pillars supported the small roof that protected the entranceway. There was an upstairs, plus an attic with a slanted ceiling above that.

The house also badly needed a paint job. The house was peeling, a dingy shade of gray instead of the desired white. The peeling was most noticeable over the front door.

The house Giuca led the others into was also not the most desirable home in the neighborhood because of what lurked directly behind it. Viewed from the front, Giuca's house was silhouetted against a dark-brick background. A huge building sat where the backyard should be, and along the backyards of all of the other houses on that side of Stratford Road. Butting directly against Giuca's practically nonexistent backyard was a huge apartment building, seven stories, and stretching the entire length of the block.

In the evenings, when a lot of homes were still in the sunshine, Giuca's house was already shaded by the huge heavily fire-escaped building to the rear.

* * *

Fisher probably noticed that Giuca was a rough kid with a really thick Brooklyn accent—a white gangsta, like Eminem or something.

Fisher might have noticed Giuca's recognizable street affectations and swollen sense of entitlement, but he probably just chalked it up to Giuca's being a "city kid."

It is doubtful he recognized the danger.

Danger didn't frequent Fisher's world, not when he was growing up in the well-manicured suburbs of New Jersey, nor when he moved out of the house and into the safe womb of the Fairfield dorms.

There were crimes on campus. Sure. But nothing with a victim. Guys got into fights. Once a drunk girl had to be saved from herself when she stumbled into a construction site. Snack and juice machines were found pried open.

But nobody had taught Fisher to distinguish predators from allies—especially when he was three sheets to the wind.

Giuca noticed Fisher, though—and he registered his threat. Fisher was big and he had muscles, and he had the kind of boyish good looks that made the ladies look away from his ample gangsta charms. Giuca could tell that Fisher was "with" Flannigan—and Giuca thought Flannigan was cute.

According to Huggins's later statements, he took Fisher aside not long after they arrived at the house in Ditmas Park. The doorbell rang and Huggins talked tough to the "rich kid."

Huggins told Fisher, "There's some guys that don't like us. Be careful. There might be trouble."

"Don't worry," Fisher said to Huggins with a wink. "I've got your back."

The doorbell turned out to be rung by a pair of friends, rather than foes. One of them was the friend who had been allowed inside the bar called Model T's when Giuca was turned away. The other was a heavyset black dude named Jimmy.

There was beer and wine. The house had a back porch and for a while they sat around a table. Joints were passed around. Mark didn't need much. Uh-oh. One toke over the line.

Fisher didn't have much fun at the party. Too many drinks, topped with drugs. Giuca gave him a pill. Said it was a painkiller. Should kick in in about five minutes. Two plus two made eight. Things were spinning. It was going to be a "one foot on the floor so you don't puke" night.

Not long after they got there, a kid with dreadlocks showed up with drugs. His name was Antonio "Tony" Russo. Some called him "Tweed" or "Anthony," too.

Russo was bigger and heavier than Giuca, but no-where near as big as Fisher. He had a girl's name, "Evelyn," tattooed on the left side of his neck.

Tweed didn't help Fisher's disorientation. Tweed called him "Yarmulke," which didn't make any sense.

Russo lived in the apartment building directly behind Giuca's house. He was a high-school dropout with a job at a fast-food place. Though of mostly European descent, Tweed had a whole Rasta thing going.

He was dark-skinned to begin with, especially during the summer, and wore his hair in braids, which resembled dreadlocks, and had borrowed terms from Jamaican culture, calling police "Babylon," and shit like that.

Russo had problems. A troubled kid. Giuca's mom let him hang around the house because she felt sorry for him. It was her belief that Russo's mom, Evelyn, was a crack-addicted hooker.

Russo had been hanging around Giuca's house since forever. What? Like since he was eight.

Giuca didn't like Fisher any more in Brooklyn than he had in Manhattan. Fisher sat down on a table and this pissed Giuca off. He told him he didn't know how it was where he grew up, but here you sat in a chair, not on the fucking table.

One of the guys was rolling a blunt and Fisher said he'd like to smoke some weed. Giuca said the free ride was over. If he wanted to smoke, he'd best ante up.

Giuca didn't like the guy to begin with and now he was on his nerves. Figuring the guy had money, Giuca told Russo to take Fisher to an ATM machine. Russo said sure, they needed beer anyway.

"Hey, Yarmulke, beer run," Russo said.

Fisher said sure. The nearest ATM was just on the other side of Coney Island Avenue. There was a convenience store that was open twenty-four hours a day. They could get cash and buy beer all in one stop.

Coney Island Avenue must have been yet another trip for Mark. It might seem impossible that one could go from manicured suburbia to urban grit in a matter of two hundred yards, but that was the way it was in Brooklyn.

Coney Island Avenue was six lanes wide and there was still regular traffic in the middle of the night. It was a major artery and it was a weekend. The wide noisy street ran on the other side of Tweed Russo's apartment building, and featured all of the businesses one might expect to see.

Between Giuca's house and the ATM was a KFC, with a drive-thru window, but it wasn't the KFC where Tweed worked. He had to trek all the way out to Ninety-second Street on Fort Hamilton Parkway every day to get to work.

The ATM was in a corner store called the 11-Seven Food Mart. It was on the southwestern corner of Coney Island Avenue and Beverley Road. The awning over the front of the store said it was a fruit-and-vegetable stand.

That distinguished it, in theory, from the standard image of the twenty-four-hour convenience store, based on the knowledge of what a 7-Eleven looked like. But this was an 11-Seven, completely different.

That awning, which stretched across the store's facade on both the Coney Island and the Beverley sides of the building, had a colorful cornucopia of fruits and vegetables painted on it.

Not that Fisher ever saw any fruits and vegetables. It looked like a decent-sized place from the outside, but once inside, you couldn't get two steps without running into a wall. That was the thing with city real estate. Everything had to be scrunched together. It was condensed, with the spaces that were normally between things simply removed.

The ATM was right inside the door, facing the entrance. The cash machine was the plastic portable variety, on wheels, with plastic buttons to push and a slot to swipe one's card. The three letters *ATM* were huge and in white, set against a blue background, and perched atop the cash machine, so that the sign became the head to the robot. The sign became the inhuman face. The cash spit out from the belly. Below the cash slot was a decal with icons of all the twelve different types of cash cards the ATM recognized. It looked like all of them.

Somehow Fisher managed to get his cash card out of his wallet and into the ATM's slot so it could be swiped. He remembered his Personal Identification Number.

But when the prompt came to select how much money he wanted to withdraw, he chose $20. That would buy smoke, right?

To the left of the cash machine were the pots of coffee, sitting on the burners of three coffeemakers, red lights lit. Nearby was the usual assortment of milk and sugar, everything needed for people to fill their own containers to go. Those who preferred tea were taken care of as well. On a rack on the wall, just above the upside-down plastic cups and coffeemakers, were a row of small boxes, each containing a different type of tea bag. Next to the tea bags was a green bottle. Maybe it contained lemon juice. The coffee machines were on the top deck of a tiered set of shelves made of wire. The center tier had extra Styrofoam cups, coffee machine filters, and premeasured packets of ground coffee. The lower shelf had big boxes that probably held gross quantities of those same items.

To the right of the cash machine were broken-down cardboard boxes resting upright against the wall, plus a three-foot pile of sacks containing potatoes. There was a large window that looked out onto an outer space, where the fruits and vegetables were, and there were already some pumpkins out. Beyond that space was a clear plastic sheet that, when standing at the ATM, provided a view of Beverley Road. Though cars went by every once in a while along Coney Island Avenue out the front entrance, to the side, on Beverley Road, it was the still of the night.

Farther to the left was the cash register. A customer had to take a left and walk around the coffee kiosk to get to the rest of the store. The beer was all the way in the back.

According to the ATM, the withdrawal was made at 4:23 A.M., but the machine's internal clock was later determined to be off. After grabbing the lone bill, and probably handing it immediately over to Russo, Fisher and his dreadlocked escort returned to the house on Stratford Road.

Fisher sure as hell didn't need any more beer. He'd only been back to the party for a few minutes when he fell out on a couch. Meri Flannigan wanted to cuddle up with him as he slept, but there wasn't room. He took up the whole couch, so she fell out elsewhere.

Later it would be discovered that around the time he'd made his ATM withdrawal, he'd also managed to call his Fairfield friends, borrowing Angel's cell phone to do it.

The call had not gone through, but Fisher's friend later received a message that said, "It's Fish. I'm wondering where you guys are. Give me a call back on Angel's phone."

The Fairfield friends, by that time, were back in New Jersey, minus one of their party.

On Stratford Road, the party wound down. The two guys who'd rung the doorbell left. Mark and Meri were out like a light. Out on the back porch Giuca and Russo were joined by Giuca's little brother.

At 4:30 A.M., Albert Huggins and Angel DiGiovanni must have decided that the party was over. That was when Huggins's mother said she heard Albert and Angel enter the Huggins home.

For almost two hours, all was quiet.

CHAPTER 3

Ditmas Park

Ditmas Park is actually a subsection of the larger geographic region known as Flatbush, because of its proximity to Flatbush Avenue, Brooklyn's version of "Main Street," which cuts diagonally across the borough from the northwest to the southeast.

The whole neighborhood today has been officially named a Historic District. Even the slightest changes to a house would have to be approved. That section of Brooklyn had been all farmland until the 1900s when the "suburban" housing development was built. So all of the houses there were approximately the same age, built between 1900 and 1910.

Since 1908, the neighborhood has had its own "association," the Ditmas Park Association, which, according to its literature, "hosts social events, publishes a newsletter and a home improvement directory, and works on numerous civic issues."

Ditmas Park was one of the neighborhoods in New

York City that often caused people's jaws to drop. Real estate agents would talk about the shock their clients expressed when they pulled off Coney Island Avenue and into the enclave of what was called, in the real estate biz, "nineteenth-century Victorian charm in postmillennium Brooklyn." Nobody expected to see that kind of quaint beauty in the middle of a borough that—although filled with people of great character, of course—was on the grimy side. Even the street names changed. All the names were clearly Anglo-Saxon and may just as well have been in the English countryside: Argyle, Rugby and Marlborough.

And they were roads, not streets. The neighborhood, when built, had been in the country.

The Victorian homes that lined the streets of Ditmas Park were beautiful, but it would have been a mistake to assume that the neighborhood was free of crime. In fact, the number of reported crimes in the neighborhood had increased dramatically since 2003.

Hollywood film crews frequently used the neighborhood as a setting for scenes, both in movies that took place in present-day Brooklyn, and period pieces, because the streets of the neighborhood had such a "land-that-time-forgot" ambience.

Between 1999 and 2003, the crime rate in Brooklyn's Seventieth Precinct had dropped, but someone flicked a switch in 2003 and since then things had been bad.

It was surrounded on three sides by neighborhoods that weren't as nice. Because it was an island of historical preservation in the midst of urban decay, the neighborhood had a "sole survivor" mentality.

Most of the crimes had not been major. There were more and more kids getting their bikes stolen. More muggings. Smart muggings, too. The kind that came seconds after the victim got paid. The UPS guy now traveled with an armed guard.

Some of the muggings were savage. One high-school sophomore was mugged three times in six months. The third time the mugger concealed box cutters in his fists and slashed the kid's face.

Had it been a gang initiation? Was the money delivered directly to a gang leader? Were the box cutters there to draw "innocent blood," a key feature to gang initiation in 21st-century Brooklyn, USA?

A community crime stoppers group had formed. Ditmas Park was a small town, an oasis in the squalor, and eyes and ears were everywhere in anticipation of trouble.

There were places in Brooklyn where residents were hesitant to talk to police no matter what kind of trouble was occurring outside their window. But that was hardly the case in Ditmas Park; it was the type of neighborhood where people were *quick* to call 911.

At 6:41 A.M., October 12, at least two people in Ditmas Park *did* call 911. Gunshots had been heard.

CHAPTER 4

The Medical and Ballistic Evidence

The autopsy on the body of Mark Fisher was performed by Dr. Charles Cantanese on October 13, 2003. The first step was to measure and weigh the body. Mark Fisher, in death, was six feet three inches tall and weighed 205 pounds.

An external examination of the body revealed the presence of multiple gunshot wounds to the torso and right arm. Specifically, there were two gunshot wounds to the right back, one gunshot wound to the right side of the abdomen, one gunshot wound to the right shoulder and two gunshot wounds to the right arm.

There was also evidence of blunt-impact injuries. There was a one-inch reddish brown abrasion on the right forehead, a half-inch abrasion on the left forehead, a half-inch contusion on the bridge of the nose, two ¾-inch abrasions on the right cheek and four ¾-inch abrasions on the chin of the deceased. There was also a half-inch abrasion on the lateral aspect (the side) of the right hand and a one-inch contusion of the right thumb.

When the external examination was complete, an internal examination was performed. The paths of the bullets needed to be determined, and the internal organs checked for abnormalities and injuries.

The gunshot wounds were numbered to be more easily distinguished from one another. There was no way to tell in which order the wounds had been inflicted. The numeration process made no attempt to put the wounds in chronological order.

Wound number one, Dr. Cantanese designated, was to the back of the right chest, located fifteen inches below the top of the head and six inches to the right of the midline, an imaginary line that bisected the body in a symmetric fashion. That bullet went through the muscles of the back, the right lung, the heart and the left lung.

The bullet that caused wound number one was recovered on the left upper front of the chest. The bullet had been traveling from back to front, right to left, and upward.

Wound number two was also a wound to the back of the right chest, just below wound one. It was located seventeen inches below the top of the head, and 5½ inches to the right of the midline.

This bullet went through the muscles of the back, perforated the right lung, the esophagus and the left lung. The bullet that caused wound two was also recovered in the left front of the chest, below the level of the other bullet.

Wound number three was a gunshot wound to the right flank, to the right side of the abdomen, located twenty-five inches below the top of the head and four inches to the right of the midline. The bullet that caused this wound perforated the liver and entered the abdominal muscle in front of the left lower part of the abdomen.

The small-caliber bullet that caused that wound was also recovered during the autopsy. The direction of the gunshot that caused wound number three was right to left, back to front, and downward.

Wound number four was a gunshot wound to the right shoulder, on the side of the right shoulder, 2½ inches below the top of the shoulder. The bullet that caused this wound perforated the muscles of the right shoulder and traveled upward. The bullet ended up in the left lower front of the neck. The direction of the gunshot had been right to left, back to front, and upward. The bullet was recovered.

Wound five was to the right arm, 5½ inches below the top of the shoulder. It involved the muscles of the right arm, the axilla and the right lung. The path of the bullet ended in the area of the ninth and tenth posterior ribs. A bullet fragment was recovered at that location. The bullet had traveled downward through the body, from front to back, and from right to left.

Wound number six was an in-and-out wound to the right elbow. No bullet was found corresponding to this wound.

Fluids and tissue samples were taken from the body, and those samples were tested for the presence of drugs and alcohol. Alcohol was found. There was also a drug found, which turned out to be a stimulant, chemically consistent with Ecstasy.

Although the quantities of alcohol and drugs found in the body had been significant—the victim had been drunk and high at the time of his death—those levels had not been large enough to be a contributing factor in the victim's demise.

Dr. Cantanese wrote that death came as a result of five bullet wounds to the neck and torso, including one in the heart. The bruising was consistent with a beating before he was shot.

There was no way for an autopsy to determine where Fisher had been when he was shot. Was Fisher shot in the house, in a car, or right there on the street where he was found? Because of statements made by witnesses, police did not necessarily believe that all of the wounds had been caused in the same place. There might have been a vehicle involved.

Perhaps he had been shot first at another location and later in the vehicle. Perhaps he had been shot first in the vehicle and then finished off as he lay in the street.

The ballistic evidence found at the crime scene was sent to the Firearms Analysis Section of the NYPD, specifically to Detective Mark Basoa. Detective Basoa was given two shell casings found near Mark Fisher's body, and five bullets (four whole bullets and one lead fragment).

Using microscopic analysis, he determined that the shell casings came from a .22-caliber semiautomatic handgun. Though the bullets were too deformed to determine if they had all come from the same weapon, the evidence did point in that direction.

In other words, there was no evidence that two different guns had been used. He could determine that the four whole bullets were .22 caliber, whereas the caliber of the small lead fragment could not be determined.

There was a discrepancy between the number of bullets found in the body and the number of shell casings found at the crime scene. Five bullets. Two casings.

There were two theories as to how this occurred. Fisher had been shot three times in one location, then twice in another, most likely the spot where the body had been found; or, he had been shot five times at the crime scene, and the killer or killers, in their haste, removed only three of the five shell casings.

Police had an early theory that Fisher had been shot as he slept on the couch in the den of Giuca's home. This theory stemmed from a suspicious stain on the carpet near the couch. The theory fell apart soon enough when samples from the stain turned out to be something other than blood.

At first, another key piece of evidence looked to be a small yellow thread that was found after a search warrant was obtained for the party house on Stratford Road. That thread potentially linked the home of John Giuca with the blanket in which Fisher's body was wrapped when it was found. The importance of the discovery was diminished, however, when both Giuca and his mom conceded that the blanket had come from their home.

The investigation made some progress during the key first 48 hours. A check of Fisher's bank records revealed that he had gone to an ATM and taken out $20 not long before his death.

The withdrawal took place at 4:23 A.M. The ATM was in a twenty-four-hour convenience store not far from Giuca's house. Some thought this might have provided the motive for murder.

The Jersey group, with whom Fisher had started the tragic evening, reported that he did call at about 4:00 A.M., saying that he was going to a party in Flatbush and that they should join him. They declined.

Police interviewed the source at Fairfield University that had tipped them off to their victim's identity and learned that Fisher had gone to a party with Fairfield schoolmate Angel DiGiovanni and some others.

Not long after receiving that lead, investigators discovered that Fisher's last party had taken place in the home of John Giuca on Stratford Road, only about two blocks from the spot where his body was found.

Detectives began to make a list of the kids who had attended the fateful party. The list, once it developed, was comprised of both kids who admitted to being at the party and kids, some not yet found, who were reported to be there by others.

After Giuca, one of the first names they put on their list was that of Antonio "Tweed" Russo.

At 9:10 P.M., on the evening of October 14, 2003, less than three days after the murder, Sergeant Michael Joyce, of the Seventieth Precinct's Detective Squad, along with two sergeants, went to the apartment building behind John Giuca's house to talk to Giuca's buddy Antonio "Tweed" Russo.

They took the elevator to the fifth floor. As police were getting off the elevator, Russo was in the hall and tried to get on. He was with his grandmother and an older male. They asked him if he would accompany them to the Seventieth Precinct for an interview. Russo came along willingly.

When John Giuca's mom, Doreen Federicci, returned home to Brooklyn from Florida, John told her about the tragedy that had occurred, and how the kid had been at a party at their house before he was killed.

"John was telling me the story and he was crying hysterically about when he found out the boy was dead. He felt really, really bad for the family. He kept saying, 'He was such a nice kid, he was such a nice kid,'" Doreen later recalled.

CHAPTER 5

The List

Despite the investigation's progress, there was early indication that this progress would soon bog down. As police tried to reconstruct the last few hours of Fisher's life, all did not go smoothly.

Angel DiGiovanni caused problems because, at first, she could not be found. According to NYPD spokesman Paul J. Browne, Angel was "hard to locate," and was "not immediately available" for police interview.

Angel, of course, was considered a key witness, because she was the social link between the Fairfield students, with whom Mark Fisher had begun the evening, and the residents of Ditmas Park, with whom Mark Fisher had ended the night.

By the end of Sunday, detectives did locate Angel and she gave a brief statement. After that, her father, attorney James DiGiovanni (pseudonym), did all the talking. He said, "She left that young man earlier in the evening. He decided to stay (at the party). My daughter left. She knew nothing about this until a day later."

The lawyer told the press that detectives had praised his daughter for her cooperation, but police spokesman Browne told a different story. He said that the very fact that she had insisted on having a lawyer present when she spoke to the police demonstrated a "lack of full-hearted cooperation."

Police eventually developed what they believed to be a comprehensive list of those who had attended Giuca's party. Although as many as fifteen people were at the party at one time or another, six were there for only a few seconds. The list of people who were at the party and stayed for substantial amounts of time counted nine, including the victim.

It wasn't long, but it was quite a list. One girl was the daughter of a lawyer who had defended reputed mobsters. One boy was the son of a former congressional candidate. All were in their teens or early twenties.

The partygoers included:

1) James Mamorsky (pseudonym), twenty years old, a portly African American. Called Jimmy by his friends. Lived not far from Giuca. Graduated from Bishop Ford High School, which was in Brooklyn, only a few blocks west of the Ditmas Park section, where the murder took place. Attended Seton Hall University. Parents owned a corner store in the Crown Heights section of Brooklyn.

2) Albert Huggins, nineteen years old. Graduated from Bishop Ford High School. At the time of the party he was a student at St. Francis College, also in Brooklyn. His father, Albert Sr., was a wealthy investment banker who had once backed

an Oscar-winning actor's restaurant venture. His mother was a Republican Party fund-raiser who had once run for Congress. Albert was the friend of Fairfield student Angel DiGiovanni and was with the girl who had introduced the victim to Meredith Flannigan at the time of the murder. Mark Fisher's body was found only a few houses down from the Huggins house.

3) Meredith Flannigan, nineteen-year-old college student who had met and befriended the victim earlier in the night at the Ships' Harbour in Manhattan. She was a high-school friend of Angel DiGiovanni's. Meri, as she was called, and Fisher had gone to the party in the first place because the night had grown late and they did not want to separate. She told police that she was awoken as she slept lightly in Giuca's house by a slamming door. She said that she had slept until 10:00 A.M. and woke up wondering where Mark Fisher had gone.

4) Angel DiGiovanni, nineteen-year-old daughter of the prominent lawyer James DiGiovanni. Angel supplied the social bridge between the victim and the host of the party. She was a friend of Fisher's from Fairfield University. And she knew Giuca through Al Huggins, her boyfriend's college buddy. She was also the one who introduced Fisher to Meri Flannigan. Without Meri's presence, Fisher, no doubt, would have returned to New Jersey with his friends. Angel's lawyer father defended reputed mobsters (such as Colombo associate Armand "Chips" DiCostanzo, a career criminal who was active during the bloody Colombo war, and Joey

Ida, a Genovese soldier who whacked Antonio "Hickey" DiLorenzo).

5) Antonio Russo, seventeen years old. He was a high-school dropout who worked at a KFC in the Fort Hamilton section of Brooklyn, not far from the Verrazano-Narrows Bridge. Police believed he held the key to solving the murder. He told police that Mark Fisher was still alive when Russo left the Giuca party for the last time. Antonio lived around the corner from John Giuca, and Russo went with Fisher to an ATM hours before the murder. Following the murder, Russo's behavior was the most suspicious.

6) Thomas "Tommy" Hassan (pseudonym), twenty-one years old. Another one of Giuca's Bishop Ford High School buddies. He had been in the city with Giuca and Huggins earlier in the evening. A student at Brooklyn Polytechnic Institute. Lived in Brooklyn with his parents.

7) Matthew Federicci (pseudonym), fifteen years old. John Giuca's half brother. Police, the papers reported, believed him to be an innocent bystander. He attended a prep school in the Bay Ridge section of Brooklyn and had been described by investigators as a "good kid."

8) John Giuca, twenty years old. Host of the party and social leader. According to some witnesses, Giuca was a leader of a fledgling club called the Ghetto Mafia. "Gang" name: Slim Shady Loc. He was a graduate of nearby Bishop Ford High School and attended John Jay College.

The name Ghetto Mafia, or GM for short, came from a music act the group listened to. The original Ghetto

Mafia was a hip-hop act from Atlanta, hard-core rappers in the NWA mold.

Many of the rap group Ghetto Mafia's compositions were ultramilitant, ultraviolent calls for revolution. They chanted lyrics that urgently called for death to white people and police officers. In 2002, they had a hit with "Money Murda and Muzik." The music group GM had been around since 1994.

Interestingly, Assistant District Attorney (ADA) Josh Hanshaft would later say that Giuca was kind of "slight and weak-looking."

Quite a cast of characters, indeed.

CHAPTER 6

"Wangstas"

Many of the kids at the party had been students at Bishop Ford Central Catholic High School, which, since 1962, has sat on a slender parcel of land sandwiched between the Prospect Expressway and Greenwood Cemetery. The school had been named after Maryknoll bishop Francis X. Ford, who was martyred in China in 1952. The school building was designed to resemble the Chinese mission of Bishop Ford. Atop the school is a cross sitting atop a pagoda, and the school's colors, red and black, are symbolic of the Chinese artistic tradition and the Maryknoll Fathers. In previous incarnations, the plot of land upon which the school was built held a trolley barn and, during the Civil War, a federal prison.

Although police were actively investigating all of those whose names appeared on "the list," they took a special interest in two of the names: Antonio "Tweed" Russo and the host himself, John Giuca.

According to some, Giuca was a cross between a gangsta

and a gangster, part Eminem, part Tony Soprano. And he was a leader of the Ghetto Mafia, a neophyte gang looking to establish itself on the bad streets of Brooklyn, which were only a few blocks away from the upper-class neighborhood where Giuca lived.

GM was made up of mostly white kids with money who, witnesses said, sought "street cred" in Brooklyn's gangsta world. Giuca listened to music written by black males lashing out at the white world.

It may seem to some an unusual social phenomenon that white kids with money would emulate the behavior of black kids who were poor and lived in harsh, sometimes dreadful conditions.

Strange, maybe, but not unheard of. There were enough white kids seeking to be gangstas in Brooklyn that they had acquired a name. The parochial girls who floated in and out of their lives called them "wangstas," a blending of "white gangstas."

Fisher's wallet was found tossed into a sewer drain at the corner of Turner Place and Stratford Road—just steps from Russo's high-rise apartment building and Giuca's home, equidistant from the boys' respective front doors.

The wallet contained Fisher's New Jersey driver's license, an Old Navy credit card and his bank ATM card—but no fingerprints.

Reporters canvassing the neighborhood learned that the party house was notorious on the street. There was frequent late-night activity and noise there, neighbors reported.

"It's young guys that do hang out, and like I said, [it's] until the wee hours of the morning. Not sure what's going on over there," said one neighbor.

CHAPTER 7

Antonio Russo:
Unusual Behavior

In the hours and days following Mark Fisher's murder, among the partygoers, Antonio Russo behaved the most suspiciously. He'd always been very proud—vain even— about his braids, his practically Rastafarian dreadlocks.

Yet within an hour of Fisher's death, Russo went to an acquaintance and asked him to cut off his braids. Since it was dawn on a Sunday, the usual barbershops were not open. Tweed, however, wanted to alter his look *now*. Police knew that sudden attempts to change one's appearance is evidence of guilt.

So is flight. Guilty parties often attempt to distance themselves from the crime. In the days following the murder, Russo went to California. He had an uncle there.

After a week, though, Russo returned to Brooklyn. He was back by the end of October.

Russo had also been the only one of the partygoers to try to lay responsibility for Fisher's death on someone else. If they said anything at all, the others said they didn't know what happened.

Russo tried to convince police that it was another person who had been at Giuca's party who had killed Fisher, and that he'd had nothing to do with it.

Not totally without justification, Russo felt somewhat stalked by the police during the weeks following Mark Fisher's murder. Seemed like Tweed saw a cop every time he turned around.

Russo's friend Linda Brown said that Russo used to enter and exit his apartment building on Turner Place through the main entrance, like everyone else. Now he went around to the back and accessed his fifth-floor apartment via the fire escape.

With its entrance on Turner Place—between Stratford Road and Coney Island Avenue, on the south side of the street—the apartment building was directly behind Giuca's house.

Then, of course, there was the location of Fisher's wallet. Though his body had been found a couple blocks away, the victim's wallet was found in the sewer on the corner, midway between Giuca's house and Russo's apartment building.

John Giuca's mom was later asked about Russo. She said she thought from the get-go that Russo had been behind Fisher's death. She knew from experience that it was difficult to believe a word Russo said.

"Antonio was a good storyteller," Doreen Federicci recalled. "One day he was a pilot. Another day he climbed mountains. Another, he was in a submarine. They were so far-fetched. All he did was lie.

"I'd say to John, 'Don't you call him on it?' He'd say, 'No, Ma, he has nothing in his life. If he wants to be a pilot, we just laugh.'" Disturbingly, according to Giuca's mom, Russo's lies became increasingly violent.

"It stopped being about adventures and turned into the number of people he'd hurt," Doreen Federicci said. "He would claim to have beat up and stabbed hundreds of people."

CHAPTER 8

Mark's Funeral

Byram Township, located forty-five miles west of Manhattan, is just shy of 22½ square miles in size. The ancestors of the Lenape Indians were the area's first residents. The origins of that people date back as far as 11,500 years. The Lenape were not egotistical as a tribe. Loosely translated, the word "Lenape" means "ordinary folk."

The first Europeans to settle in the area were the Dutch in the 17th century. Their colony had a population of six hundred by 1753. Byram Township was established in 1798, named after the Byram family, surveyors who'd lived in the area since Colonial days.

By modern times Byram Township was considered one of the nicest places to live in all of New Jersey. The area was proud of its long history. One small section had been preserved and restored to its Colonial appearance, and was populated by actors wearing the garb of early settlers.

It had a nickname, calling itself "The Township of Lakes" because of the area's two dozen lakes—Lake

Mohawk, Lake Lackawanna, Cranberry Lake, etc.—most ringed with cottages and summer homes. In the summer, boats hummed upon the lakes, often pulling water-skiers, and the air was filled with the smells of barbecue.

One out of every twenty acres was water. The current population of the township was nine thousand, although it fluctuated. The number went up in the summer.

The township was 96 percent white. About half of the remaining percentage were Native Americans. Three out of four homes had a married couple living in them, and a little less than half had children under eighteen running around inside. The average income per household was close to $90,000 a year. Only 1 percent of the residents lived at below the poverty level.

It was like heaven, especially in October with the autumnal foliage, even as the town gathered for the grim task of saying good-bye forever to young Mark Fisher.

Mark's body was prepared for burial and laid out for visitors at Goble Funeral Home in Sparta, New Jersey. The family received their friends there on Thursday, October 16, 2003, from 2:00 to 4:00 P.M., and from 7:00 to 9:00 P.M.

The funeral mass was held at ten in the morning on Friday, October 17, 2003, at Our Lady of the Lake Church, in Sparta. Family and friends packed the church. Interment followed in the Gate of Heaven Cemetery in East Hanover, New Jersey. In lieu of flowers, the family asked that memorial contributions be made to the Mark Steven Fisher Foundation.

After her son's funeral, Nancy Fisher said, "We have to pick out a tombstone for our son. It doesn't matter how much crying you do or how sorry you are. Everything is excuses, excuses. Everyone can find excuses, even to kill."

Asked about Mark, Nancy continued to refer to her dead son in the present tense.

"He is always smiling," she said.

Michael Fisher read a statement about his son: "Most kids learn a lot from their father. I learned a lot from him," he said.

A girl came up to Michael Fisher after the funeral and told him how she had moved to New Jersey from California, and that at first, no one at her new school had treated her well. Mark was the only one who had welcomed her with open arms.

Michael later commented: "People expect parents to say nice things about their children, so it was better coming from someone else. He was a good person. He showed so much kindness and open-mindedness to people."

Mark's dad said that his late son was the most unselfish person he had ever met.

"As a high-school freshman, he was a big kid, six-five, and he was the quarterback. In his junior year the coach asked him to play the line. I told him, 'Don't be crazy, you're going to go to college to be a quarterback.' He said, 'I gotta do it.' He wound up being the MVP. He was very good at turning bad situations into good ones. He was the most unselfish person I ever met."

And another example: "When the kids were small, it was Christmas and my wife was in the hospital for surgery. All three kids were upset. Mark said, 'Don't worry, Mom, we will be all right.' He put her comfort before his own.

"When my daughter, who is younger than Mark, would get in trouble, he would tell her, 'Tell Mommy that I did it.' He had a goofy, fun-loving nature that doesn't measure to height and weight. He would take the guilt for anything because he felt comfortable with himself that he didn't do it."

As for Mark's legacy, Michael said, "One thing we really want is for people to remember him. If we know that other people are thinking of him, it will make us feel better."

Not long after the funeral, a letter was placed at his grave site by some of his friends and schoolmates. It read: "Mark, . . . You were a friendly 'Good morning' every day and a smile seen from all the way down the hall, a humble star who was willing to step back for someone else to shine in the spotlight."

On the day of Mark Fisher's funeral, Police Commissioner Ray Kelly commented on the state of the investigation: "The victim left that party with at least three other people, perhaps more.

"He went to a location in Brooklyn, they used an ATM machine at around five-forty in the morning, for twenty dollars. We are now in the process of talking to some of the people who left that establishment," Kelly continued.

"Investigators do not believe that the motivation was robbery, or that it was a random act. Other than that, I don't want to go further, because no arrests have been made in this case," the commissioner concluded.

The investigation, Kelly said, was focused on the house on Stratford Road, where the victim had spent time just before his murder, and the attendees of a party that went on at that home that night.

The single-family frame house—with a center hall, double parlor, fireplace and private driveway—was built on a forty-eight by one-hundred-foot lot. It had 3½ bathrooms and seven bedrooms. It had last been refinanced in 1991.

Ray Kelly said, "We know that there was a party, there was a gathering, we executed the search warrant."

All of the Argyle Road residents who lived near the crime scene had been interviewed. Police said a white vehicle, possibly an SUV, had been seen pulling away from the scene soon after the shots were heard.

Some of the neighbors heard the shots but, like Mr. Feldman, were too frightened to look outside right away, for fear that a bullet might come whizzing their way.

One earwitness was Lowell Rubin, who said, "We were sleeping. It was six-thirty, six-forty A.M. It woke us. Originally, we did not even know what it was. Unfortunately, when the police came, we saw the body."

CHAPTER 9

Hot Guns

Russo was interrogated for days. Although closed-lipped at first, info did start to leak out of him little by little. Yeah, he and his crew were known to have guns.

What did they do when a gun got hot—that is, when they used it for a crime and didn't want it traced back to them? They took it to the Wenninger brothers (pseudonyms), who lived in Bensonhurst.

Did Russo think the Wenninger brothers had hot guns at their house right then? Maybe, Tweed said. Let's go for a ride, police said.

On October 18, 2003, "gun charges" were filed in connection with the murder. Police arrested Jesse Wenninger, twenty-one, a friend of Giuca and Russo's, for possession of unregistered weapons. Police did not say if Wenninger's arrest was linked to Fisher's murder.

"Right now, he's just been charged with weapons possession in the third and fourth degree," said a spokesman for the Deputy Commissioner of Public Information Office.

By October 23, police were still not willing to name a suspect, but they did go so far as to say that they had evidence pointing to "specific people" and a "specific location." They said they had interviewed the suspected triggerman, but the youth had gotten a lawyer and had stopped cooperating with the investigation.

More evidence was needed, police said, before an arrest or arrests could be made. The location police referred to was the house on Stratford Road.

Police sources told *Newsday*, the daily newspaper that served both New York and Long Island, that Fisher and another man at the party were interested in the same woman. Detectives thought Fisher and the man who shot him may have fought over the woman.

If John Giuca was actually on the scene when Mark Fisher was murdered, as police suspected was the case, it was not the first time he had allegedly been around during alleged gunplay on a Brooklyn Street.

His name showed up on an incident report from several months before Fisher's murder. Story was that Giuca and another man had gotten into an argument at 5:35 A.M. on June 28, 2003.

The argument had taken place on Twenty-third Street in the Greenwood Heights section of Brooklyn. That was between Third and Fourth Avenues, east of Ditmas Park, on the other side of the huge Greenwood Cemetery from where Giuca lived.

On the Third Avenue end of the block stood the elevated platform that held the Gowanus Expressway, a major thoroughfare that ran directly above Third Avenue for many blocks. Third Avenue was a street in perpetual shadow, and the area had long been a hot spot for vice of all sorts.

On the other end of the block was the subway, the BMT line running under Fourth Avenue.

According to a friend of Giuca's, who had just been dropped off before the trouble started, the shooting took place following an evening of nightclubbing and, as he understood it, a subsequent drug deal gone awry.

According to another friend, there had never been any gunplay at all, just some firecrackers designed to scare the shit out of some kids.

The police report didn't mention firecrackers. It said that Giuca menaced the man verbally and then fired a handgun at a car holding three of the man's friends. Nobody was hit. Neighbors called 911, but Giuca and the group he was arguing with were all gone by the time police arrived.

Not long after the shooting, Giuca was picked up and questioned by police about it. Police were pretty sure that Giuca was the guy who had fired the gun, but there was no one to make a complaint, so he was released.

CHAPTER 10

Wall of Silence

Police had learned some things in the first week of the investigation. They'd made the list of partygoers and were fairly certain it was complete. They had located and questioned everyone on the list, and they'd learned a few things. But that flow of information—never really more than a trickle—had run dry by the time Mark Fisher had been dead for a week. The eyewitnesses had closed the ranks. Mum was the word.

Some of the partygoers refused to be asked questions unless they were with their lawyers. Nobody saw anything or heard anything. No one had a clue as to what might have happened to Mark Fisher. He had left the house not long after he'd arrived and had gone to an ATM to withdraw money. Then he'd returned to the party.

Some of the witnesses really didn't know anything. The party, police believed, had thinned to four by the time Fisher met his demise. The last thing several of the partygoers remembered, Fisher had fallen asleep in the den. Someone had thrown a blanket over him. He was still asleep as of 6:00 A.M., only forty minutes before gunshots were reported.

Among those whom police wanted information from most was John Giuca. Like the other survivors who'd been at his house that night, he'd gotten a lawyer, Lance Lazzaro.

Antonio Russo had lawyered up as well. He had retained Neil S. Ruskin to represent him. Ruskin, who had his office in Downtown Brooklyn near the courthouses, told the press that the police were barking up the wrong tree and that his youthful client was "a very decent young man" who was being "threatened and intimidated by the police."

Before getting lawyers, some of the eyewitnesses had suggested that Fisher must have left the house on his own in an attempt to stumble home, and that he had been the victim of a random robbery/murder, but Police Commissioner Kelly wanted them to know that the police did not believe this to be the case.

"We believe it wasn't a random street crime, and it emanated from a dispute," Kelly said in October. "We believe Fisher was jumped by a group as he left the house and thrown into a white car or van. As an investigative premise, I would say more than one person was involved."

Police believed that out of the nine names on their list of partygoers, three were present at the time of the murder and watched Fisher die.

And police learned that Giuca had been known to ride around in a white SUV. Giuca's mom conceded that John's friend Tommy Hassan drove a car like that, but she doubted if Tommy would let anyone borrow it.

Antonio Russo couldn't stay out of trouble. A month after Mark Fisher's death he was arrested for menacing.

Trouble had started when he and a friend had gone out to throw rocks through windows.

When the friend said that he didn't want to join Russo in this act of senseless vandalism, Russo threatened to shoot him with a gun. The friend reported Russo to the police and he was arrested. In January 2004, according to a *New York Times* article citing court records, Russo pleaded guilty to a lesser charge of disorderly conduct.

CHAPTER 11

The Fishers Search for *Hows* and *Whys*

On December 8, 2003, Michael and Nancy Fisher visited the Fairfield University campus. They distributed posters offering a $40,000 reward for any information leading to an arrest.

"We are destroyed by this, especially with the holidays coming up," Michael Fisher said. "We believe Mark's murder was a setup. It wasn't random. Why was he murdered? I have no idea."

To the Fairfield community, Michael Fisher said, "We believe students might be withholding information. We're asking you to please help . . . give the police some information or give it to us."

In remembrance of Fisher and his happy, optimistic character, Fisher's family set up the Mark Steven Fisher Foundation. "We have not decided completely on where all the money will go," said Michael Fisher. "We would like to award a scholarship every year to Mark's high school, and we may do something with Fairfield University depending on the money available.

"We would like to urge students to never forget Mark since it's all we have left. He was always a good kid, and he was very close with my wife. The police found a paper in Mark's dorm room that he wrote about his mother. We all read it, and we all cried. It is really starting to settle in that he's not coming back. He's never coming back."

The presence of Mark's parents served as a forum for Mark's friends to gather and talk to each other and reporters about their frustrations. Fisher's friend Mary Boehmer said, "The worst thing in the world is not knowing . . . the feeling of the unknown. We feel like there are students here who do know exactly what happened but are too scared to come forward. If there are indeed students who know what happened or have a piece of what happened, then they should share, because eventually the truth always comes out. If there is a student here who knows something that we don't know, and if they are keeping a secret because they are scared, I want to tell them not to be scared. They should tell the truth because if there is no truth in this world, then there is really no basis for anything. Don't be afraid, and do what is right. I want them to give the Fisher family some peace. They cannot give the Fishers Mark back, but they can give them peace of mind at night and a sense of finally knowing what happened. There is a void in my daily life; when someone you love dies, there is a before and after. There is life before they have died, and then there is life after they have died, and you are never ever the same."

Friend John Mahoney said, "Everyone here wants justice, and if they know what happened, they would come forth and tell whatever they knew to put this matter to rest. If anyone is withholding information, it does bother me some because it is selfish. They could be withholding something that can bring closure to this whole thing and put the Fisher family at some ease. I really hope that the horrible person who did this is caught."

Friend Tim Savage added, "It's really frustrating knowing that whoever did this hasn't been arrested, and that someone has to have information about what happened, but they haven't come forward. It's hard to swallow what happened to 'Fish,' knowing that no one has been arrested for what they did. Being with all of our friends has really helped me out a lot. We're always thinking about Mark, and we still miss him. Our friends have really rallied together to help everyone out, and we're trying to keep Mark and his family in our thoughts and prayers. We hope that someone will come forward with details on the case."

The reward eventually grew to $100,000. Cops posted a reward poster in the lobby of Russo's building asking for information about the crime. Another was placed near the sewer opening at the corner of Turner and Stratford, where police had found Mark Fisher's discarded wallet. Other copies of the poster were put up around the neighborhood.

Much of the reward money came from Fisher's parents, a desperate attempt to coax information from the stubborn witnesses.

Mark's parents visited Ditmas Park many times during the two months after their son had died there. Sometimes they asked questions of people and sometimes they just drove around, just trying to get a feel for the *hows* and *whys* of their son's death.

Michael Fisher tried and tried to envision what had happened to Mark during his last hours and minutes of life, but no revealing vision came to him, no matter how many times he and his wife visited the Brooklyn neighborhood.

"The only thing I see in my head all the time is him lying down, facedown, dead," his father said. "It's haunting."

By December 2003, Mark Fisher's parents' impatience with the lack of answers they were getting from law enforcement turned to aggravation. They decided to take a little action on their own.

They got in touch with Meredith Flannigan, the girl Mark had followed to Brooklyn. They begged her to meet with them in person, and she agreed to do so. The meeting took place in the lobby of a New Jersey hotel.

Meri, now twenty, brought along her own mom for the meeting. Meri told Mark's parents that Mark had made quite an impression on her during the short hours that they had known one another. She also told Michael and Nancy Fisher that their son had been thinking about them during the last hours of his life.

The young girl seemed well-meaning, but she was nonetheless unhelpful. The information Meri gave the Fishers was touching, but not really revealing. They already knew that Mark was a great kid and a great son. It was what happened to him on that fateful night in Brooklyn that they wanted to find out.

The problem wasn't that Meri was afraid to talk, but rather she did not know anything. She had been asleep during the crucial hours when Mark left (or was taken out of) the house and murdered. The Fishers wanted more, but Meri had said all she was going to say.

Like the Fishers, police were not completely certain of Meri's sincerity. She had agreed to be interviewed by the police only with a lawyer present. Although it was not unusual for kids whose parents had money to bring a lawyer with them to a police interview, it was uncommon when the young people in question were merely possible witnesses to a crime and not suspects.

Although police repeatedly stated to the public that the witnesses in the Fisher murder case had been uncooperative, not one of the witnesses had admitted to giving law enforcement anything less than full cooperation.

"I've been completely cooperative," Meredith said, for example, when asked by a *New York Times* reporter. She was on the phone with the reporter, talking from her New England sorority house when she said, "I have done all I can."

CHAPTER 12

First Crack in the Wall

By February 2004, police were getting aggravated as well over the lack of progress in the case. The *New York Post* reported that the key witnesses in the case seemed to be Giuca, his younger half brother and Russo. They were, as far as police could tell, the last to see Mark Fisher alive—and they weren't talking.

The *Daily News* published the list of young people who, as far as police knew, accounted for everyone who was at the Giuca party during the early morning that Fisher was killed.

The paper also reported that police had an informant who was pointing his finger at Antonio "Tony" Russo, the guy with the street name of Tweed. Russo was, according to the *News*, "the man [police] believe may have pulled the trigger."

The informant was a teenager named Gregg Cunningham (pseudonym), who was awaiting sentencing for an unrelated shooting. Cunningham was Russo's childhood friend and former neighbor. He was also looking to make friends with law enforcement to hopefully get himself a more lenient sentence. He'd told cops that he had seen Russo near the murder scene shortly after Fisher was killed.

Regarding the informant's information, a key police investigator said, "Everything we have points to Russo. He changed his appearance the day of the murder. He went to California for a while. He gets arrested for menacing someone with a gun. We believe he's the guy."

The investigator said there was disagreement among the ranks as to why Fisher was killed. "We don't have a solid motive," he said. "They could have planned to rob him, thinking he was some really rich kid from Jersey, or it could be just a thrill kill, a spur-of-the-moment thing."

Law enforcement sources said that it appeared that Fisher, wrapped in a yellow blanket that had come from John Giuca's home, was lured into a car, where he was shot three times.

The source added that Fisher was either pushed or fell out of the vehicle and was still alive when he hit the ground. There was evidence that he had made an attempt to crawl, but he hadn't gotten very far.

One investigator working on the case said, "The shooter jumped out of the car and pumped two more bullets into his back, killing him. We only found two pieces of ballistics (from a .22-caliber handgun)."

Russo himself was approached outside his apartment building by a reporter asking about Cunningham's statements.

"I didn't do nothing. Get away from me" was Russo's only comment.

Russo's mother, Evelyn Jennings, was also asked for a comment by the press.

"My baby didn't do this. He's no killer," Jennings said.

"I know who did this. It wasn't my son." She did not elaborate on who she thought was the actual murderer.

Police said publicly that they thought at least three people witnessed the shooting, and that those three people were John Giuca, Antonio Russo and a third male whom they would not identify. On February 13, the *New York Post* reported that the third male was Giuca's half brother.

The *Post* reported that an anonymous police source specified that Giuca and his half brother, whom they still were not naming by name, "held the key" to the case. However, it was reported, they were "stonewalling" the detectives investigating the case. The *Post* had checked property records to verify that the home where Mark Fisher's last party took place was owned by Giuca's mom, Doreen Federicci.

On February 4, police held a press conference right on Stratford Road, only a few yards away from the home where the victim attended his final party. The blinds were closed tight at the house, and when reporters knocked on the door, no one answered.

Fisher's parents spoke at the press conference. They aimed their comments squarely at the eyewitnesses who wouldn't share what they knew.

"I don't understand how people can keep their kids quiet and hide behind lawyers," said Michael Fisher. "The only thing I know is that my son Mark died after coming to this house. You don't shoot someone with five bullets at the spur of the moment. Someone wanted him dead."

To the members of the press, police said that they were there to drum up new leads and to send a strong message to those who were not cooperating with the investigation.

Michael Fisher named Meredith Flannigan and John Giuca as two individuals who knew more than they were saying—who had been in the cab with Mark from Manhattan to Brooklyn, and who were still at the party when their son left.

Michael Fisher said, "It's taken away half my life that he's gone. I'll never be the same without him. My family will never be the same."

He then pleaded to the parents of the eyewitnesses: "From what I've been told [by police], it's been very difficult getting people to talk about Mark's murder. If it was my kids, I'd tell them to tell the truth and cooperate."

Also at the press conference was a friend of Mark's, Christopher Deneen, who said, "It's not fair to the Fishers and Mark's friends that certain people are withholding information. If you're withholding information, wise up. Think about your old friend Mark."

Speaking to DiGiovanni, but without using her name, Michael Fisher said, "Mark was part of your Fairfield family. Whoever you are, you should be more than willing to try and help and reach out."

By this time police were willing to state publicly that they believed Fisher had been taken from the party in a white SUV, that he'd been shot three times in the SUV and had been subsequently dumped on Argyle Road inside the yellow blanket, at which time he'd been shot twice more. Police said they thought Fisher's wallet had been dropped in the gutter away from the body so that Fisher would not be quickly identified. They no longer believed that robbery was the motive, they said, although they admitted that they were not certain what the motive was.

"The motive is completely unknown," said Inspector Raymond Ferrari, commander of Brooklyn South Detectives. "The crime is completely senseless."

In response to the Fisher's Ditmas Park press conference, the *Daily News* printed an editorial on February 6. It called the witnesses in the case who were not cooperating with police "beyond pathetic.

"You don't throw away a human being like trash," the article read. "Or maybe you do, if you're part of a certain Brooklyn party scene."

The paper said that Fisher had been tossed out of an SUV and tossed into the gutter "like so much garbage." The real garbage, the editorial said, were the "sorry excuses" the witnesses were using for their continued silence.

"Pass the clothespins, please," the editorial concluded. "The stench is intolerable."

CHAPTER 13

Angel's
Cry of Innocence

The New York/Long Island newspaper *Newsday* printed the names, as they believed them to be, of those who were "not fully cooperating" with the investigation. On that list were the names Al Huggins and Angel DiGiovanni, the girl who had introduced Mark and Meri at Ships' Harbour. Angel immediately protested loudly and often that her name did not belong on that list.

Angel's dad, attorney James DiGiovanni, told the *Daily News* that his daughter was cooperating with law enforcement "one hundred and fifty percent." She didn't know anything, however, so there was nothing for her to say.

Angel told the *Fairfield Mirror* that her whole family was refuting that report, that she'd been questioned twice and had told police her entire story.

Replying to Angel's cry of innocence, Michael Fisher rebutted, "Mark went to Brooklyn with Angel DiGiovanni, that's all I know. The only reason he went to that party is because he knew Angel; they were her friends. He didn't know anybody in Brooklyn. And Mark went with Al Huggins and they found Mark's body on Argyle Road. That house is across the street from where Al Huggins lives."

Continuing the dialogue via reporter, Angel took on the notion that she had been friends with the people who attended John Giuca's party. She replied to the latest statement from the victim's father with, "That is not true. The only person I knew was Al Huggins."

Reporters found Huggins's mom as she was walking her dog outside her home. She also took issue with reports that her son was stonewalling the investigation.

"My son has been as cooperative as possible," she said. "He has told all he knows. My heart goes out to those parents."

Angel said that after they all arrived at Giuca's house, she left with her friend Al. At that time Mark and Meri were still at the party.

"I called Meri in the morning (after the murder)," Angel said, "and she said that Mark went home all right. I expected to see him back in Fairfield the next day."

Angel added that, although she strongly refuted the things Michael Fisher was saying about her, she had great sympathy for Mark's dad.

"I can't imagine losing a son and not having any answers," Angel said. "The last time I saw Mark, he was safe in a house with one of my girlfriends who he wanted to be with. Mark was one of my friends also. A lot of people forget about that."

CHAPTER 14

The Elite
Investigative Team

During May 2004, Brooklyn district attorney Charles Hynes and New York police commissioner Raymond Kelly put together an elite investigative team to work the Fisher case twenty-four hours a day. Members of the team were Detectives Thomas Byrnes, James McCafferty and Steven Grafakos, from the NYPD; Michael Vecchione, chief of the District Attorney's Rackets Bureau; his deputy, Patricia "Trish" McNeill; Anna-Sigga Nicolazzi, senior trial attorney from the Homicide Bureau; and Josh Hanshaft, senior trial attorney from the Rackets Division. Nicolazzi's boss was Ken Taub, chief of the Homicide Bureau. Hanshaft and McNeill reported to Michael Vecchione, chief of the Rackets Division.

McNeill was in her midthirties, a single redhead from Long Island. She had a bachelor's degree in poli-sci and sociology from Hofstra University, a school built on the runways of old Mitchell Field between Hempstead and Uniondale on Long Island. In 1994, she received her law degree from Brooklyn College, the campus of which was located only eight avenue blocks south of where Mark Fisher lost his life.

There are many parts of the country where police do the investigations and the district attorney's office prosecutes the accused—and those roles seldom overlap. But that was not the case in Brooklyn. Befitting her new assignment, Trish McNeill was an investigative prosecutor. She was an assistant district attorney who also investigated the crimes she was to prosecute, much like the ADAs on the television drama *Law & Order.*

Trish was second-generation law enforcement. Her father, Al McNeill, headed the federal government's Witness Security Program (WITSEC) under Howard Safir and later served as Safir's deputy commissioner of administration when Safir was the NYPD's police commissioner.

For as long as she could remember, McNeill wanted to be a prosecutor.

"I grew up in a law enforcement environment, so I knew it was exciting and fulfilling work, especially doing Mob cases," McNeill said in a later interview for this book.

There may be some ADAs who would find the role of investigative prosecutor doubly stressful, but not McNeill. "I find it very rewarding to take a case and build it. Merging the two worlds together is the best aspect of the job. Few people have both. We're very lucky, but many people in New York don't stay as long as we do (as relatively low-paid prosecutors). We build very strong cases, because we are with it every step of the way.

"The work is very time-consuming. It might take one full day just to get bank records and fill out subpoenas. So much research goes into everything we do before you can even write subpoenas or warrants."

McNeill interned with former U.S. attorney Charles

Rose, a man upon whom Anthony "Gaspipe" Casso once put a contract during a big money-laundering case. She sat at Rose's trial table. Her first murder case was a federal Eastern District of New York case against a mobster named Joey Flowers. She didn't prosecute, but was involved in the investigatory aspect.

Josh Hanshaft looked like he came from Central Casting. Forty years old, he was movie-star handsome with a thick crop of jet-black hair. He was born and raised in Staten Island, New York, the oft-forgotten borough of New York City, just across the Verrazano-Narrows Bridge from Brooklyn.

Hanshaft traveled across the state of New York to go to college, graduating from the State University at Buffalo with a business degree. He received his law degree from City University. He started out as a Bronx assistant district attorney in 1993, but then took a job working for a Connecticut judge. But prosecuting cases was his first love. He got back to that during January 1996 when he took the job in the Brooklyn DA's Office. Josh has been prosecuting homicides in the trial division ever since. He has also indicted many homicides, as well as conspiracies and attempted murders.

How much did Josh love prosecuting murderers in Brooklyn? Well, a lot, but he conceded that there were plenty of jobs with less stress—maybe all of them.

"There is a high burnout factor," Hanshaft said. "For three weeks at a time, you have no life and a lot of stress. You can do six trials in one year. There's so much preparation involved before the trial even begins. Most people don't last more than five years. Doing trials is consuming pressure."

Still, there isn't anything he'd rather be doing. He just wished he could be doing it for more money.

"I'm happy with my job," Hanshaft said, "but might get to the point where I have to make money."

Six months had passed since Mark Fisher's murder, and the NYPD investigation hadn't learned much new since the initial forty-eight hours. It wasn't the detectives' fault.

According to Trish McNeill: "The detectives did outstanding work, but were stonewalled every step of the way."

The detectives had run into the same stone walls too many times. The case was given to McNeill, Hanshaft and Nicolazzi to get a fresh perspective. They decided to look at it as if no one had ever looked at it before.

They immediately broke the players into three groups: 1) the Garden City Girls, 2) the Ghetto Mafia and 3) the Fairfield University group.

"Their three worlds came together and collided that night," said McNeill. "The Garden City Girls came back from college for Columbus Day weekend, the Ghetto Mafia was hanging out in the city and the Fairfield students were home from college. Certain members of the group knew each other, and as the night progressed, it became a question of who ended up with who."

Without input from all of the players in that night's activities, the three prosecutors could only come up with a best-guess theory of who was where and when. By their tally there were somewhere between eight and ten people at John Giuca's party. By the time Fisher was killed, that number was down to four, and one of those was Meri Flannigan, who was probably asleep on the couch.

One witness told investigators that the Ghetto Mafia was an offshoot of the gang known as the Crips. Trish McNeill described the Ghetto Mafia as "a mixture of everyone and anyone."

The prosecutors were told that members of the Ghetto Mafia had to go through an induction ceremony, which involved fighting with other members of the gang, or with members of a rival gang.

Like any secret society, they had fashion statements (in this case, special beads) and secret handshakes in common, little things that separated with a distinct line those who belonged to the gang from those who did not. Witnesses said that Giuca was one of the leaders of the Ghetto Mafia and that Antonio Russo was more of a follower.

During the first half of 2004, the investigators' big question remained, how to deal with the wall of silence that had been built up around those suspected by the investigators of killing Mark Fisher.

"There was not a lot of physical evidence," Trish McNeill later said. "Most of the kids from the Ghetto Mafia knew what went on. The others were not so informed. The friendship (of the Ghetto Mafia) gave strength to a very limited group. Every group cooperated with the exception of the Ghetto Mafia. They had the most reason not to."

The investigative team went back and reinterviewed a lot of the witnesses. They used psychological techniques to get one witness to turn on another witness. Each new piece of information that was learned was worked into the questions for another witness, until no one knew just how much the investigators knew, and who was and wasn't spilling their guts.

Thousands of hours of hard police work went into making the case. Cops sorted through boxes of telephone records. The idea was to monitor the phone conversations of that night's partygoers, to see who was talking to whom. It was an investigative technique often used in organized-crime cases, where witnesses tend to be less than forthcoming with authorities.

They learned that Russo and Giuca had called each other dozens of times in the hours and days following the murder, just as you would expect from two guys who were trying to get their stories straight.

More than one hundred potential witnesses were interviewed. That included both people who had seen Fisher at the Brooklyn house party and those who had observed his actions in the Upper East Side bar earlier that night. Among the witnesses who were reinterviewed were the several neighbors who called 911 after hearing gunshots and seeing Mark Fisher's body by the side of the road.

The girlfriends of Giuca and Russo—Lauren Conigliaro and Crystal Guerrero (pseudonyms)—were interviewed repeatedly. Though they were very different women, and investigators used very different techniques when interrogating them, both showed signs of being helpful.

During May 2004, Fairfield University was once again traumatized by an untimely death. The valedictorian of the senior class, Francis "Frank" J. Marx V, who had already written his valedictorian address, had been killed.

And his death had been violent. Frank, as he was known, was killed when he was run over by a bus during a confrontation with other students in Newport, Rhode Island. There had been a crowded corner, some pushing and shoving, and Frank had fallen beneath the wheels of the bus.

The second tragedy rekindled memories of Mark Fisher, that he was murdered, and that the murder had not been solved. And so, during the last days of the Fairfield school year, the tight-knit campus community began a second cycle of mourning.

CHAPTER 15

Giuca Arrested in Florida

Giuca spent the summer of 2004 in Palm Harbor, Florida—a small town in the Tampa Bay area, where his folks had bought a condo. With him were his brother, Matt, and his friends Scott Powers and Jennifer Baker. Powers was one of Giuca's best friends since they were kids. They grew up only one block from each other. Jennifer, a raven-haired beauty if there ever was one, had been Scott's girlfriend for about a year. She lived with her parents and one sister in the Windsor Terrace section of Brooklyn, which was between Ditmas Park and Park Slope, very close to Bishop Ford High School.

Palm Harbor was a quaint village overlooking the Gulf of Mexico, with an Old Palm Harbor section that dated back to the 19th century with streets wide enough for pedestrians and horse-drawn carriages, but only barely for automobiles. Old yet young, Palm Harbor was a college town, as well as a rural center with strong ties to the citrus industry. As in Ditmas Park, there was an abundance of trees—and tree-lined streets. The area in which Palm Harbor had been built had long been known as Sutherland, the vernacular form of Southern Land Development Company, which planned the community in 1888.

Getting away from Brooklyn had been a relief for Giuca, Powers later recalled. In Brooklyn, cops were jumping out of the woodwork to accost Giuca on a regular basis.

"I was with John at least twenty times when cops would run up on us and search me, give me a pat down, for two seconds. John—they'd make him take off his shirt, open his belt, shoes, everything."

In Florida, Giuca had hoped to find a little peace—but it was not to be.

Although the young people had been enjoying the relative quiet of the Florida summer, Giuca never totally forgot that he was a kid in trouble.

Jennifer Baker later recalled, "The whole trip he'd say, 'I'm just waiting for them to pop out of the palm trees.' Every time we were sitting somewhere, he'd curse or say something stupid and say, 'Oops, they're listening.'"

Back in Brooklyn, police had decided to make a move on Giuca. They had always found it compelling that one of the last people to see Mark Fisher alive, before Mark Fisher was shot with a pistol, was a suspect in the firing of a handgun only a few weeks before.

Very compelling. It was unknown if it was the same gun, but it was the same guy—John Giuca. And both crimes had occurred just before dawn, when only a handful of people are up and about—even fewer in a shooting mood.

Giuca's rap sheet wasn't impressive. He got caught

jumping a turnstile once (that is, entering the subway without paying the fare), and was accused of stealing a CD in school, when he was a teenager. Not exactly "Most Wanted" material.

But the shooting incident was something else. Here's a kid who was suspected of having a gun in his hand, in the city, and to have discharged it. Luckily for the cops, even in Brooklyn, even among young men, that kind of behavior wasn't common.

Compelling, yes, but for a time there wasn't much the NYPD could do about it. The young men at whom Giuca had allegedly shot wouldn't talk. That is, not until now. Suddenly one of those men had come forward and had identified Giuca as the man who'd shot at them.

Police had a reason to pick him up and arrest him and hold him long enough to have a long chat with him, hopefully a long enough chat to get him gabbing about the murder of Mark Fisher.

If he was subsequently arrested for the Fisher case, the additional charge would encourage a judge to refuse bail or to make the bail prohibitively high, because Giuca was considered a high-profile bail risk. Give him half a chance, police believed, and Giuca would flee.

The only complication was that Giuca was down in Florida, so an expedition of NYPD officers was sent down to pick up Giuca and bring him back to Brooklyn.

Giuca was arrested in Palm Harbor on Monday, July 5, 2004. It was a hot sunny day. Giuca was walking with his brother, Powers and Baker to a convenience store. They couldn't use Giuca's mom's car because she was asleep.

Jennifer Baker later said: "We hadn't seen a soul outside on the whole trip because it was so hot. That morning all these people were out on lawn chairs to see what was going on. Suddenly I see cars swerving and guys with guns out. I said, 'Oh, my God.'"

Scott Powers believed that the arrest was far more dramatic than it needed to be. The police, he opined, were clearly trying to get maximum media attention. And they did get media attention, even if most of it was inaccurate. For some reason the Florida newspapers got the idea that Giuca was being arrested for a shooting in a Florida nightclub.

Powers and Baker may have been startled, but Giuca seemed to take it in stride.

"He was totally normal. He knew it was going to happen," Baker recalled.

Scott Powers, on the other hand, was taken by surprise. "I didn't think they'd be down there in Florida," he said. "They had us on the ground in the grass. Passersby were looking at us. The police said they'd been watching us for three days."

Giuca was immediately brought back to Brooklyn for arraignment.

The arrest was news enough to make the New York papers. Police in New York verified for reporters that the John Giuca who had been arrested in Florida was the same man who was "a possible witness" in the murder of Mark Fisher.

Giuca was charged with attempted assault, weapons possession, menacing and reckless endangerment stemming from the 2003 dispute. His lawyer, Lance Lazzaro, said that the police spoke to Giuca shortly after the shooting, and that he was released. Lazzaro declined to comment on the nature of the charges.

Lieutenant Robert Casazza, of the Brooklyn South Homicide Task Force, explained that no charges had been filed against Giuca at the time of the Greenwood Heights shooting because, having responded to a 911 call, the first policemen on the scene had found all of the participants in the shooting to have left the scene. Police said that the men who had been fired upon had recently come forward and made a complaint against Giuca, which was why NYPD officers traveled to Florida to pick him up.

The official story was, although it was interesting to the police that Giuca was also a potential witness in an unsolved murder in Ditmas Park, that was just a bonus as far as they were concerned. It had nothing to do with the official reason for the timing of Giuca's arrest down in Florida.

On July 7, a senior law enforcement official who did not wish to be named admitted to a reporter from the *New York Times* that investigators hoped the new arrest would advance the eight-month-old Fisher investigation.

Giuca and his friends, however, had no trouble seeing through the police's scheme. According to Giuca's good friend James Petrillo, "At the time the Greenwood Heights shooting happened, the police didn't deem it important at all. He didn't get arrested. Once the papers came about Fisher, they said he was arrested before for shooting a gun and that John was nothing but trouble. After Mark Fisher the police said they found a witness on Twenty-third Street who said they saw him firing a gun at a car, blah, blah, blah."

On June 23, 2004, Al Huggins's attorney arranged for his client to take a lie detector test. According to the examiner, the polygraph examination was given for the "purpose of determining the truthfulness of the answers to the following questions."

The examiner noted that the subject—that is, Huggins—had signed statements "releasing all parties concerned and empowering this examiner to disclose to those in authority his opinions, as well as information elicited during said test."

The lie detector to be used was a "four-pen Lafayette Polygraph," which registered changes in the subject's blood-pressure rate and strength of pulse-beat, galvanic skin response, and the respiratory pattern. The stated purpose of the examination was to determine if Huggins's statements regarding the murder were truthful.

Huggins was hooked up to the machine and told to relax. He took a deep breath. The examiner then began to ask questions, getting the subject adjusted to the pace of the questioning. The only questions that were transcribed were those pertinent to the case.

"Regarding the murder of Mark Fisher, do you intend to answer truthfully each question about that?"

"Yes."

"Do you know who murdered Mark Fisher?"

"No."

"Do you know any information about Mark Fisher's murder that you are holding back from the police?"

"No."

According to the examiner, who studied the test results, "no deception was indicated in the subject's recorded responses."

This exam would later strike the friends of John Giuca as significant, taking into consideration the fact that Huggins would one day be a witness at Giuca's murder trial—a witness for the prosecution.

CHAPTER 16

Anniversary
of the Killing

In October 2004, the tristate area newspapers ran one of the saddest forms of feature, the anniversary-of-the-tragedy piece, in this case the first anniversary of Mark Fisher's death.

Steven M. Andrews, of the *Fairfield Mirror*, said that the police had a "mounting pile of evidence and short list of suspects." Andrews also noted, "Authorities believe some of the people at the house not only know what happened, but are withholding critical information."

William K. Rashbaum and Ann Farmer also wrote a piece in the *New York Times* noting the sad anniversary, saying that the murder of Mark Fisher had developed into "something of an enigma" for the NYPD.

The *Times* noted that the closed mouths of witnesses had "stymied" the homicide investigation. The paper characterized those witnesses as "young people who have refused to tell what they know about the killing." The presumption that they knew something was clear. Why else the silence?

There were reasons for hope. Police Commissioner Kelly had recently cited progress in the case—implying movement, if not genuine momentum, toward solving the crime. Things, at the very least, were not at a standstill.

"We believe that the people who have information about this case got together early on and had a pact, you might say, where information was simply not going to come forward," Commissioner Kelly said. "They were very careful in speaking about it to others. But we're hopeful now—as I say, there have been some developments—we're hopeful now that we'll see some progress in that case."

Kelly refused to be more specific and instead changed the subject to his department's security preparations for Ramadan.

Plus, it was publicly revealed for the first time that a Brooklyn grand jury was hearing evidence in the Mark Fisher case. Several police officials were asked if an indictment was imminent, and all said no.

As always, no one from the NYPD would name a suspect in the case, but now routinely pointed out that the host of Fisher's last party, John Giuca, was someone they thought could provide key information.

On the anniversary, for the umpteenth time, Fisher's mother was asked her feelings and she complained about the state of limbo she and her husband felt trapped in.

"We have no results," she said. "We're hoping that soon we'll hear something. We just want closure." Regarding the wall of silence, she added, "I believe time will tell what happened. I don't know if they can go their whole lives without telling. How could they protect a criminal?"

And about the police, she said, "They're working very hard on the case right now. They have three detectives working full-time. I would give anything to find out what happened that night. The reward is up to one hundred thousand dollars, but we don't know if money will make someone talk. We just want to prove a point. If everyone you were with is a stranger, and you don't come forward, it's one thing, the people involved know more than they are sharing. I don't know who is really holding all the cards in this case. I don't think they will just volunteer this information. The only people who I think are holding back information are those with lawyers."

Mrs. Fisher said that she and her husband were planning to hold a memorial service right on the spot where their son's body had been discovered one year before.

Giuca's mother, Doreen Federicci, told the press that she believed her son to be completely innocent. In fact, she thought police were treating him unfairly—harassing him. The media was doing it, too.

Mrs. Federicci said the pressures of the investigation had forced her son to quit attending classes at John Jay College. He was only a few credits shy of his associate's degree.

John had always been a kid with a lot of anxiety, but now it was worse than ever. He was seeing a therapist. And it wasn't just John, either. It was the whole family. Everyone was affected.

They felt like they were under a microscope, hunted like that guy in *Les Misérables*. It was impossible to stay in Ditmas Park. The family had to move.

A police spokesman was subsequently notified of Federicci's charges of harassment and categorically denied that there was any truth to them.

As promised by the Fishers, a memorial service was held on Argyle Road. To show their support for the victim, Ditmas Park residents, some of whom had been among the first to report Mark Fisher's shooting, helped out with the memorial service.

One neighbor laid bouquets of white lilies at the curb where Mark Fisher was dumped. Another neighbor brought red roses to place at the spot. Fisher's family— his mom, dad, brother, sister and others—brought many baskets of flowers on their own.

They'd had program notes printed up and these were handed out to those who attended the service. Family members took turns speaking to the gathering. Some discussed Mark's promising future, the huge part of his life that would never be realized. Others spoke of Mark's killers, and how their desire was very strong to see that justice was served.

Mark's aunt, Ruby Bonanno, said, "The family is not seeking revenge. We pray for those who know how it happened. We pray they receive and accept the strength to overcome their fear to tell the truth."

Mark's father was emotional throughout the service, and when it was his turn to speak to the gathering, he sent out a message to the police. He did not want the investigation into his son's murder to be focused too narrowly.

"I just hope that the police and everyone are looking in the right direction," he said, "And not just at one or two persons. Because there were a lot of people there that night."

That same month, one year after Fisher's murder, Giuca was arrested for a second time, this time on drug charges. He was wearing a bulletproof vest at the time of his arrest. Police asked him to explain the garment and he said it was to protect him from "terrorists."

CHAPTER 17

The Case
Against Tweed

The Brooklyn grand jury was making progress. They were utilizing what prosecutors called "evasive contempt proceedings." These types of proceedings were used infrequently, only when it was necessary to get a group of otherwise silent people to open up and tell the truth.

The witnesses who wouldn't talk were subpoenaed and questioned under oath. Some were granted limited immunity, but they were not made exempt from perjury or contempt charges if they lied or tried to avoid questions.

The case against Russo was developing more quickly than the one against Giuca. After more than a year of maintaining their uncooperative behavior with authorities, Russo's friends finally broke their wall of silence. Witnesses now said that there had been a lot of drugs and alcohol at the party. Fisher wound up going with Russo to an ATM.

First one witness talked, then another; then an avalanche of information came. The most damaging testimony given for the grand jury came from Crystal Guerrero, Russo's ex-girlfriend, with whom he'd had a baby. She said that Russo repeatedly admitted to her that he had been the one to shoot Mark Fisher. Those admissions had come during the days following the murder.

Then came the fact that Russo had made a somewhat desperate attempt to change his appearance only minutes after Fisher was shot. The braids that Russo had been so proud of were lying on the floor of a friend's apartment, even while police were still processing the crime scene a couple blocks away. Soon after dawn on a Sunday morning was not a typical time to get a haircut.

Phone records showed that there had been a flurry of calls between Russo and Giuca during the hours and days following the murder, and there was the fact that he'd changed his story during his long, long interrogation.

Plus, there was the matter of flight. According to Commissioner Kelly, Russo only returned to Brooklyn because he could not find a "permanent residence" in California.

The grand jury decided it was enough.

During late November 2004, the grand jury indicted Antonio Russo for the murder of Mark Fisher. There was no indictment passed down for John Giuca at that time, but the grand jury remained impaneled and testimony continued to be heard.

CHAPTER 18

"*Tranquilo*"

On Tuesday, November 23, 2004, at 7:00 A.M., thirteen months after the murder, police began to gather around the apartment building on Turner Place. It was quite a production.

When a dangerous suspect is wanted for murder, you don't just casually knock on his door and ask if he is home. There was a cop stationed in the hallway outside Russo's apartment, between the door to his fifth-floor apartment and the elevator.

There were five more cops in the stairwell, in case he went out the window and exited via the fire escape, as they already knew he was prone to do. Another detective was posted on the roof. Two uniformed cops were stationed in the yard behind the apartment building with their eyes on Russo's apartment windows and the fire escapes.

They knew Russo was home. When he came out of the apartment he shared with his mom, they'd nab him.

A policeman knocked on the door and told Russo's

grandmother that Antonio had been indicted and the police were there to get him, so she called Russo's lawyer, Neil S. Ruskin, and asked if it was true.

Ruskin called the grandmother back and confirmed that it was true. She asked what she should do. She had tried to warn Antonio, but he was sleeping.

"Wake him up and tell him to get dressed and get ready to surrender," Ruskin said.

Once it happened, it happened in the blink of an eye. Russo stepped out of the apartment door and into the hallway. Police were on him instantly. Before he could utter a protest, his hands were cuffed securely behind his back. He was taken directly into the elevator, then through the lobby, where the poster still hung showing Mark Fisher's face and the bold-lettered offer for a $100,000 reward. Russo was marched out of the building, and into a waiting unmarked car.

One cop described Russo as trying to act like "Joe Toughguy" during his apprehension. Another characterized the suspect's demeanor as "stoic."

A neighbor who witnessed Russo being led from the building said he looked "*tranquilo*," Spanish for "calm" and "untroubled."

Reportedly, Russo's only words during his arrest were: "What do you want? What am I arrested for?"

The arrest went so smoothly that the woman who lived in the next apartment didn't know that anything had occurred at all until later in the day when a reporter knocked on her door.

The neighbor, thirty-three-year-old Linda Brown, said, "I knew him since his mother was pregnant. I remember Anthony as a tyke, coming to a Halloween party dressed as Superman. We have pictures and videos of him in his tight pants.

"I worked in a hospital and used to get free condoms,

which I gave to the young people in the building. When Anthony was thirteen, he was cute and becoming good-looking, and he came to me for condoms. Girls liked him.

"Sure he was at that party. Sure he knows what happened. But I don't think he killed him."

Brown said that Russo's buddies liked to go nightclubbing in Manhattan and spend money, but Anthony didn't do that. He had to save his money. He had a lot of girlfriends and that cost money.

Brown might not have noticed, or maybe chose not to mention, that Russo's friends probably had more money than he did in general. They lived in nice houses and had parents that made a lot of money. Russo lived in an apartment and did not have responsible parents. He had a job at KFC.

It didn't matter how many girlfriends Russo had or didn't have. He probably could not have gone nightclubbing with his more well-to-do buddies anyway.

She said that she once asked Russo about the Fisher murder and he said to her, "Don't even worry about that because you know I didn't do that."

She recalled a time when she was on her way to the store and she saw Russo was being followed by policemen. He pointed his tail out to her. She told him, "I can't believe this is going on."

"Man, Babylon is everywhere," he said, a Rastafarian-like comment that went with his formerly braided hair, if not his European heritage. "Babylon" translates loosely as "The Man," or, in this case, the police.

Brown asked Russo, "Why are they following you all over the place?" But he did not answer.

Brown said that she last saw Russo at 7:30 P.M. on the Monday before his arrest when he'd knocked on her door to bum a cigarette. He seemed unconcerned.

Ten minutes later, Brown heard police radios in the

hallway and she assumed that Russo's mom must have called the cops on him over a minor matter or something like that.

Brown left the building and ran into Russo outside, who was approaching with a girl. Brown said, "Don't come back to the building, because they're in there looking for you."

Without saying a word, Russo steered his girlfriend into an about-face and headed away from the building. As it turned out, the police were back the following morning, but this time they had their radios turned off so as not to attract attention.

Working with a new stealthiness, this time the police successfully caught Russo unaware. They'd caught Linda Brown unaware, too. She'd been watching a TV movie at the time and missed the whole thing.

In the middle of the afternoon after Russo's arrest, Paul, Russo's little brother, came home from school and asked Brown why all the newspeople were around.

"He thought maybe they had won the lottery or something," Brown recalled.

Brown told Paul that his brother had been arrested. He wanted to know when and she told him late morning. With that, Paul disappeared into his apartment next door. Brown heard the grandmother arrive at the apartment soon thereafter. After that, she heard shouting for a while. Then it was quiet.

On the night of Russo's arrest, Mark Fisher's parents said that the news gave them little comfort.

"It gets worse every day," said Mark's dad, Michael Fisher. "Our family is hurting a lot. The only thing that makes us feel good is that Mr. Hynes (the DA) said more arrests will follow."

"It's been sad and painful. It feels like a hundred years have passed already," said Nancy Fisher. "We miss Mark."

Police Commissioner Raymond Kelly announced after the arrest: "The wall of silence surrounding the murder of Mark Fisher has finally been breached. But this case is not closed."

Kelly refused to reveal the investigatory strategy or the sequence of events that led to the grand jury's indictment of Russo. He said, "There are other aspects of this homicide that are still under investigation, and for that reason, we can't give you all the details about how the silence was broken or how our detectives put the pieces of the puzzle together."

"People do strange things for money," said Brooklyn DA Charles Hynes. "Twenty dollars doesn't seem like a hell of a lot, but that's the thing that set it off."

Cops said that there was a possibility of further arrests. An anonymous source inside the police department told the *Daily News* that he believed Giuca and possibly others witnessed the killing.

Someone asked what would become of the $100,000 reward and police said it would probably go uncollected.

The next day the tabloids were full of opinions about the case. There was: "Thank goodness, Babylon (meaning 'police' in Russo-speak) is not easily deterred." And, "Now that the (alleged) triggerman is in custody, perhaps the wall of silence will crumble. If only because Russo's comrades in silence will now want to save their own sorry butts."

CHAPTER 19

"Evelyn"

Russo's arraignment hearing was held November 24, 2004, the day after his arrest. Russo had a quick meeting outside the courtroom with attorney Neil S. Ruskin, his grandmother and several reporters.

Russo was asked by a reporter about the word "Evelyn" that was tattooed on the left side of his neck. Russo said that that was his mother's name.

He had not changed his clothes since his arrest, but his belt had been taken from him, and his hands were cuffed securely behind his back. He had to hook a finger through a belt loop to keep his baggy trousers from falling down.

Ruskin and Russo entered the courtroom together, and once they had taken their position before Judge John P. Walsh at the front of the courtroom, they had a brief conversation. Ruskin, at that point, picked up his briefcase and left.

Mark Fisher's mother and father sat in the back row

of the courtroom, as close to the exit as they could get. Finally, after a brief delay, defense attorney Jonathan Fink said he would stand up for the defendant and take Ruskin's place.

"I just happened to be in the courtroom when they were looking for counsel to be assigned to him," Fink later said. "Judge Walsh asked if I wanted to represent him and I said I would."

Fink became Russo's legal defense attorney as per what was known as the 18B program, an extension of the Legal Aid program, whereby defendants who can't afford legal representation are given free legal services, compliments of the taxpayer.

Jonathan Fink was a youthful thirty-eight, in great shape. Married with one child, he had offices on the twentieth floor of an Exchange Street office building in Manhattan. He was of average height and weight, maybe five-nine.

Though he was just starting to go gray, he radiated energy, enthusiasm and intelligence—a can-do attitude. He was a man of confidence. He knew he was good at what he did and that he did not have a lazy bone in his body.

Not a poser in any sense, he was just as confident addressing a jury as he was pouring his breakfast cereal.

Fink was born in New York City, but was raised upstate in Columbia County in the Berkshires, an area that borders New York State, Connecticut and Massachusetts. After earning a political science degree at the University of Pennsylvania, he got his J.D. at Brooklyn Law School and became a lawyer.

After his first year of law school, he received an internship at the Brooklyn District Attorney's Office. He began his legal career as an assistant district attorney in Brooklyn in 1992. Fink worked for the Kings County Prosecutor's Office for five years. While there, he tried numerous felony drug, robbery and homicide cases.

He was not assigned to the Homicide Bureau, but to the Green Zone, which included the following precincts: the Six-Oh (Coney Island), Six-One (Brighton Beach), Seven-Oh (Flatbush), Seven-One (Crown Heights) and Seven-Two (Sunset Park). Because of high crime in the early 1990s, Brooklyn prosecutorial areas were divided into zones.

During his time working for the Kings County DA, Fink personally tried or was the "second seat" for about five homicide cases. Some were retrials from hung juries.

In 1998, he switched sides of the fence and became a defense attorney. Because he had seen justice from both sides, he tended to understand his opposition better than many defense attorneys, who, preoccupied with the rights of their clients, cannot fathom the schematic processes of the prosecution.

He was once asked which he'd rather do in a murder case, prosecute or defend. Not answering the question, he said, "Some homicide cases can be very easy to prosecute. It all comes down to the evidence. If the evidence is there, homicide cases can be very easy to prosecute. Same thing with the defense. If the DA has the evidence, it makes it much more difficult to defend."

Russo pleaded not guilty to the second-degree murder, robbery and weapons charges. Jonathan Fink asked that bail be set for Russo, who was a local youth with family living in Brooklyn.

But the prosecution didn't think Russo's roots were sunk that deep, certainly not deep enough. Anna-Sigga

Nicolazzi argued that Russo was a flight risk, having flown to California days after the shooting.

Nicolazzi characterized Russo as a high-school dropout. She characterized the crime as a robbery gone wrong. Judge Alan D. Marrus ruled on the side of the prosecution and Russo was ordered to be held without bail. His next court appearance was scheduled for December 8.

Russo's mother, Evelyn Jennings, was in a surprisingly pleasant mood outside the courtroom following her son's arraignment on murder charges. She had a smile for reporters as she said, "My only comment is that he is innocent, and I want to thank everyone for their support."

After the hearing was over, DA Hynes said, "Detectives are still trying to determine if anyone saw Mr. Fisher being shot and whether there was a cover-up after the killing."

Fisher's mom said, "Hopefully, this is just the beginning. We hope there are more arrests to follow, we think about three or four arrests in the next week or so."

Russo's grandmother Mary Jennings, who was outside the courtroom, said, "He had no reason to rob anybody. I'm going to trust in the Lord with all my heart, and lean not to my own understanding. In all of my ways, I'm going to acknowledge Him and I know He's going to direct my path."

"Did Mr. Ruskin leave the case because of a problem paying his fee?" a reporter asked.

Russo's grandmother said that money had nothing to do with the change in Antonio's representation.

"They can't say that Antonio going to California makes him a flight risk. The police knew he was going to California before he left. It wasn't flight, it was a planned trip," she said.

"How is your grandson doing?"

"He's okay. I'm not okay," Mary Jennings replied.

Mary Jennings would stay by her grandson's side

throughout the process. According to defense attorney Jonathan Fink, there was not a single day in court over the next months when Russo did not have his grandmother nearby, lending her love and support.

Investigators had not been idle during the twenty-four hours since Russo's arrest. With Russo in custody, they had descended upon the Turner Place apartment building.

A thorough search was carried out of four locations in the building: the compactor room, the boiler room, the yard and the apartment Russo had been living in.

Publicly, Russo had denied all involvement with Fisher's death. But *Newsday* had sources "on the street" that said Russo had frequently bragged about the "hit"— that is, the murder of Mark Fisher—among his friends.

The Associated Press had a street source that said Russo had claimed the murder was over money, that Fisher had failed to hand over his wallet and the twenty dollars he had just withdrawn from an ATM, and this started the dispute that led to Fisher's death.

The *Fairfield Mirror* spoke to Fairfield University students who'd been friends of Fisher's. One friend, from the Class of 2006, said, "It was about time they made an arrest. It's good they're moving deeper into the case and that people are going to pay for what they did."

On the day after Russo's arrest, Fisher's parents allowed a *Daily News* reporter into their home in Andover. Michael Fisher said, "All we have are memories. We would like everyone who was involved to be arrested. We go through the motions and routines of life like zombies."

Nancy Fisher added, referring to Mark's two siblings, "Their life is not the same. It's not the same for anyone." About Mark, she said, "I used to say that he'll be the future president of the United States. He was a humble, simple kid, but was very bright."

"When you're a parent, your kids are what you dream about," Michael Fisher said. "I've lost a lot of hope in life."

At a court hearing on December 8, Russo arrived in court with bruises on his face. He'd been in jail for a little more than two weeks. When the judge asked what had happened to him, Russo explained that he had been beaten by a group of fellow inmates at Rikers Island.

Jonathan Fink explained to Judge Marrus that his client's life was at risk as long as he was kept in the general prison population. He also asked that Russo be granted bail.

The judge agreed and ordered Russo to be placed in protective custody. The judge said that the matter of bail would not be considered until Russo's next court appearance, scheduled for January 21.

After the hearing concluded, Russo's grandmother was asked about Russo's beat-up appearance. She told reporters that he'd been beaten by quite a crowd, as many as thirty fellow inmates.

Newspapers reporting on the court hearing were still going with robbery as the motive for Mark Fisher's murder, frequently reminding their readers that the depraved killing had been "over $20."

As 2004 drew to a close, the investigative grand jury had developed a case against John Giuca worthy of an indictment.

There had been some bad blood between Fisher and Giuca.

Some remembered that Fisher had been drunk and

had sat down on a table. Giuca said that this was disrespectful, that the chairs were for sitting in, not the tables.

Among those who spoke up now were Albert Huggins, the son of the investment banker who was a friend of Angel DiGiovanni's. Huggins, as it turned out, had legal problems of his own involving a bar fight—a fact that allowed investigators to lean on him a bit.

Huggins now said that Giuca had admitted to them after the crime that "we might have" been involved in the murder. He said that Giuca told him that he had given Russo a gun on the night of the killing and had told Russo to teach the kid (Fisher) "what's up." He said Giuca's girlfriend had helped dispose of the murder weapon.

Huggins said he talked to Giuca early on the afternoon after the murder and Giuca was worried about Meri's location. He thought she was spending the night at his house, but when he woke up, she was gone. Giuca asked Huggins if Meri was at his house. Huggins told Giuca that he didn't know where Meri was. Angel had tried to call Meri but had been unable to get in touch with her.

According to Huggins' testimony, Giuca had stressed the importance of locating Meri and that Huggins should get in touch with him as soon as he learned something. Huggins said he asked Giuca about Mark, and Giuca said Mark had left the house early in the morning and had caught a subway home on Church Avenue.

That night Giuca had again called Huggins and was now curious about the murder victim found on Huggins's block. Where exactly was the victim found? Was the victim still alive? Huggins told the grand jury that Giuca had gotten rid of his guns with the help of his girlfriend, Lauren, who had taken the gun in a plastic bag, removed it from the house and driven it away. Giuca told Huggins that if he happened to be questioned by the cops about anything, he should keep his mouth shut and just ask for his attorney. By this time Angel had gotten in touch with Meri. Meri had said that she'd left Giuca's house on Sunday morning and had caught a cab home. Giuca, for some reason, was reluctant to believe this. How could she find a cab home when she didn't even know where she was? Giuca wondered.

Also testifying was twenty-two-year-old Lauren Conigliaro, who had been Giuca's girlfriend for five years, at the time of the murder. According to John's mom, her son and Lauren were not on the best of terms at the time of the murder because Lauren had caught John cheating on her. According to Doreen Federicci, it was this wedge between her son and his girlfriend that caused Lauren to turn on John. Another theory was that Conigliaro was studying for a career in law enforcement and was afraid her future would be hindered if she was perceived as uncooperative with the Mark Fisher investigation.

Whatever the reason, when it was John's ex-girlfriend's turn to testify before the grand jury, Lauren corroborated Huggins's statements that Giuca had been talking about his involvement in the crime after the murder. She testified that Giuca had admitted to supplying the murder weapon. She said that Al Huggins lied when he said that she was the one who disposed of the murder weapon.

Doreen and Lauren were of one mind on that count. They believed Huggins was probably the one who got rid of the gun that killed Mark Fisher. Why else lie? Why else try to ditch the blame?

CHAPTER 20

The Sexy Photos

Doreen Federicci believed Lauren was telling the truth and that Albert Huggins was a lying son of a bitch. Lauren had become like family. She'd been around for years. She was always over to their house. They loved Lauren. When they went on vacation, Lauren came along.

"When Lauren and John fought, I used to stick up for her," Doreen Federicci recalled.

Why had Lauren been so angry that she had turned on John and lied when she said that he admitted having a hand in Mark Fisher's death? Several mean tricks were played on Lauren, Doreen believed.

It had to do with some photos, the stuff of blackmail, photos that John had taken of Lauren so he'd have something for under his pillow when she couldn't be by his side.

According to Doreen, during an execution of a search warrant, police discovered the erotic photos of Lauren in Giuca's closet. The police then took the photos to Lauren.

Doreen freely admitted that she already knew that the photos were in the closet. She'd found them while snooping. That was how she knew where the police had found them.

The police, Doreen claimed, told Lauren that they had gotten the photos from John's friends, that he had been passing the photos around, letting his buddies drool over Lauren as she posed for the camera in a variety of alluring poses.

In Doreen's scenario, Lauren believed the police and thought Giuca, in addition to cheating on her, was betraying their trust in yet another fashion, by allowing his friends to see images so intimate, so sexy, so naked, that they were clearly intended only for the eyes of herself and her longtime boyfriend.

She knows because Lauren came to her after the police confronted her with the erotic photos. She was crying. John was showing the dirty pictures to all the boys.

Doreen believed that it was this scheme on the part of the police that angered Lauren sufficiently for her to lie about him under oath. After Huggins implicated Lauren by saying that it was she who got rid of the gun, she had to talk, just to defend herself. After that, Doreen said, it was just a matter of getting Lauren hostile enough toward John so she would say what they wanted to hear.

Although Doreen loved Lauren for all those years that she dated her son, she did realize over time that Lauren had a knack for getting her son in trouble.

"I finally realized that she was the type of girl who would try to get John into fights with someone who was checking her ass out. She wanted him to profess his love for her," Doreen later said.

CHAPTER 21

Christmastime in the City

On Monday evening, December 20, police, some of whom had been working on the case for more than a year, surreptitiously surrounded John Giuca's house on Stratford Road. John wasn't home. He was in Manhattan—"in the city," as Brooklynites refer to Manhattan—Christmas shopping. As he walked up the walk to enter his home, he was carrying bags of things he had bought. Neither he nor the bags ever made it inside his home. Police surrounded him and cuffed him. He was placed under arrest for the murder of Mark Fisher.

In New York's war of the tabloids, the *New York Post* won this skirmish and was first to get on the newsstand with news of Giuca's arrest.

It was the third time Giuca had been arrested since Fisher's death. The first had been the arrest in Florida.

The second had been the drug bust, during which Giuca had been discovered to be wearing a bulletproof vest.

On the morning following Giuca's arrest, newspapers reported that Police Commissioner Raymond Kelly said, "The other shoe has dropped in the Mark Fisher case. While we long suspected that John Giuca abetted Antonio Russo in the murder of Mark Fisher, it was only recently that we developed enough information to arrest him last night. Based on facts uncovered in a pain-staking investigation by our detectives, we now know that Giuca provided Russo with a .22-caliber gun that was used to kill Mark Fisher. We believe that, prior to the departure of Mark Fisher from Giuca's residence, Giuca retrieved the gun from an upstairs bedroom and gave it to Russo."

It was Commissioner Kelly's theory at that point that Giuca had not been present when Mark Fisher was shot. He was being charged with supplying the murder weapon to the killer, a weapon that had never been found.

It was unknown, Kelly said, if shooting Mark Fisher was the object all along, or if the shooting had become necessary when the attempt to rob him had not gone as smoothly as Russo had hoped.

The difference between planning ahead of time to kill Mark Fisher and only shooting him in a panic was important—the difference between first- and second-degree murder.

Commissioner Kelly discussed the process by which the case had been broken, and the wall of silence investigators had to break through: "Cracks in the wall of silence finally emerged. Once put before the grand jury, witnesses realized that by keeping silent, they could deny justice in this case."

In case the reason for those witnesses' enlightenment was unclear, District Attorney Hynes drove the point home when he said, "Charges will be brought against those who did not tell all they knew about that night.

Every one of them stands to face charges of the felony of perjury or the felony of evasive contempt. We used a classic investigative technique, the power of the grand jury, to put pressure on people who thought they were going to get away with what they had done because they had lawyered up."

There were attendees of the Giuca party who still had not agreed to cooperate. The DA just wanted to make sure that those young people did not think that he had forgotten about them.

The indictment brought by the grand jury against John Giuca, once unsealed, revealed that Giuca was charged with second-degree murder, first-degree manslaughter, first- and third-degree robbery and multiple counts of criminal possession of a weapon.

Giuca was arraigned in the Brooklyn State Supreme Court on December 21, the day after his arrest. For his arraignment Giuca wore a green jacket and a plaid sweater.

His mother, Doreen Federicci, was at the courthouse alone. She was a slim and attractive forty-two-year-old blonde. As her son huddled with his lawyer, James A. Kilduff, an associate of Lance Lazzaro, in a hallway outside the courtroom, she approached rapidly and loudly. Heads turned. The approach was so aggressive that it required intervention.

Giuca's mom was stopped by security.

Federicci indignantly explained who she was and, after showing ID, was allowed to pass. She tried to embrace her son, but was thrown off-kilter when she saw that his wrists were cuffed behind his back.

"I love you," she said with quivering lips. She ended up giving him a slightly off-balance hug and a kiss just before he was led into the courtroom to be formally charged.

Her brain was racing. How was she going to be able to

get through this? she wondered. All the heartache. It piled up. And now it all flashed back on her, the pain she carried.

Even though her eyes were open and part of her brain registered the scene outside the courtroom, inside her head she was forced to endure the grimmest of all possible slide shows.

It was 1980. Her brother was stabbed to death in a street fight nearly a quarter of a century before. She was eighteen. He was twenty. They were hanging out at a bar on Fifth Avenue when it closed in the wee hours. Brother was a bodybuilder who didn't drink booze, but smoked pot. He also always drank milk. He was on the corner with a container of milk in a bag. Everyone else had a forty in a bag. A guy passed by and asked if he had a joint. Words were exchanged. The guy left and came back with more people. Her brother was stabbed in the heart. The guy who allegedly stabbed her brother, a white guy named Charley, was acquitted. The guy who handed him the knife, a Hispanic named Negron, was convicted. The guy who did the actual stabbing walked. The other guy got fifteen years for acting in concert. Doreen remembered that throughout the trial her mother felt terrible for the parents of Charley, even though she'd lost her own son. Doreen came from a large family, a lot of men, and they just wanted to strangle the guy. But her mom was so hurt that Charley's parents were suffering so much, too. They were good people. The father was a fireman. She kept saying, "Let the law take care of it." Doreen's family had a meeting—all the men in the family were there. Doreen's mom said, "I don't want any of you to say or do anything bad to the parents. They are not responsible for what their kid did." Doreen heard that a year or two later, Charley, who was from a good family in Staten Island, was found shot, stabbed and strangled outside his mom and dad's house.

Causing more pain for Doreen, her cousin and close

*friend, Jackie, was burned to death in a house fire. Her
two best girlfriends, inseparable since they were fourteen,
died of AIDS. Her mom died suddenly right in front of her
from a heart attack.*

Then came the worst of all, a slide that lingered. In
1989, she gave birth to Mallory, a daughter who was di-
agnosed with cerebral palsy when she was six months
old. Mallory only lived to be three. Her daughter died,
too young, in her arms. . . .

And now they wanted to take her eldest son. When
did the living hell end?

I can't take the pain any longer, Doreen Federicci
thought. She entered the courtroom and took her seat.

She sure hoped no one tried to make John sound like
a racist or a bigot or anything like that, because if they
did, they would be wrong. She knew John didn't have a
bigoted bone in his body. John appreciated the gorgeous
mosaic that was Brooklyn.

They lived in a mixed community. John had friends
from every ethnic group. He brought them together. He
didn't care what color or religion they were, especially if
they were down on their luck.

She remembered when a teenage John would get in
trouble with her for stealing food from the refrigerator
to serve to a homeless black man on Church Avenue. On
several occasions he also fed the homeless at a local soup
kitchen.

How could they think a young man like that could kill
someone? It was outrageous.

What was it about John that got him set up? she wondered. Her best guess was that it was her boy's thing for
guns. Loved them. It was almost like a gun fetish. That
was why she had encouraged him to become a cop.

She figured he was going to get involved with guns
one way or another, no matter what he decided to do

with his life. So if he became a cop, he would at least be dealing with guns in a positive way.

"Why would they want John?" she would later say. "This kid, maybe he had a three-eighty, maybe other kids looked up to him, but he tried to interfere with the investigation. How dare he?

"Because he wouldn't cooperate, they made him pay a very high price for it. He had a lifelong dream of being a cop. Maybe, maybe, he had an infatuation with guns. When you are a mom, you know this about your child. You keep pushing to the other side of the line, make sure you use that in a productive way. If the guy likes guns, make sure they become a detective and use it properly."

The gun fetish thing, it was mostly talk anyway. It was just part of survival in the city. One had to talk tough. A person never knew when the kid he invited into his kitchen might be a thug. A guy didn't want anyone to think they could take advantage of him.

"Anytime people would come to our house—girls, guys from other neighborhoods—to hang out, drink and smoke, John and Matthew had a plan to say they had all kinds of weapons, so more of those people would not get the idea they could rob the house. They tried to act like tough guys. Oh, yeah, we got sixteen guns upstairs, we got a machete . . . ," Doreen said. "When I heard they'd talked about their weapons at the party, I said, 'You stupid, friggin' idiots.' They might have had a party and said, 'Oh, yeah, me and my brother have guns in the house.'"

How did she know John was innocent? Easy. He proved it. When he first had told her about what had happened, no one had located Meredith Flannigan yet, Doreen recalled. John had been frantic.

He figured that Mark Fisher and Meri Flannigan had left the house together. So, he figured, if something bad had happened to Mark, then there was a chance something bad had happened to Meri, too.

That was his reaction—hardly what one would expect if he knew exactly what had happened the night before. John had acted like a kid who didn't have all the facts. Which he didn't, his mother believed.

"John was worried to death about Meri," Doreen would later recall. "He said, 'I'm afraid Russo did something to her. She fell asleep on the couch.' When John woke up in the morning, she was gone. He was afraid that crazy fuck did something to her."

And he'd felt so bad about Mark Fisher's death. No one who saw how distressed John had been could ever think he had anything to do with the murder, Doreen recalled.

He worried about Fisher's mom and dad, who had lost their child, but he was most worried of all about Fisher's siblings.

According to his mom, John would say, 'What would I do without my brother?'" referring to Matthew.

Sitting there in the courtroom, she felt like she had to go down swinging. She had to fight the system, the system that was trying to take her son's freedom away. She was a battler. She wouldn't give up. One of eight kids, Doreen was born and raised in Brooklyn. Downtown Brooklyn. That was only a few blocks from the courthouse to the west.

She was half Irish, half Native American. She'd met John Giuca's father, also named John Giuca, when she was eighteen. She had John when she was twenty-two and left John's father when she was twenty-three.

John Giuca Sr. had been damaged by the needle. His heroin addiction made the marriage impossible. Doreen left the elder John when her son was two, and young John didn't see his biological father again, until he was thirteen.

Doreen lost touch with her ex-husband as well. When later informed that the elder John had been in prison during many of those years, Doreen said that it was news to her.

"Big John," to his credit, always tried to communicate his love for his son whenever they spoke. He never held back the words "I love you."

Big John had never consciously abandoned his son. Doreen would be the first to admit that. She had separated her son from his father because her ex-husband was a druggie.

Even as a boy, young John dreamed of being a cop, and, although he didn't know the whole story, he knew that his dad was troubled. According to Doreen, this caused anxiety.

John would dwell on unlikely scenarios sometimes—like, what if he became a cop and he had to arrest his own father? What if? What if? What if? It would keep John up nights.

Three years later she was with a building contractor named Frank Federicci (pseudonym) and had a son named Matthew. Frank became a stepfather to John, and they got along pretty well—although there were the usual difficulties when John was going through adolescence.

"Frank and John bumped heads when John was fourteen, fifteen. At sixteen, they were best friends again," she recalled.

Frank Federicci was a construction developer, and there were some lean early years. Doreen called those years "very challenging financially." They passed on a big wedding and lived in an apartment until they could afford a house.

Doreen always felt that the house was lucky. It had a lucky number. The address on Stratford Road was the same as the house she'd grown up in on Huntington Street in Downtown Brooklyn.

They were poor and there were a lot of them—eight kids and a single mom—but young Doreen and her family had been lucky enough to grow up in a house.

Now her sons were just as lucky and the street number was the same. They had lived practically, and when the time had come, there was enough money to send her sons to Catholic school.

Her mom had loved the boys. John was her favorite. John could sit with his grandmother and talk about anything. Matthew would just say, "I need this and I need that."

They weren't rich, but their lives had some structure. Every night was a sit-down dinner. Six o'clock. Whatever the kids were doing—manhunt, kick the can, whatever—they had to stop and come in right away when dinner was ready.

It was good to have that kind of order in a child's life, Doreen felt.

John said something about that just the other day, he'd mentioned the sit-down meals. He missed that, the whole family sitting down and eating together, a half hour every day for everyone to be together. It wasn't much, but it was a lot.

According to Mrs. Federicci, the relationship between her sons was typical. The younger brother wanted to hang around with his older brother and his friends. Much of the time, the older brother, John, and his friends wanted nothing more than for Matthew to get lost.

"Matthew followed John all around. John had all the friends and Matthew looked up to his brother. He always tried to play with John and his friends. John would say, 'Ma, call Matthew, he can't hang out with us.' Matthew would start trouble with John's friends, hoping that John would stick up for him. He wanted so bad for John to make him number one. John wouldn't do it. John now says, 'I feel terrible about it.' I say, 'John, you were a teenager.'"

Mrs. Federicci's version of the crime was simple. Antonio Russo did it and now he was trying to lay the blame on her John. John's only crime was that he was, as she later put it, "compassionate, loyal and a little naive maybe."

She struggled with the guilt. It was really her fault. She could have prevented John from hanging around with Russo, if she had put her mind to it. She underestimated the problem.

Russo had been around for years—since the boys were little. She felt sorry for Russo. She knew that Russo was a troubled kid, and yet she had actually encouraged John to play with him.

How long had Russo been bouncing in and out of her house? Since the boys were about twelve. And she did mean *bouncing*. Russo was hyper. He couldn't stand still.

"If you were standing and talking to other kids, he'd be jumping off a car. He'd do cartwheels on someone's car," Doreen Federicci later said.

Everyone knew who John was and who Antonio was. Ask anyone. Russo started trouble and John stopped it. She later recalled, "John was no pushover, but I know for a fact that he defused fights."

She remembered the time John dragged Russo out of a bar. It had something to do with a girl, or maybe it was the time Russo tried to swipe money that had been left on the bar.

Since all of this had happened, she'd been out talking to all of John's friends, and not one of them had contradicted her. John was a peacemaker. Murder wasn't in his vocabulary. The crime had Antonio Russo written all over it.

"John was the type of guy who went over to the kid on

the corner who was left out. That's the John I know. He was a big believer in karma," Giuca's mother later said.

Mark Fisher's parents, Michael and Nancy, were there. Just as they had done for Russo's arraignment on December 8, the Fishers chose to sit in the very rear of the courtroom, close to the exit.

Giuca appeared calm as he pleaded not guilty to all charges. Speaking in an attempt to get bail set for his client, Kilduff argued that Giuca was not a flight risk. He said to Justice L. Priscilla Hall, "If John Giuca had wanted to flee, he could have fled."

Despite Kilduff's argument, Judge Hall had Giuca remanded without bail. Giuca closed his eyes while the judge spoke. The judge said that she would postpone her decision of whether to set bail until Giuca's next court appearance.

That appearance was scheduled for January 21, 2005, to coincide with a hearing already scheduled for Antonio Russo. This was customary in cases where more than one defendant was charged with the same crime. It was done to save the friends and relatives of the victim an additional trip to the courthouse.

After the arraignment ended, Giuca's mom told reporters, "The truth will set him free."

"We haven't given up," Michael Fisher said in a very low tone, implying he felt there were further arrests to come. "We feel that justice will be served."

CHAPTER 22

Arrest of
Hassan and Petrillo

In January 2005, there were two other arrests that were associated with the case. Some heavy-handed techniques, allegedly, had been used to assure that everyone who knew anything about Mark Fisher's demise kept their lips buttoned.

Two longtime friends of Giuca's were arrested for "threatening a witness." One was twenty-two-year-old Brooklyn Polytechnic Institute student Thomas Hassan—who had been in Manhattan with John Giuca at the time Giuca first encountered Mark Fisher, and was later at the party at Giuca's house. The other was twenty-one-year-old construction worker James Petrillo.

Petrillo was an old friend of Giuca's. Even though John had gone to Bishop Ford and Petrillo went to Xaverian—a jock school on Shore Road overlooking the bay—they'd met through mutual friends when they were sixteen.

Petrillo lived alone with his mother, but he had a big family—mother, sisters and aunts. Giuca used to sleep over at Petrillo's house all the time, and according to Petrillo, everyone loved Giuca like he was a part of the family.

Petrillo—a soft-spoken young man of average height but burly build—was a bit of a contradiction. Though he worked in construction, and had aspirations toward working for the city sanitation department one day, he was also a computer whiz.

Petrillo saw himself as a soldier in the cause to free John Giuca. His pursuit was sincere. He believed wholeheartedly that Antonio Russo—and Antonio Russo alone—was behind the death of Mark Fisher, and that John Giuca had nothing to do with it.

Russo was a troublemaker, Petrillo knew.

"I spent time with Russo out at bars and he always had to be the one to cause some kind of trouble for no reason," Petrillo later said. "He was always getting into a fight. He'd even start fights with people he hung out with."

Now Russo was lying to make his buddy Giuca look guilty, and maybe that was understandable because he was scared and he was looking to save his own ass. But Petrillo didn't want anyone else lying about John Giuca.

John, on the other hand, was a peacemaker. That was Petrillo's experience. Russo started trouble and Giuca smoothed it out.

Petrillo later recalled, "One time we were at a bar and I got into words with him. Antonio started with me. I really wanted to hit him. John broke it up."

Petrillo knew that John was a far more compassionate man than he was. The burly young construction worker didn't see himself as a guy who went out of his way for people. He just didn't bother.

But John was different. He was like his mom in that sense. Doreen was the mom who was always giving people rides places, doing favors for people, and John was just like her.

Petrillo knew that if it had been up to him, Russo wouldn't have been anywhere near that party that night. But Russo was John's friend, John's friend for a long time, so what was he going to do?

Hassan lived on Ocean Parkway, about eleven blocks south of the crime scene in the Kensington section of Brooklyn. Petrillo lived farther away, near the corner of Bay Ridge Avenue and Fifteenth Avenue in the Dyker Heights section.

On January 20, 2005, a grand jury voted to indict Hassan and Petrillo on charges, including intimidating a witness in the third degree, tampering with a witness in the third degree and attempting hindering prosecution in the first degree. Additionally, Petrillo was indicted on two counts of perjury in the third degree. If convicted, Hassan and Petrillo faced $1\frac{1}{3}$ to four years in prison.

Regarding the arrests, DA Charles Hynes said, "Every single person who was part of or otherwise involved in the murder of Mark Fisher should be on notice that this investigation continues and will not be completed until every person is given their measure of justice."

According to Sandy Silverstein, at the Kings County DA's Office of Public Information, the actions of Hassan and Petrillo were "indicative of the apparent agreement in existence by Giuca's and Russo's close-knit circle of friends, who dub themselves 'GM,' or the 'Ghetto Mafia,' to obstruct the ongoing investigation."

On January 22, Hassan and Petrillo appeared before Judge Marrus in Kings County Criminal Court for their arraignment. Both had military-style haircuts and stood with countenances of unflinching seriousness as they entered their pleas of "not guilty." These were the first criminal charges ever brought upon either of the young men. Unlike Giuca and Russo, Hassan and Petrillo were granted bail, which Judge Marrus set at $25,000 each.

The charges were based upon allegations that they they took a female witness aside during the previous fall and had threatened her with retaliation if she cooperated with the grand jury.

Assistant district attorney Anna-Sigga Nicolazzi did not want to give details of the crime—not at that time—but Judge Marrus said that the charges required elaboration.

So, begrudgingly, Nicolazzi said: "They picked up an individual and made very clear references to an episode of *The Sopranos* where a witness who cooperated was taken up to the country and killed. Then they discussed the individual's cooperation with authorities. They drew a clear parallel between the character's death and the witness's situation. They made their message clear."

Nicolazzi did not identify the witness, a woman, but she did identify which episode of *The Sopranos* was mentioned to the female witness.

"It was the one in which the character Adriana La Cerva was driven to a secluded spot and shot because she planned to cooperate with prosecutors," Nicolazzi said.

She added that Petrillo and Hassan went directly from giving their own grand jury testimony to the female witness, at which time they committed the crime. The female witness had not testified yet and the defendants wanted to make sure that they all had their stories straight.

The encounter terrified the female witness, Nicolazzi said. "She was in fear of her safety, she legitimately was in fear, and it had to be a significant fear because she came forward."

The woman had already talked to authorities by the

time Petrillo and Hassan warned her not to talk to the grand jury, the assistant district attorney explained.

Almost twelve months had passed between the murder and when the woman first gave a useful statement to investigators. Her statement had come four months after the formation of the special police/prosecutor's office task force.

Judge Marrus ordered all the lawyers in the case to file their various motions in a timely manner. "I want to be prompt in bringing the case to trial," he said. "This is a case of the highest priority and it is on the fast track, as far as I am concerned."

Representing the men was Lance Lazzaro who was Petrillo's lawyer, and was representing Hassan only until he could find another attorney. Lazzaro was also Giuca's lawyer. Outside the courtroom Lazzaro told a reporter that he was "shocked" by the charges against his clients.

"The first I heard of this story was in court," Lazzaro explained.

"The number of defendants may continue to grow," DA Hynes said. The grand jury wasn't done yet, he said. But, as it turned out, law enforcement had made their last arrest in the case—a point that would become a lifelong frustration for the parents of Mark Fisher.

Petrillo had a lighter version of the events that led up to his and Hassan's arrest: "I picked up Tommy Hassan's girlfriend in the city (Manhattan). Her name is Sarah. While we were in the car, he asked if the detectives ever came to speak to her.

"He kept asking her and finally she said yeah. He got upset, not because they went to see her, but because she lied to him. They started to argue. I didn't say two words.

"After the argument she's in the backseat flipping out, saying, 'Where are we going? Where are we going?' We were looking for gas, but in the city there is only one gas station. We were running out. Flipping out, 'where we going?' I said, 'We're going upstate, where do you think we're going?' She made it out like I was threatening her," Petrillo said.

Petrillo admitted to being a big *Sopranos* fan and owning all the DVDs, but said that he never made the connection between what was said in the car and the TV show.

Eventually both Petrillo and Hassan were acquitted of witness intimidation, but Petrillo was convicted of misdemeanor perjury. Petrillo's perjury conviction stemmed from what Petrillo called a question of semantics. John's loyal friend supposedly lied to the grand jury about having an agreement with the other kids about what to say to the police. He said they never had an agreement about that. The only agreement was that no one would talk to the cops, and the cops would be referred to their lawyers.

Petrillo's jury deliberated for three days before acquitting him on the witness intimidation charges. Doreen commented about that jury, "They did their job. I was very proud of that jury."

Petrillo himself felt that the police seemed a little desperate when it came to this case. The newspapers were following the developments, and the police and the prosecutors all acted like they were under a microscope. They seemed to be even more eager than usual to make mountains out of molehills.

"Look at my case," Petrillo later said. "They made that into a big showcase, like the Sopranos looking to kill this girl. One statement in a car, joking around. It was blown out of proportion. I said, 'We're going upstate' in a joking manner.

"When I said that, I wasn't even thinking of *The Sopranos*. It's so ridiculous. Why's she thinking, 'Where are we going?' I made much worse jokes than that, that I should have gotten arrested for."

CHAPTER 23

Russo's Mental Health

On the same day as Petrillo and Hassan's arraignment, January 21, 2005, Antonio Russo appeared in court. Russo looked bad. His hair was disheveled. He had trouble standing up straight, and when the judge asked him questions, he either made no response at all or mumbled under his breath. His responses were inaudible or unintelligible. One reporter described him as "confused and almost catatonic"; this after appearing alert and coherent when first led into the courtroom moments before.

"Do you know why you are in this courtroom, Mr. Russo?" the judge asked.

Silence.

"Are you familiar with the charges against you?" the judge asked.

Russo mumbled something, all but inaudible. Maybe he said, "I dunno," someone guessed. No one understood him.

"Could you please speak up so the court can hear you, Mr. Russo?"

Russo mumbled again, making no attempt to turn up the volume.

"Can you identify the man standing next to you?" the judge asked.

There was a long silence before Russo muttered the word "Lawyer."

"Do you know where you are?"

"Court," Russo said.

Russo's court-appointed lawyer, Jonathan Fink, intervened on his client's behalf: "Your Honor, I would like to have my client's mental health evaluated."

"I think that's a good idea," the judge concurred. Then, with an amused expression on his face, he added, "I don't think an exam is necessary, but I am going to order one anyway, since you asked for it."

The judge scheduled a hearing to assess Russo's ability to stand trial—and distinguish right from wrong.

After the hearing concluded, Fink explained to a reporter, "I was unable to effectively communicate with him, and that's why I requested a psychiatric exam. You can take that for what it's worth."

The whole scene started speculation that Fink and Russo were planning an insanity defense.

As Russo was led from the courtroom, his grandmother Mary Jennings called out, "I love you, baby."

Russo stopped briefly and turned slightly when he heard his grandmother call out, but he did not respond to her.

Later the grandmother firmly told a reporter, "I love him and he is innocent."

As usual, Mark Fisher's parents were in the courtroom. On this day Helida DiGiacomo, Nancy's sister, was with them, providing moral support. The three relatives of the victim were escorted from the courtroom by employees of the DA's office.

Outside the courtroom they were crowded by a cluster of scribbling and mike-toting journalists. The Fishers showed the reporters their palms, politely refused to answer any questions and headed home to New Jersey.

Doreen Federicci was later asked if she thought Antonio Russo looked up to John, and if she believed that it was Russo's need to impress her son that led to the death of Mark Fisher. Her answer was a definitive maybe.

Although she agreed that Russo admired her son, she didn't see him as a kid robbed of self-will by the intensity of his idol worship. Not at all. Russo, she believed, never forgot to look out for number one.

"He could have looked up to John," she later said. "The court might say he looked up to John and he did what John said, but Russo had an agenda of his own. He was always out to prove himself."

She said that Russo, in his hyperactive way, was constantly involved in a game of one-upmanship, both with everyone else in the world and with himself.

"He was always doing bigger things, better things," Doreen Federicci said. "I don't know if he looked up to John, per se. It could have been anybody, but because this incident happened with John, the courts are gonna say he looked up to John. Did he look up to Fred and Harry and everyone else that was older than him? Yes! Maybe!"

During the months leading up to the trial, the Brooklyn DA was critical of the young people at the party who had known what had happened but had chosen not to cooperate with the law. "They thought they could wait us out and thumb their nose at us," Brooklyn DA Charles

Hynes said. "Anyone who saw pictures of that kid lying on the pavement with all the bullet wounds, and not feel a tinge of empathy, is a cretin."

In the long run, however, the police had won the war of wills. "They thought they could tough it out," said Commissioner Kelly. "They were proven wrong."

On February 8, a hearing was held in Brooklyn to determine if Giuca should be given bail. Bail was denied.

Outside the courthouse Mark Fisher's father, Michael, told a reporter, "They're expecting two more arrests." Asked about this, a police source said that no arrests were imminent.

CHAPTER 24

Preliminary Hearings

On March 22, 2005, a pretrial hearing was held regarding the *People of the State of New York* versus *Antonio Russo*. Hynes, Nicolazzi and McNeill appeared for the people, Fink for the defendant. Judge Marrus presided. The hearing was held in the courthouse on Schermerhorn Street in Downtown Brooklyn.

The prosecution's first witness was Sergeant Michael Joyce. Questioned by McNeill, Sergeant Joyce said he'd been with the NYPD for twenty-two years, the last fifteen of them as a sergeant. He was currently assigned to Brooklyn South Homicide, but at the time of the murder, he was assigned to the Seven-Oh's Detective Squad. Joyce told McNeill that on the evening of October 14 he'd gone to Russo's apartment house and picked him up for a meeting of partygoers at the station house. Russo, he told the court, had come along willingly. He identified Russo as the individual "sitting in the front row in the gray sweatshirt."

Joyce said that Russo was taken to the precinct in a police car, and that, at that time, he had no reason to suspect that Russo was any more involved in Fisher's murder than any of the other young people who were at the Giuca party. That concluded Joyce's direct examination.

In cross-examination Fink asked Joyce if he had taken any notes at the time he picked up Russo and took him to the precinct. The sergeant said he carried no memo book and kept no notes. Joyce said that Detective Dennis Murphy had been the one to speak to Russo during the car ride, but that he did not remember what was said, nor the tone in which it was said.

Fink asked if Joyce remembered who the older male was with Russo and his grandmother in the hallway of the apartment building, and Joyce said he seemed to remember that the man's name was Lew, but he couldn't recall if Lew accompanied Russo to the precinct.

Joyce knew that he himself said nothing to Russo during the ride in the car, and couldn't recall if Murphy had said anything to him. Joyce, in fact, was not even sure if he rode in the same car as Russo during the ride back to the precinct. He did, however, have the impression that Russo was not frisked before being put in the car. Since he was not a suspect at that time, he probably would not have been frisked.

Joyce told Fink that he was at the precinct for several hours after Russo was brought there that night. Although he did not partake in any of the questioning of Russo himself, he knew that Russo was still there at the precinct when he reported for work the next day.

Joyce told Fink that there were about ten personnel on the second floor of the precinct when Russo was brought there and that different members of law enforcement questioned Russo at different times. When Joyce reported for work the following day, Russo was sitting in a chair in the corner, but he was no longer being questioned.

Joyce said that he recalled Russo being fed during his lengthy stay at the precinct, and that he was free to use the bathroom. Joyce didn't recall if Russo was escorted back and forth to the bathroom on those occasions.

Joyce did not recall Russo ever saying that he wanted to leave. Joyce said that he was not present when police learned that Russo had been at the Giuca party and did not know how that information was obtained.

On redirect, Nicolazzi asked Joyce about Lew, if the sergeant knew anything about him. Joyce said that he did, he knew he was an NYPD detective, who was not there in his official capacity but rather as a family friend. Lew was frisked in the elevator. Regarding Russo not asking to leave the precinct, Nicolazzi now got Joyce to testify that Russo *didn't want* to leave the police station.

"I think he said he was afraid to leave," Joyce said.

The next witness called was Detective James Gaynor, of the Brooklyn South Homicide Squad. He was questioned by Nicolazzi. Gaynor stated that he had been with the NYPD for 18½ years and had been on the Homicide Squad for the last "two or three" of those.

He stated that he became involved with the Mark Fisher murder investigation early on Sunday morning, October 12, that he had been the homicide detective assigned to the case. Gaynor testified that on the evening of October 14 a witness (who was to remain anonymous at these proceedings and who would be referred to as "witness one") was shown a photo array that had been prepared by Detective Chris Garbarino. The witness had been someone who attended the Giuca party. Among the photos in the array was one of Antonio Russo. The witness was asked if there were photos of anyone in the array who had also been at the party. Witness number one picked photo four, the photo of Antonio Russo. The witness said that was a picture of "Tony," who had been at the party. Gaynor testified that police had previously talked to other witnesses who had placed Tony at the party, which was how Russo's photo got in the array in the first place.

Gaynor said he interviewed Russo later that night on the second floor of the precinct house, that Russo was not wearing handcuffs at that time and—because he was not a suspect—was not read his Miranda rights.

"What, if anything, did Russo tell you about the case?" Nicolazzi inquired.

"He told me that on October twelfth he had a phone call from his friend, John Giuca, saying that he was having a party. Russo lived right around the corner and went over. It was about four A.M. When he got there, he met his friends Al, Tommy, John and John's brother, Matt. He said that at the party were two girls he didn't know and a guy he didn't know," Gaynor testified.

Russo told Gaynor he'd wanted beer. At the same time the guy he didn't know said he needed an ATM, so the pair walked together to a Coney Island Avenue convenience store. Russo said that when they got back, the same people were at the party as when they had left.

Russo said about twenty minutes later he had lain down to take a nap and woke up at about 6:00 A.M. At that time, Russo said, only he and the guy he didn't know were in the house. Russo told the guy he had to leave. The guy wanted to know where the girls, Angel and Meri, had gone. Russo said maybe to Al's house. The guy said he didn't know where that was, so Russo gave him directions and walked him to the door. The guy he didn't know then left the house and he never saw him again.

Soon thereafter, Russo went back home. Gaynor asked Russo if he had cut his hair recently and Russo said that he had, that he'd cut it earlier that day. Gaynor said that his interview with Russo lasted for about an hour. Russo never said he didn't want to talk and never asked to leave.

Russo, he believed, did not leave the precinct until the evening of the next day. After he was through asking Russo questions, another detective took up the questioning. Russo was fed at least twice during the time he was being questioned, once on the first night when his grandmother brought him something to eat, and again the following day when detectives fed him.

At some point Russo was asked if he had any idea where the murder weapon might be. Russo said he couldn't be sure, but it might be at a house on Eighty-sixth Street in Brooklyn, where two individuals named Billy and Jesse Wenninger lived. During the early morning of October 15, Russo and detectives went together to the Wenninger house. Russo was in no hurry to be turned loose, Gaynor said, after giving police information regarding the Wenningers. But eventually, on the evening of October 15, Russo was driven home by Detective Murphy.

Fink then cross-examined Gaynor, seeking details on how the photo array was shown to "witness number one." Gaynor, who referred to the anonymous witness as "she," said that the witness had come to the precinct on her own and had not been provided transportation by the police, and that, as far as he knew, no notes were taken as the witness identified Russo from the array. Gaynor said the other photos in the array, those that were not of Russo, were picked out of a computer photo-generating system. Gaynor admitted that Russo was hesitant to speak with the police and "seemed guarded in his answers." Gaynor said he did not recall Russo using the restroom during the interview, but noted that if he had gone to the john, he would have been escorted. Gaynor said that at the time he interviewed Russo, he had been up for three days working on the case and was very tired. Gaynor said he'd asked Russo if Mark Fisher had taken a blanket with him when he left the house at six in the morning, but didn't remember if that was the last question he'd asked. Following the interview, Gaynor said, he had typed up a synopsis of what was said on a form called a DD-5. That DD-5 was introduced. The typed statement was based on notes Gaynor had taken during his interview with Russo. The DD-5 may have been typed the following day, Gaynor said, despite the fact that it was dated the fourteenth. The date would have been the date of the interview, not the date it was typed.

"During the course of your interview, did you ever say to Mr. Russo that his statements didn't make any sense?"

"I may have."

"Did you ever say to him I think you are lying about something?" Fink asked.

"I don't remember calling him a liar, but I may have," Gaynor replied.

Gaynor said he didn't know if Russo had been given a place to sleep during the night he spent at the Seven-Oh, but he assumed that since Russo had been in the same office the next day as he had been the night before, he'd been in that office all night. Gaynor reiterated that he was not there when Russo was taken to the house on Eighty-sixth Street, and didn't know exactly when that occurred.

Fink asked if Gaynor spoke to Russo the day after their interview, when Russo was still in the police station. Gaynor said he had, and that it was at that time that Russo expressed nervousness, telling Gaynor that he'd given up info on some guys and thought he might need protection. Gaynor said that he last saw Russo that day at about 8:00 P.M. Then Gaynor had to split to New Jersey to do another interview regarding the case.

On redirect Nicolazzi had Gaynor clarify his statement that Russo would have been escorted to the restroom if he had had to go. Gaynor said that this wasn't because Russo was a suspect, but because that was the policy for all visitors.

Going back to the anonymous "witness number one," Nicolazzi asked if Russo's was the only photo array that had been prepared for the witness. Gaynor said that an array had been made for Giuca as well. The only question the anonymous witness was asked regarding each array, Gaynor testified, was if she saw anyone she recognized as having been at the party on Stratford Road.

Regarding the trip to Eighty-sixth Street, Gaynor said that despite the fact that he had not been there, he had later been told that, in addition to taking Russo to the house on Eighty-sixth, detectives had also entered the home and had made an arrest.

That concluded Gaynor's testimony. Court reporter Lois Civelia then indicated that she needed a break. Since the noon hour approached, Judge Marrus recessed the hearing until 2:15 P.M.

After lunch Nicolazzi called Detective Peter McMahon to the stand. McMahon said he was with the Brooklyn South Homicide Squad, twenty-four years with the NYPD, twenty as a detective, ten with the homicide squad. McMahon said that he, too, had been one of the men to question Russo on October 14. His interview started at eleven-twenty that night, and had followed Gaynor's interview.

As a formality McMahon identified Russo in the courtroom as the one with the long-sleeved sweatshirt. Detectives Bobby Sommer and Frank Byrnes had been in the room with him as he questioned Russo. McMahon said that he'd spoken to Gaynor and knew the statements that Russo had already made.

McMahon understood that Russo was not in custody and did not read him his Miranda rights. McMahon, as had Gaynor, began by asking what happened that night. Russo pretty much repeated the story he had told Gaynor, except he referred to Giuca as "Shady."

Russo listed everyone he could remember who was at the party: Shady, his brother, Matt, Al, Angel and another girl, Jimmy and Tommy, and a guy he didn't know who turned out to be the victim.

McMahon told Russo flat out that there were some aspects of his story that didn't make sense to him and he was hoping Russo could explain. For example, Russo was not in his own house and yet, according to his story, he was the last one there and was responsible for locking up.

And another thing, Russo said he kicked the stranger out of the house. How did he know that the stranger didn't have permission to spend the night? Who was he to kick him out?

Russo started to tell the story again, but now there were changes. There had been a problem with the stranger, who ended up dead. Everyone was drinking and smoking weed. After the stranger and Russo got back from their beer/ATM run, the stranger had fallen asleep on the couch. That was when Shady started talking to Meri, and when Russo got the idea Shady and Al were planning something.

Asked what Russo had said to him at that point, McMahon replied, "John and Albert were planning something because they kept going back into the room and looking at this guy who was again laying down on the couch sleeping. He said that it was something with Angel's girlfriend involved."

Russo said he left the house at that point and went home. At 5:30 A.M., Shady called him and told him he had some "work to do." Asked about that phrase, Russo said he thought it meant that Shady was going to shoot the guy who was asleep on the couch.

Russo said he went back to sleep. The next day he

talked to Shady on the phone and Shady told him that he had shot the guy. Giuca told Russo that, should the police ask, Russo was to say that he had been the last one in the house, that he'd shown the stranger to the door and had never seen him again.

Nicolazzi asked if Russo claimed Giuca had given him any details regarding the shooting. According to Mc-Mahon, Russo said that details were forthcoming, that Giuca had said Tommy was with him when it happened, that Tommy had been a lookout and getaway driver.

When Russo was asked why Shady would want to shoot the stranger, Russo said it had to do with a girl. Russo said he'd overheard Shady asking Angel's girlfriend, "What are you doing with this guy?" After that, Russo knew that Giuca and Huggins were planning something.

Asked about the gun, Russo said that it was probably hidden in Shady's bedroom closet. Although, there was another possibility. Then Russo began to talk about the gang they were all involved in and how, whenever a gun was involved in something they did—and the gun was hot—that it was routine for them to leave the gun at the Wenninger brothers' house on Eighty-sixth Street.

Russo said that their gang was called the Ghetto Mafia and there were a couple previous shootings that Shady had been involved in, one involving John Giuca "shooting up a bar."

The Ghetto Mafia, Russo had told McMahon, was feuding with another gang. He couldn't remember the exact name. It was called something like the South Brooklyn Boys.

McMahon left Russo and spoke to his supervisors about the statements Russo had just made. It was agreed that an immediate trip to the Wenninger house was in order. By that time it was the early-morning hours of October 15.

While other detectives went into the Wenninger house, McMahon stayed in the car with Russo. The car then returned to the Seven-Oh and Russo was again placed in an office.

It was McMahon's understanding that one of the Wenninger brothers had been arrested and he thought he'd better keep Russo on hand in case the district attorney wanted to talk to him.

McMahon didn't talk to Russo much after that, and noticed that Russo put his head down on the desk for a few catnaps during the hours that followed. McMahon told Nicolazzi that he did type up notes following his interview with Russo, but those notes had been misplaced and, as of that date, had not been located.

In cross-examination Fink got McMahon to admit that he had gone over his testimony a couple times before taking the stand, once with Detective Gaynor just before the hearing began, and once with the prosecutor's office.

McMahon said that he was aware, when questioning Russo, that this was a continuation of an interview started by Gaynor, and that Gaynor had needed to be replaced because he was tired. Gaynor had quickly briefed McMahon before McMahon's portion of the interview commenced. Gaynor said that there were elements of Russo's story that he did not believe. Gaynor thought that Russo was covering up for some of his friends. Gaynor, however, was not specific.

McMahon said that during his questioning of Russo, Russo was argumentative, but did not yell. Russo never asked for a lawyer, never had to get up to use the bathroom. McMahon remembered that he had had to pause their four-hour interview a couple times to go to the bathroom, but he had no memory of Russo ever leaving his chair. Russo never used the victim's name when describing him.

During a brief redirect examination of the witness, Nicolazzi asked McMahon if he had made any promises to Russo during the long interrogation. McMahon said that he had not.

* * *

Next on the stand was Detective Samuel Ortiz, of the South Brooklyn Homicide Task Force, twenty-four years with the NYPD, fourteen as a detective, six on the task force. Ortiz said he'd been assigned to the investigation into Mark Fisher's murder and in that capacity encountered Antonio Russo during the midafternoon of October 15, 2003. He had been briefed by McMahon and then interviewed Russo.

According to Ortiz, Russo told him that during the late afternoon of the Monday following the murder, he had gotten a call from John Giuca on his cell phone. Giuca told Russo he was going to Gregg's apartment—referring to his friend Gregg Cunningham—and to meet him there.

Russo told Ortiz that he went to Gregg's apartment, just as he had been told, and heard Gregg ask John if he had "taken care of the burners on the roof." Giuca said everything was okay. Gregg asked him what had happened. Giuca told him that "he had killed the guy."

Russo said that he left Gregg's apartment at that point. Ortiz said that Russo made these statements without anyone having to yell at him. Russo may have used the bathroom once while Ortiz was questioning him. Russo seemed completely calm and unconcerned as he made his statements.

During cross Ortiz admitted to Fink that he and Detectives Gaynor and McMahon, the three detectives who were testifying at the hearing, had all come to the courthouse that day in the same car. In theory this gave them the opportunity to go over their statements with one another to make sure no one contradicted anyone. Ortiz, however, said that although they discussed the case in general terms that morning, they did not get into specifics.

Ortiz said that he took notes in a spiral notebook

during his interview with Russo, but it was established that no one knew the current whereabouts of that notebook. That brought to two the number of missing sets of notes regarding interviews with Russo.

Ortiz said that he had started questioning Russo on his own volition. No one had instructed him to interrogate the witness. He was there, Russo was there, so he began asking questions. He admitted that he spoke to McMahon about the specifics of the interrogation of Russo up to that point, although he did not know that a trip had been made to the Wenninger house, that an arrest had been made and that guns had been confiscated. Ortiz said that Russo appeared neither fired nor scared, but was thirsty at one point and was given a soda. Russo left the precinct at about 9:00 P.M. on October 15. He was driven by Detective Murphy to the home of his then-girlfriend, Crystal Guerrero.

On redirect Ortiz admitted that judging from the fact that his notes could not be found, he was no longer certain that he kept notes during the interview. He did, however, type up a DD-5 form with his recollections from the interrogation the following day. He remembered that for certain.

The next witness was Detective Thomas Byrnes, twenty-two years with the NYPD, fifteen as a detective, for the previous 2½ years assigned to the Major Case Squad. McNeill did the questioning for the people.

Byrnes testified that it was he who had arrested Russo on November 23, 2004. Russo was taken to the precinct house. Russo subsequently asked Byrnes if he could use the phone. He wanted to talk to his grandmother. Russo was in a cell. Byrnes provided the phone.

At that time Russo asked him, "When are you going to arrest the other guys?"

Byrnes asked which "other guys" he was referring to.

Russo replied, "I'll talk to my lawyer first."

Byrnes had another conversation with Russo later that day, in the Major Case office. Russo was sitting in a chair with one hand cuffed to the chair. He asked when the police were going to pick up the other guys.

When asked to whom he was referring, Russo said, "We'll talk, but I need to talk to my lawyer first."

The next time Byrnes spoke with Russo was on November 24, at the Brooklyn Supreme Court Building, for Russo's arraignment. Russo at that time said, "I'm the only one arrested?"

Again Byrnes asked who else should be arrested, and again Russo said he needed to talk to his lawyer.

On cross Fink asked Byrnes when he first became involved in this case, and Byrnes said it was May 2004, about seven months after the murder. He had Byrnes name the other policemen who were there when Russo was apprehended. Then he got Byrnes to admit that, to his knowledge, no one read Russo his Miranda rights, even though they knew Russo had a lawyer named Ruskin. Byrnes also admitted that Russo's statements about arresting others came solely from Byrnes's recollection and not from notes, as he kept no notes.

On redirect McNeill asked one question. She wanted to know if Byrnes was aware that he was not the only Detective Byrnes connected with this case, and the witness said yes, he was aware of that. There was another, but he spelled it "Burns."

Giuca's preliminary hearing was held the same day in the same courtroom, again with Judge Marrus presiding. McNeill and Nicolazzi represented the people and Giuca was represented by Sam Gregory, Lance Lazzaro's former partner. Sitting at the defense table throughout the court proceedings would be Gregory and Lazzaro's associate, James A. Kilduff.

The fifty-one-year-old Gregory was a tall, slender man with piercing blue eyes. He radiated intensity and intelligence. His manner, as well as his physical demeanor, suggested a man who enjoyed extreme sports and extreme activities. Not that he'd always been a clean liver. He had given up smoking ten years before. Although he didn't drink anymore, he'd only been religious about it for about a year. Now, instead of drinking and smoking, he jogged. A resident of Brooklyn, he'd been married since 2001 and had two children, a boy and a girl.

Gregory was a well-known presence in both the state and federal courts of New York and New Jersey. For years he had been a partner in the firm of Lazzaro and Gregory. But he'd recently struck out on his own, opening his own law offices in the DUMBO (Down Under the Manhattan Bridge Overpass) section of Brooklyn. The new digs were in the shadows of the Brooklyn Bridge in the same building that housed Gleason's Gym, made famous by the many champion boxers who had trained there. (For readers unfamiliar with New York City geography, the Brooklyn Bridge and Manhattan Bridge are side by side, connecting Brooklyn to Manhattan over the East River.)

Gregory had a practice designed to keep things interesting. He handled a wide range of clients, involving not only criminal cases, but civil rights litigation, corporate fraud and other white-collar cases as well.

He was born in Orange, New Jersey, and raised in Summit, New Jersey. His father owned a contracting business and Gregory worked there on and off from the time he was a teenager. He received his undergraduate degree from Boston University in 1980. While working in construction, he attended New York Law School, from which he graduated in 1984.

That same year he began working for the Legal Aid Society. As a public defender he had an astounding 85 percent acquittal rate. He started out as a staff attorney handling misdemeanor cases.

Within one year he was handling felony cases. Within eighteen months he was trying cases and within three years he was assigned to the Major Offense Bureau in Brooklyn, the youngest person ever to be appointed to that position.

"For four years I handled nothing but cases with people facing life sentences," he said. "I did a lot of heavy serial type crime and heavy drug cases." As a Legal Aid attorney, Gregory tried about thirty to forty cases. Since most cases result in plea bargaining, that is a large number.

It was not a matter of temperament or politics that led Gregory to stay on the defense side of the justice fence.

"I never had a political philosophy that prevented me from doing prosecuting," he said. "I always felt as though defense work was more challenging. It was easier to be creative and artistic as a defense lawyer than a prosecutor."

In 1991, he entered private practice, where he has remained ever since, first with Lazzaro and Gregory, and then on his own. Now his firm was known as The Law Offices of Samuel Gregory.

"I made my reputation doing drug cases in Brooklyn," he said. "In the mid-to-late '80s a lot of buy-and-bust operations were being conducted at the street level by the Narcotics Division of the New York City Police Department. They were military-type operations that were very carefully strategized and executed with precision. My thought was that those cases were attackable because of some of the problems within the department. I put together some other lawyers and we broke down the paperwork. I started trying those cases with great success. That was the beginning of where I started to stand out as a lawyer."

As his reputation increased, Gregory got bigger clients and bigger cases. He defended one client who was coined "the Bicycle Thief." In that case he got seven to eight rapes severed into three separate cases. He got the defendant acquitted in two cases and went against prosecutor Star Jones, now a television personality, in the third. He also handled several of what he called "notorious city cases" because of the intense media attention.

Star Jones, the former panelist on the ABC morning talk show *The View,* who was once a Kings County prosecutor, wrote repeatedly about Gregory, as a tough adversary, in her book *You Have to Stand for Something, or You'll Fall for Anything.* She had faced Gregory not only when he was in private practice, but back in his Legal Aid days as well. Jones wrote that defense attorney Sam Gregory was at that time Legal Aid's biggest star.

Gregory's practice had evolved just the way he'd hoped. Instead of handling a lot of cases, Gregory now only handled a few. However, they were complicated cases, cases that presented the maximum challenge, cases that required all of Gregory's skills.

In 1995, Gregory had been one of the first lawyers to be certified in New York State to handle death penalty cases. He became the first New York attorney to win an acquittal in a first-degree murder case after the death penalty had been reinstated in New York State.

Folks who watched a lot of all-news TV on cable sometimes recognized him. He'd been a talking head on CNN, MSNBC and Court TV discussing a variety of legal topics. He'd been written about in the *New York Times* and *People* magazine.

Gregory was also an amateur pilot who often flew over New Jersey, and frequently visited Byram Township, where Mark Fisher grew up. He had landed his plane plenty of times at Trinca Airport in nearby Green Township. Looking at him, it was obvious that he had no aversion to hard work and was not afraid to get his hands dirty.

In 2001, Gregory defended a restaurant busboy accused of using the Internet and the *Forbes* list of the richest people in America in a scheme to steal millions from such figures as Steven Spielberg, Warren Buffett, Martha Stewart, Oprah Winfrey, Ross Perot and Ted Turner.

After years at the old firm something had to give. Gregory was not happy with what he was doing and decided to take a sabbatical in 2001. He headed off to Alaska, Mexico and Panama on his own to clear his head and reconsider his priorities. He wound up buying a log cabin in Alaska, which he still visits with regularity. He is currently trying to establish a program where he or an organization he would form would take ten to fifteen inner-city kids to the wilds of Alaska for a few weeks each summer in order to get a different, more positive perspective on life.

"I didn't like the direction the firm was taking," he said. "I felt as though if I didn't leave the firm, that would be my legacy. Rather than just accept the fact that I was making money and doing well running a lot of cases, I decided to leave. I'm glad I did. I enjoyed the time off."

While in Alaska, Gregory met the woman who is now his wife and the mother of his two small children, a girl and a boy. They live comfortably in Brooklyn, about one mile from where the murder of Mark Fisher took place.

Gregory was a busy guy. In addition to his legal practice, he was also a trial advocacy professor at St. John's University, and a frequent guest lecturer on theories of defense at various organizations at Brooklyn Law School, the New York Law School, the Brooklyn Criminal Bar Association and at the DA's office.

Prior to taking the Fisher case, Gregory had met Giuca briefly while representing a friend of Giuca's family. "He was very quiet, reserved, and always polite and respectful," said Gregory, referring to that initial meeting. "When we met in this case, my initial impression was reinforced."

Gregory knew that the prosecution was going to attempt to paint his client as the "brains" behind Mark Fisher's murder. However, when he talked to his client, he found that notion hard to believe. Months later, Gregory said, "John's definitely not a criminal mastermind. He's a kid living at home who had a couple of run-ins with the police—nothing particularly major. To me he never had homicide on his mind. I still don't believe it."

At Giuca's preliminary hearing, the people's first witness was Detective James McCafferty, who became involved in the case in May 2004.

"As part of your involvement in that case, did you arrest anyone pursuant to a Kings County Supreme Court warrant on an unrelated shooting back in 2004?" Nicolazzi asked.

McCafferty said that he had, and that the arrest was made July 5, 2004, and he identified the man arrested at that time as John Giuca, who was sitting in a chair in a gray sweatshirt.

He testified that the arrest had been made at 6:45 P.M., with assistance from the Pinellas County Sheriff's Department, at a location on Cypress Pond Road in Palm Harbor, Florida.

McCafferty said that with him in the police car when Giuca was apprehended was Lieutenant Brady, with the local sheriff's office. McCafferty said that Brady was instructing his men to search the area for another individual.

When Giuca heard that the area was being searched, Giuca asked if there was a warrant for his brother also. No other arrests were made and Giuca was taken to an interview room on the second floor of the sheriff's headquarters.

McCafferty testified that Giuca was allowed to make phone calls and called his mother, who was also in Florida. Giuca made the call on his own cell phone, which had been taken away from him at one point but returned to him so he could place the call.

Giuca, the witness said, used his cell instead of the sheriff's phone because he wanted to call his mom's cell and it was agreed that it would be easier. While talking to his mother, McCafferty overheard him telling her that he was under arrest and that she should be sure to call Tommy and Lauren. At the time Giuca made that request of his mom, McCafferty said, he had not been informed of what he was under arrest for.

In cross-examination Gregory established that McCafferty had a copy of the arrest warrant with him when he went to pick up Giuca, and that McCafferty never went inside the target residence on Cypress Pond Road. Giuca was apprehended outside the residence, the witness said.

Gregory asked McCafferty to describe the circumstances of the apprehension, but Nicolazzi objected on the grounds that the question was outside the scope of the hearing.

Judge Marrus overruled the objection and McCafferty said the police had staked out the outside of the residence and picked Giuca up when he was leaving. Giuca had been with three other people: his brother Matt, and friends Scott Powers and Jennifer Baker.

According to McCafferty the police said to Giuca, "Don't move. Let me see your hands."

Giuca was handcuffed, but McCafferty could not remember if anyone specifically said that Giuca was under arrest. Giuca did not ask what the warrant for his arrest was for.

In other words, he was being arrested for the shooting

incident unrelated to Mark Fisher's murder, but he didn't necessarily know that.

Gregory asked if the whole object of the exercise was to get Giuca to believe he was being arrested for murder so that he would make incriminating or otherwise revealing statements.

That was objected to, although Gregory did get the witness to deny discussing with the local law enforcement any such strategy as Gregory suggested, then admit that he had discussed with other members of the NYPD the plan to not tell Giuca what he'd been arrested for, hoping he would assume—and assume wrong. If he asked what he was under arrest for, the plan was to say "a warrant" without specifying what the warrant was for.

Gregory asked about the search that had been ordered for another individual at the time Giuca was apprehended. Gregory asked point-blank who the other individual had been and McCafferty replied it had been Matthew Federicci, Giuca's brother.

Gregory asked how much time passed between local law enforcement ordering a search for another individual and Giuca asking if there was a warrant for his brother, too. McCafferty said that about ninety seconds elapsed between those two events.

The witness stated that it was a ten- to fifteen-minute ride from the site of Giuca's apprehension to the sheriff's headquarters, where he was taken to be questioned. Asked if he had any conversation with Giuca at the sheriff's office, McCafferty said that there was only light conversation, why John was in Florida and things like that, but nothing regarding the case.

Regarding the phone call between Giuca and his mom that McCafferty overheard, Gregory asked why McCafferty had been close enough to eavesdrop, had he purposefully been listening in? McCafferty said he had not, but had stayed close for Giuca's protection. If the young man had started to hurt himself, McCafferty wanted to be in a position to stop him. He also wanted to make sure Giuca didn't try to escape. The door to the room had been left open despite the fact that it was video-monitored.

Next on the stand was Detective Gaynor, who testified that on October 14, 2003, he was involved in the investigation into Mark Fisher's murder. In that capacity he had shown a photo array to a witness referred to as "witness number one" and that among the photos in the array was one of John Giuca. A computer chose photos of people who resembled Giuca. Six photos in all were shown to the witness, but only photo number five was actually of Giuca. The witness correctly picked number five, Gaynor said, identifying Giuca by name, calling him "John." Gregory had no cross-examination and that concluded the hearing.

CHAPTER 25

Dual Trial

Russo and Giuca were to be tried together, but each defendant would have his own jury. Often, both juries would be in the courtroom. Sometimes one jury would be allowed to hear testimony, while the other had to leave the courtroom and wait.

It was tedious for the juries and could cause lengthy sidebars regarding which jury could hear what, but it was still kind to the taxpayer in the sense that it was a lot quicker than holding two separate trials during which much of the testimony would be duplicated. The dual trial was to be held in the New York Supreme Court building in Brooklyn, with Judge Alan Marrus presiding.

Both of the defense attorneys in the case, Sam Gregory for John Giuca, and Jonathan Fink for Antonio Russo, were opposed to the idea of their clients being tried together.

Fink felt that it was difficult to keep one jury from knowing what the other jury was hearing. Even if the juries were kept separate from one another, there was so much media attention given to the case, Fink felt, that the juries were bound to find out bits and pieces about what was going on when they were not in the courtroom.

But Judge Marrus ruled that this would be one trial, held before two juries, and that was that.

By rule, only two assistant district attorneys would be allowed to participate in the prosecution. Three prosecutors had been involved in the investigation: Patricia McNeill, Anna-Sigga Nicolazzi and Josh Hanshaft. Hanshaft volunteered to sit it out, although he was equally capable of handling the courtroom duties.

The trial, because of its nature, had to be held in the largest courtroom in the building. There had to be room for thirty jurors, twelve jurors and three alternates for each defendant.

There was a sign on the courtroom wall that occupancy by more than 164 persons was a violation of the fire laws, and throughout most of the trial the room was filled to capacity.

Although the double-jury trial was extremely rare, not all of the lawyers involved in these proceedings were completely unfamiliar with the process. Jonathan Fink not only had worked a double-jury trial before, this was his second one in a row—a strange coincidence.

When Giuca was brought into the courtroom for the jury selection of his trial, on the morning of September 12, 2005, one of the court officers recognized him. Sergeant Billy S. Sullivan (pseudonym) of the fourteenth-floor security operation at the courthouse was closing in on thirty years on the job.

Sullivan took one look at Giuca and the lightbulb went on over his head. Sullivan's wife worked in educational publishing, but years earlier she had been a grade-school teacher, and had taught Giuca when he attended St. Sav-

iour School on Eighth Avenue and Seventh Street in the
Park Slope section of Brooklyn, just west of Prospect Park.

The thing that made Giuca memorable was that he
had been a disruptive kid, but every time his mother was
called in, she would turn a deaf ear to complaints about
her son's behavior.

John's mom, Doreen Federicci, would make it clear
that the real problem was the fact that John was brilliant
and everyone else—including the teachers—was not.

"My wife thinks everyone is good. Of course, I don't
know why she married me. But she didn't like this kid's
mom," Sullivan recalled.

Sullivan's daughter was in her early twenties at the
time of the trial, and a private first class in the army stationed in Iraq. When she got out of the service, she
planned to join the NYPD. She'd known Giuca and his
pals growing up, and told her dad that they were a
"bunch of jerks."

Before the trial was over, DiGiovanni, Angel's dad, a
lawyer who defended reputed mobsters, wanted to
attend the trial to oversee his daughter's testimony, but
he didn't want any publicity. So, he attempted to be-
friend Billy S. Sullivan, the longtime court officer.

"Could you get me into the courtroom without the
papers seeing me?" DiGiovanni asked.

"Are you kidding me?" Sullivan replied.

Jury selection began on September 12, 2005. Outside
the courtroom Fisher's mom told the press that she
would be there every day of the trial carrying a teddy
bear made out of Mark's football jersey.

To avoid confusion, the juries were color coded. The
jury determining Russo's fate would be known as the

*R*ed Jury. Giuca's would be called the *G*reen Jury. *R* for Russo, *G* for Giuca.

Judge Marrus addressed the new juries and gave them their instructions: "The first rule is that you are the judges of the facts. That's why you are here. You have been selected to decide what happened in this case."

He told them the rules of evidence and warned them to keep an open mind until all of the evidence had been heard. When together in the jury room, they were allowed to be as social as they pleased. They should talk to one another, but they couldn't talk about the case. That was forbidden.

They were not allowed to go to the crime scene. They could not watch or read media reports involving the case. They were obligated to report anyone who tried to improperly influence them.

No newspapers at any time. No cell phones in the courtroom—and that applied to everyone in the courtroom . . . turn 'em off. If they should coincidentally run into someone involved in the case, they were not allowed to have a conversation with that person.

Judge Marrus's last rule was a dress code. Men were to wear a tie if they owned one. Women were to dress as for "an important job." He then explained the unusual nature of the trial, two defendants, two juries, one courtroom.

After the juries left, Nicolazzi noted to the judge that she would be mentioning the Ghetto Mafia in her opening statement, and she wanted to make sure that it was okay. Judge Marrus said that it was, as long as she promised to call a witness that could corroborate each of her references to John Giuca's alleged gang.

CHAPTER 26

Nicolazzi's Opening Statement

On the morning of September 15, 2005, the dual trial began. On the wall behind Judge Marrus's head, in large letters, it read: "IN GOD WE TRUST." The victim's immediate and extended family were there in numbers, and they promised to be there throughout the trial—a promise they kept without fail. Mark's mom always had her teddy bear.

Two opening statements were made by the prosecution, one for each jury. One each by assistant district attorneys Anna-Sigga Nicolazzi and Trish McNeill.

New York Times reporter Alan Feuer noticed that, despite the fact that it was an unusual trial with two juries, and the fact that both defendants had made statements that implicated the other, the courtroom was not divided up into three distinct camps, as one might imagine. The courtroom, rather, Feuer noted, was divided into two camps, just like more conventional trials with one defendant and one jury. The friends and family of the victim sat grim-faced in the center section of the courtroom, while friends and family of the defendants sat together only a few feet away.

During her opening statement to the Green Jury, Nicolazzi described how Mark Fisher had been drawn into a world he didn't understand, a world he was unable to cope with on the night of October 11, 2003, and during the early-morning hours of the following day.

She said that the evening featured a collision between three worlds, a collision with tragic results. The three worlds were Fairfield University, lovely suburban Long Island and the Ditmas Park section of Brooklyn.

"Angel DiGiovanni was the thread that connected those worlds," she said. "She was born in Brooklyn, raised in Garden City and went to school at Fairfield."

She told in detail how Mark had come to the big city, for the first time without adult supervision, and had run into a schoolmate named Angel DiGiovanni at a bar on the Upper East Side.

"Angel was in the city with her own friends from Garden City, on Long Island, for the night," Nicolazzi said.

She described how Mark had been introduced to one of Angel's Garden City friends, Meredith Flannigan, and the two hit it off, talking, drinking and eventually heading to a nearby pizzeria for a slice.

They went to another bar, Model T's, where they met Angel DiGiovanni again, along with John Giuca, a childhood pal of hers.

"That's when the worlds very slowly began to collide," Nicolazzi said, "and fate began to play its unfortunate hand."

It had grown late, well after midnight, and Mark

Fisher had become separated from his friends. The girls had missed their train to Long Island. Mark Fisher had lost his phone and was short on cash.

When John Giuca suggested that they all hop in a cab and go to his house, where his parents were not home, it had seemed like an excellent idea to everyone.

Mark Fisher, she added, had become a fish out of water when he left the Upper East Side bar and went to Brooklyn, to Giuca's home on Stratford Road.

"After that," Nicolazzi said, "slowly but surely the night just got bad. Everything was fine when they first went to the house, but Giuca, this defendant, now had the home court advantage. They were at his house, in his area. His friends were on their way to join the party. The girls, these attractive young women, were now at his house. And Mark was left a stranger in an unfamiliar place . . . and at some point Mark made the mistake of sitting on a table rather than a chair. This defendant made it very clear that he didn't like that."

At some point during the party Giuca decided he needed beer and money, so he told Russo to take Fisher. Russo obeyed orders. Nicolazzi explained that the relationship between Giuca and Russo was more than one of friendship. They were members of a gang—the Ghetto Mafia, or GM as it was called. Giuca was leader. Russo was a soldier. Giuca gave orders. Russo obeyed them.

She said Giuca fancied himself to be like Tony Soprano. The evidence would show, Nicolazzi said, that while Russo and Fisher were going to the ATM, Giuca said to the remaining group in his backyard, "I want that kid out of my house, I want him gone."

Then it got to be early morning and the party started to break up. Angel and Al left, and gone was the thread that had held the group together. Left were Giuca, his brother, Russo, and Mark and Meri, who had fallen asleep in separate rooms.

Nicolazzi then gave the prosecution's scenario of the murder: "This defendant gave Tony Russo an order, to take Mark Fisher and show him 'what's up.' In their fantasy gangland world those words had meaning. Russo understood because, after saying those words, this defendant armed Tony Russo with his gun."

Giuca was a guy who liked to be in control, she said, and the murder caused him to lose control. Now he had to worry about who knew what and the implications of what had occurred.

She said the evidence against Giuca wasn't there right away. Gathering the evidence to prosecute him had taken time.

Giuca, the evidence would show, contacted many of the people who had been at that party that night and he instructed them as to what to say and what not to say. The partygoers got lawyers, she said, and they all said the same thing when they were interviewed by the police. The police kept interviewing the witnesses, over and over, keeping the pressure building, until finally a few of the witnesses broke and the truth came out.

This defendant, Nicolazzi said, had admitted his involvement in the murder. "He spun his role," she said. "He told those close to him bit by bit what he had done. When you're involved in something so big, so bad, you can't keep it to yourself."

Not everyone got precisely the same story. Giuca's girlfriend Lauren Conigliaro got one version. He knew he had to tell her something. He knew it was going to come out that there'd been a party at his house and there were other girls there. Lauren was going to want an explanation. He admitted to her that he gave Tony the gun.

The angle was different with his lifelong friend Al Huggins, whom Giuca had called later on the day of the murder. "Where's Meri? Where's Meri?" Giuca asked frantically. Last Giuca knew, Meri had been asleep in his house. Now she was gone. (Giuca had no way of knowing that Meri, unaware that anything bad had happened to Mark, left the house, wandered over to Coney Island Avenue, got money from an ATM and caught a cab home.) Huggins told Giuca that he had spoken to his mom, and she said someone had gotten shot on his block. According to Huggins, Giuca replied, "We may have had something to do with that."

Nicolazzi told the jury how the people believed the murder went down. Giuca led Fisher to Russo. As soon as they got Fisher to the place where they wanted him, Russo attacked Fisher.

"But Mark was a strapping young man," Nicolazzi said, "and started to fight back. And then Tony shot him, not once, got him on the ground, continued to beat him, continued to show him what's up. He fired five bullets into him until he was left lifeless, a promising future ripped away from him, there on the ground. That showed him what was up."

Giuca told Huggins that Russo returned to Giuca's house after the shooting and returned the gun.

"It's done," Russo reportedly said to Giuca.

Nicolazzi told the jury that they would hear of another conversation between Giuca and another leader of the GM, to the effect that the gang was soft and needed to toughen up, so from then on, to be a member, an initiate was going to have to murder somebody.

She said that Giuca couldn't have acted guiltier following the shooting. In addition to trying to figure out who knew what, and what had happened to Meri, he made arrangements with another friend, Anthony

Palumbo (pseudonym), to dispose of his .22 Ruger. Then he got rid of all of his remaining ammunition for that gun.

She said it took the police over a year to put the pieces together, but they eventually did it. Though it was not this jury's job to judge the guilt or innocence of Russo, she noted briefly that he had acted guilty as hell also, cutting his braids off within hours of the murder and splitting for California.

She told the jury to pay close attention and that when all of the evidence was presented, she was going to stand before them again and "ask them to hold this defendant responsible for the crimes he chose to commit."

CHAPTER 27

Gregory's
Opening Statement

Gregory began his opening statement by complimenting Nicolazzi's opening remarks. He said that she was organized and that her story was emotional and compelling. But, Gregory reminded the jury, Nicolazzi was not a witness to the crime. All of her information came from others, and if that information was false, then Nicolazzi's case was false as well.

Gregory said, "It's like a house built on sand. It doesn't have a foundation."

Then he listed the facts that his defense and the prosecution agreed upon. They agreed that Mark Fisher's death was a tragedy, that it occurred at 6:40 A.M. and that he'd been shot with a .22-caliber pistol five times on Argyle Road.

"And we agree that at the time of his death, Mark Fisher was alone with Antonio Russo," Gregory said.

He did take exception with Nicolazzi's claim that months and months of police work had broken the case. He said that most of the so-called evidence against his client had been gathered within days of the murder.

Gregory pointed out that all of the primary evidence against his client came from two sources, Lauren Conigliaro and Al Huggins. Both of those witnesses were interviewed by police within two days of the shooting, and the reason, he said, was clear. Huggins was at the party and lived only a couple houses away from where Mark Fisher's body was found. They spoke to Conigliaro because she was Giuca's girlfriend.

He said the prosecution was going to make much of phone records that showed who called whom, and how often during the hours and days following the murder, but that these records, too, had been available to law enforcement very quickly. Months and months of tough police work weren't involved.

The prosecution had stated that Giuca was frustrated with Fisher, and Gregory admitted that this was true. But it wasn't just Giuca who was frustrated. The six-foot-five football player was too drunk to do anything and couldn't get home. He had become, as the defense attorney put it, "a bit of a burden." Others were frustrated, too, Gregory said, particularly Angel DiGiovanni.

The truth was, Gregory said, that Fisher didn't want to go home. He wanted to be with Meredith Flannigan. "They tried to get him to go back to Jersey. They tried to get him a taxi. He stated that he didn't have any money. He had an ATM card, but he didn't mention that," Gregory said.

Gregory also took exception to the story, as Nicolazzi had told it, of Fisher ticking off Giuca by sitting on a table in his house.

"The evidence is going to show that it was someone

else in the house, Tommy Hassan, who said, 'You can't sit on a table. Here's a chair, sit here.'"

The evidence, if interpreted properly, Gregory said, would show that Giuca was breaking up the party. Fisher had to go. Russo had to go. Flannigan, she could stay. Giuca woke up Fisher and told him he had to get out. Fisher complained that it was a cold autumn morning and he only had his shirt. Giuca griped that he didn't want to give him a jacket because he knew he would never get it back, so he gave him a blanket instead—a blanket with a distinctive picture of a jungle cat on it.

"He might as well have given a blanket with his name and address on it," Gregory said. Is that the way someone would act if he were planning a murder?

Gregory referred to a phone call minutes after the shooting between Giuca and his half brother, Matt Federicci, in which Giuca apparently indicated that he didn't approve of Russo's having shot Fisher.

"That phone call makes it clear that Russo acted on his own when he shot and killed Mark Fisher. My client, John Giuca, had nothing to do with it. He was outraged when he learned what Russo, who was his friend, had done. He didn't know it was going to happen and he didn't approve of what happened."

Gregory said he believed his client to be completely innocent of this crime, but that wasn't the case with Giuca's codefendant. Russo was another matter. Gregory told the jury that Russo went out into the night with Fisher and returned to Giuca's house alone, a little panicky. Russo told Giuca that "something happened" to Fisher. Did Giuca invite him in so they could hide out? No, he threw Russo out and slammed the door behind him.

"Minutes later," Gregory said, "Russo gets his hair cut." Gregory told the jury that Russo was a funny guy, a comical guy, who loved to smoke pot. That was why he'd been invited to Giuca's party—Tweed had the weed. But Russo was funny in the other sense, too. He was unpredictable.

"He could snap," Gregory said.

Gregory then advised the jury to keep a close eye on Al Huggins when he testified. "The evidence is going to show," Gregory said, "that from the moment he first opened his mouth about what happened that night, he lied. During the morning of October 12, John Giuca did not know what happened to Mark Fisher, while on the other hand Al Huggins knew that Fisher was dead and lied about it."

Gregory reiterated that it was Conigliaro and Huggins whom he wanted the jury to cast a suspicious eye upon, because those were the two witnesses upon whom Nicolazzi most relied to make her case against John Giuca.

"I'll talk about this 'gang' evidence with you," Gregory said. "I could say anybody acts like Tony Soprano, but that's just words. That's just throwing dirt. I'll dump the water on that and get the squeegee and get rid of that in about two seconds because that's just throwing dirt on him.

"The evidence is going to show [Giuca] was in a bad situation. Not because of what he had done, but because he'd had a party. Russo's a wacko. Russo went out to take something from the kid by Huggins's house and, lo and behold, the kid ended up dead."

Gregory said that one phone call the prosecution found very interesting was from Matt Federicci to John Giuca at 6:42 A.M., two minutes after Fisher was shot. Gregory admitted that law enforcement had considered—and probably still did consider—Giuca's younger brother a suspect in the case, "although not one witness ever said he had anything to do with the case." The evidence, however, would show that the call was made from the upstairs of the house to the downstairs. Matt had heard John and Tony arguing and wanted to find out what was going on. Truth was, John during that phone call told his bother that Russo was an idiot and that he shouldn't hang out with him anymore. These were obviously not the actions of someone who "condoned" what Russo had done. In conclusion Gregory said that Giuca's actions before and after the murder indicated that he neither knew it was going to happen nor approved of it happening.

After Gregory finished his opening statement, there was a one-hour break. Outside the courtroom Mike Fisher told a reporter, "I can't believe that young people like that could be such cold-blooded killers."

CHAPTER 28

McNeill's
Opening Statement

When the one hour was up, court was once again called to order by Judge Marrus. The Green Jury was gone, and the Red Jury was in place. Delivering the opening statement for the prosecution of Russo was Trish McNeill.

As had Nicolazzi during the opening statement for the Green Jury, McNeill began her remarks for the Red Jury with a synopsis of the events that led up to Mark Fisher's death. She discussed the different groups of young people and how it had all started by accident, the completely accidental meeting of Mark Fisher and his Fairfield group, with Angel DiGiovanni and her Garden City group, in Ships' Harbour, on Manhattan's East Side. And, because Angel was there to meet Al, also joining them was the Brooklyn group. McNeill called them "the Ghetto Mafia group." The party ended up back at Giuca's.

McNeill then said, "Ladies and gentlemen, you will learn that before Mark Fisher was shot that night, he was beaten up by the defendant. And the defendant took Mark Fisher's wallet and he ran from the scene of the shooting toward his home. And you'll learn that he threw Mark Fisher's wallet down a sewer that was located halfway between Giuca's and Russo's house."

The angle involving the white SUV, put forth by many police statements during the days following the murder, was now forgotten. There would be no mention of the white SUV at this trial.

She noted the flurry of phone calls between Giuca and Russo following the shooting and the fact that Russo went out of his way to change his appearance by getting a haircut. Russo had been seen with Fisher earlier in the night at the ATM machine and didn't want to be recognized.

Russo's barber that morning, Alfredo Bishop (pseudonym), said Russo was nervous, and when he heard sirens, he acted paranoid. Russo reportedly told Bishop that he'd been mugged walking home from the subway; there was a struggle. "It was him or me, so I shot him." The hairstylist asked Russo if he killed the man. Russo said he didn't know.

According to the haircutter, Russo kept repeating, "I'm going to jail. I'm going to jail. I fucked up my life." Russo had said he was splitting for California. He asked Bishop to alibi him, say he'd been there with him all night.

The jury would learn that Russo, like the other party-goers that night, was repeatedly interviewed by the police, but unlike the others, he changed his story over time. He started out with the "I was the last one in the house and I showed the stranger to the door" story to the "I went home but got a call from John Giuca" story. Russo eventually ended up believing that his best bet was to point his finger at Giuca and keep it pointed there. Russo quoted Giuca as saying, "I got the guy. I banged him."

Since flight is evidence of guilt, McNeill mentioned that soon after the shooting, Russo did get on a plane and go to California, just as he had told the man who cut his hair.

And along the line Russo admitted what he had actually done. Among those who would testify was Crystal Guerrero, Russo's girlfriend, who would say that he repeatedly admitted to her over time that he had killed Mark Fisher.

Russo had made admissions to other witnesses that the jury would hear from as well, McNeill added. McNeill asked the jury, after they had heard all of the evidence, to hold Russo accountable for his actions. After about thirty minutes of speaking, that concluded her opening statement.

CHAPTER 29

Fink's
Opening Statement

Russo's defense attorney gave his opening statement next. Fink had joined Russo's case late, but had come up with a solid strategy. For one thing, Fink was going to try to keep out of the trial some of the things Russo allegedly said before Fink became his lawyer.

Some of the things Fink wanted to suppress were statements allegedly made by Russo that it had been Giuca who killed Mark Fisher. Now that Fink was Russo's lawyer, there would be no more direct accusations.

One of the problems with dual-jury trials was that they often turned into two-on-one contests. A defense team would not just have to battle the prosecution, but the other defense team as well.

Allegations of Russo pointing the finger at Giuca were, according to Fink, "allegedly made to the police." Fink later explained, "Those were statements I attempted to keep out of the trial. I don't know if he made those statements. I wasn't there when the police spoke to him."

Russo's grandmother Mary Jennings was there, as she would be every day throughout the trial. Russo also had frequent attendance from other members of his family—with an aunt, two uncles, both grandparents from the other side of his family, being regular faces in the courtroom while Antonio was tried for murder.

Fink began his remarks by giving the jury a reminder. At that moment Russo was presumed to be innocent, and until the prosecution met its requirement of proving beyond a reasonable doubt that Russo had killed Mark Fisher, then he was still presumed to be innocent.

"The murder weapon was never found," Fink reminded the jury. "In order for you, ladies and gentlemen of the jury, to find my client guilty, the prosecution must prove their case beyond a reasonable doubt. I say you will find an abundance of reasonable doubt." The case was filled to the brim with reasonable doubt, most of it was the product of lack of evidence. Fink reminded the jury that there were no witnesses to the crime.

Fink promised, "You are going to hear that the police tried to find a way to link Mr. Russo to Mark Fisher and his death and they were unable to do so."

The jury, Fink said, would hear about the DNA. Police took some from Russo, found some on Fisher. No match. That's lack of evidence. All of the "evidence" came from so-called witnesses who claimed Russo told them this and Russo told them that. Fink urged the jury to weigh the credibility of those witnesses.

"Ladies and gentlemen, it was John Giuca who had a problem with Mark Fisher—not Antonio Russo," Fink said in conclusion. "I ask you to decide this case based on the evidence, and the lack of evidence. And when you do that, you are going to find Mr. Russo not guilty."

That concluded the opening statements. The Red Jury was allowed to take a break. With the jury out, the court took care of some small business. Fink moved to prevent the photos of Mark Fisher's body from being introduced as evidence.

He said they were too graphic and inflammatory. It was okay to show the jury photos of the crime scene after a tarp had been thrown over Mark Fisher's body, but not the photos taken without the tarp.

Nicolazzi argued in response that the photos showing the body were important to her case. She agreed that there was one photo that was truly horrific—the one that showed the victim's face. She had no problem with that one being excluded.

She said the photos were needed to show the location of the wounds, where the body was left, how Fisher was clothed and the position he was in when found. There were six photos in all and she wanted to introduce five of them.

Judge Marrus ruled that the prosecution could introduce two, one showing the location of the wound and one showing the position of the body. The position photo would serve to show the manner of dress as well.

CHAPTER 30

First Witnesses

The Red and Green Juries were in the courtroom together. Relatives of both of the defendants and of the victim felt their muscles tighten a little bit. It was time for the prosecution to call its first witness. As is customary in homicide cases, the prosecution first established that there had been a murder.

Fulfilling the prosecution's corpus delicti was Detective Joseph Lupo, of the NYPD's Crime Scene Unit, seventeen years on the force, the last three as a detective working for the CSU. Nicolazzi did the questioning.

"If you could tell the members of the jury what are the basic duties and responsibilities of the Crime Scene Unit?"

"It's a citywide unit that responds to serious crimes: homicides, pattern robberies, sexual assaults. At those scenes we recover, document and photograph evidence, including latent fingerprints and DNA."

Detective Lupo said he'd been to several hundred crime scenes during his career. At 9:00 A.M., on October

12, 2003, he'd arrived at the scene of a homicide on Argyle Road in Ditmas Park.

He described for the juries the procedure he undertook at the crime scene. He identified photographs he was shown as those he'd taken at the crime scene. The photos were introduced into evidence, at least the two photos that Judge Marrus had agreed to allow.

Diagrams that Detective Lupo had drawn were also identified and introduced. He explained that the body had been found on Argyle Road between Beverley and Albemarle.

Argyle was a one-way street, Lupo told the jury, with all traffic going north, in the direction of Albemarle. If driving up the street, one would have seen Fisher's body on the left. The body, to be specific, was found at the conjunction of the west sidewalk and the driveway at the house address on Argyle.

Lupo then identified the shell casings from a .22-caliber pistol that had been found at the crime scene. These were introduced into evidence.

"I have no further questions at this time," Nicolazzi said.

"Cross-examination, Mr. Fink?" Judge Marrus asked.

Fink asked Lupo if when the shell casings were sent to the police lab for testing, had he requested that they be fingerprinted? Lupo said no, that he had processed the shells at the scene. No report was ever written up for that processing, however, the witness said, because no fingerprints were found.

This struck Fink as curious. Lupo explained that there would have been a report written if a print had been found, and although there were occasions when reports were written even when no prints were found, this wasn't one of them. Fink had no further questions.

During cross-examination Gregory asked Lupo if he

was still at the crime scene when the medical examiner arrived, and Lupo said that he was.

Gregory asked if there had been neighbors watching from their porches while the crime scene was being processed. Lupo said he didn't recall. Gregory then directed the detective's attention to exhibit number 1-B, a photo, taken by Lupo, that apparently showed neighbors in the background, watching the activity from their porches. Lupo looked at the photo and suggested that these were not neighbors at all, but rather police personnel who were on those porches for their overhangs, trying to get out of the rain. That concluded Gregory's cross.

In redirect Nicolazzi elicited two points from her witness. One, to the best of his recollection, no pedestrians were stopped from approaching the scene, because none had tried. And two, the shell casings discovered at the scene had been tested for fingerprints, but to no avail.

That concluded the examination of Detective Lupo, and court recessed for lunch.

At the start of the afternoon session, Nicolazzi called Edward Feldman, the first person to call 911. He told the jury that he lived on Argyle Road, very close to where the shots were fired.

He'd been reading the newspaper online when five shots rang out, seemingly just outside his window. He'd hidden under the desk for a time before making a dash for the phone to call 911.

After placing the phone call, he hid some more. He later estimated that only "ninety seconds, two minutes" passed before the police pulled up out front. They rang his doorbell and he answered a few questions.

During Gregory's cross, Feldman said that the shots seemed so close that he feared one would come crashing through his front window and hit him. Gregory then shifted gears and asked if Feldman knew the Hugginses, who were his neighbors.

The jurors had heard the name Huggins during the opening statements. The witness said he did know the family, that they lived four houses away on his side of Albemarle.

Questioning over, the witness was then allowed to step down.

CHAPTER 31

Testimony of
Meri Flannigan

The prosecution called Meri Flannigan to the stand. Both the Red and Green Juries were in their seats. Under Nicolazzi's questioning, she identified herself as Meredith Anne Flannigan, twenty-one years old, a senior at an out-of-state university, who grew up in Garden City, Long Island.

She said that she was home from school during Columbus Day weekend, 2003. On that Saturday night she had gone "into the city" with a group of her Garden City friends, whom she identified as Maggie Albanese, Jill Gentry, Lauren O'Shea, Karen Clancy, Michelle Rocco and Angel DiGiovanni (all pseudonyms). The evening had started late. They had arrived in Manhattan at around 11:00 P.M.

They went to a bar called Ships' Harbour and there she met a man named Mark Fisher. Angel knew Mark because they went to college together. He was there with a group from school and quickly the two groups joined together. Nicolazzi showed Flannigan a photo of Mark Fisher and had her identify it. The photo was then offered into evidence.

"And after you met Mark Fisher, who did you spend time with after that?" Nicolazzi asked.

"I was with him," Flannigan replied.

"And where were you?"

"Still at the Ships' Harbour."

"What were you doing?"

"Talking and drinking."

She said that her friends went on to another bar, Model T's, and that she and Mark, preferring to be alone, had gone to a nearby pizzeria to get a slice. At first, she said, there were some of Mark's friends from Fairfield in the pizzeria with them, but then they left and she and Mark were alone.

"Did you know where Mark's friends went after they left the pizzeria?"

"No."

"And where did you and Mark go after the two of you left the pizzeria?"

"Went to Model T's."

"How did you get there?"

"We walked."

"When you got there, who did you see, if anyone?"

"When I got there, Angel was there with three men. They met on the street in front of the bar." Meredith said she was introduced to the men as "Al and John." She either forgot or left out the name of the third man—which was Tommy Hassan. Prosecution didn't mention it.

She was asked if the man she met named John was in the courtroom, and she said he was. She then identified him as the man sitting in the front row wearing the black suit jacket and glasses.

"And what happened when you got to Model T's and met Angel and these men?" Nicolazzi asked.

"I was informed that Angel didn't get into the bar because her ID was denied by the bouncer. We were standing there and I tried to get in, but they were over their maximum. They were not letting people in any longer."

"How old are you now?"

"I'm going to be twenty-two in October."

"How old were you back then?"

"Twenty."

The legal drinking age in New York State, of course, is twenty-one, a point Nicolazzi felt didn't need mentioning. Instead, she asked the witness what happened after she, too, wasn't allowed in the bar.

"We were on a street corner trying to decide where we were going to go." She and Angel had considered going back to Garden City but then realized that the trains ran at "odd times after a certain hour."

Mark Fisher called his friends and they were already on their way back to New Jersey. Mark had said that he was supposed to spend the night at the house of a friend of his, but he couldn't remember what town it was in.

"John said his parents were away and we could go to his house," Flannigan said. So, all of them—Al, John, Angel, Mark and herself—got in a cab and went. Everyone rode in one cab. She said she didn't know exactly where the cab took her, but it was John's house and it was in Brooklyn.

She had never been to Brooklyn before. She didn't know who in the cab was and wasn't from Brooklyn. She said that after they got to John's house, they went in the front door and went into the first room on the left, the living room, and they sat around talking.

John told the group that they shouldn't be in the living room. His mom liked that room a lot, so they should move. So, they went through an alcove and into a nearby room, which John called the den. John then opened a bottle of wine and began to pour it into paper cups.

Nicolazzi had the witness verify that she had been drinking earlier in the night at Ships' Harbour, and Flannigan agreed that she had. "Did the alcohol have any effect on you, as to your knowledge, while you were there?"

"No."

"How much did you drink, if you remember?"

"Probably two to three drinks."

"How about Mark Fisher?"

"He seemed intoxicated at Ships' Harbour."

"And what about Al?"

"He didn't strike me as drunk, no."

"And what about the defendant, Giuca?"

"Not drunk, no."

She then learned that they weren't alone in the house. John's brother, Matthew, was there, too. She assumed that Matt had been home when they arrived because he wasn't wearing shoes when he first entered the den.

Then the party was joined by two others. A heavyset "Hispanic" male with braids and a white guy in an orange shirt. She was asked if she saw the man who wore braids in the courtroom. She said she did, and identified Antonio Russo as the man sitting in the front row wearing a blue shirt with a tie. She was asked if she saw any difference in his appearance and she replied yes, his braids were gone.

"What happened while this group was together in the den?"

"Mark sat down on a table. John asked him to move. Mark did not move. John asked him again to get up, and this time Mark did get up and moved."

After that, the party moved gradually through a set of sliding glass doors to an outside porch. Eventually she and Mark, John and Al, the guy with braids and the guy in the orange shirt, all moved to the porch.

"What was going on out there?"

"Someone was rolling a blunt, and people were smoking marijuana."

"When you say a 'blunt,' you are referring to a marijuana cigarette?"

"Yes."

Meredith recalled that she went to the bathroom, made calls on her cell phone, and when she returned to the porch, Mark and the guy with the braids were gone. John told her they'd gone to an ATM. Russo and Fisher returned.

Then John, she recalled, said he wanted Mark to leave. She didn't remember his exact words. It was suggested to Mark, she didn't remember by whom, that Mark get a train back to New Jersey. But Mark didn't leave.

In the meantime she talked to John a bit. She told him that she had never been to Brooklyn before, but that it was a lot nicer than she thought it would be. John told her that Brooklyn was very nice, but there were bad areas.

"And what, if anything, did he do or say after that?"

"He said that you have to protect yourself and that his younger brother had a gun in the house."

While going over Meredith's testimony with the prosecution during the days before she was called to the stand, it had been discovered that her recollection had been more complete during the days after the murder than it was now. A taped conversation between her and investigators, made not long after the murder, had been played for Flannigan, so that she would be able to testify not just to what she remembered, but to everything she had remembered when the occurrences were fresher in her mind. This fact helped to explain the following exchange.

"Do you recall anything else that was said about a gun in the house?"

"From listening to the tape of myself this morning, I said that John had said that he had a gun in the house as well." That gun was in addition to the gun he'd said his brother had. Two guns.

Nicolazzi then noted that the tape to which the witness referred had been made on October 15, 2003, three days after the murder. The witness verified that her statements on that tape were truthful.

Nicolazzi had a question involving Giuca's personal charm and flirtation technique: "Did John show you anything with respect to himself?"

"Yes," Flannigan replied. "He removed his shirt and showed me his tattoo. It spelled out 'Brooklyn.'"

"You said earlier that you were making cell phone calls while at the house?"

"Yes."

"And who were you making calls to?"

"I called my friends, the girls that I was in the city with earlier in the night besides Angel, because she was with me, and I was calling them to ask them if they would come get me."

"Did you mention the girls you were calling, to John Giuca?"

"Yes, he said he would give them Ecstasy pills if they showed up."

Flannigan said that when Russo and Fisher returned from the ATM, there was only one seat left out on the porch, and Russo took it. That left Mark to stand, so he leaned on a railing. She didn't think Mark smoked any marijuana. Al was smoking. Angel wasn't.

Nicolazzi asked the witness what happened next.

"Mark asked John when it was going to kick in. I asked Mark what he had taken. He said either a Clozapine or a Darvocet. I'm not sure, but a painkiller. He mentioned it."

"What did the defendant reply to Mark's question?"

"John said it would kick in, in like five minutes."

"What happened after that?"

"People started to leave. Al and Angel left. The guy in the orange shirt left. Mark went inside the house and fell asleep on the couch. I got up from sitting out there and was going to sleep next to Mark, but he was taking up the length of the couch. I went into the living room and sat on the couch calling people to pick me up."

At that hour no one wanted to come and pick her up. Since she got no takers, she fell asleep. Last she knew, John, his brother, Matt, and Russo were still outside, on the other side of the sliding glass doors.

"What happened next?"

"I woke up at around ten or eleven."

"Do you recall the approximate time when you fell asleep?"

"My cell phone died while I was making calls. I think I fell asleep around six A.M."

"How did you know what time it was when you woke up?"

"I went into the kitchen to use the phone and looked at a clock."

"From the time you fell asleep till the time you woke up, did you hear anything?"

"It was pretty quiet. I heard a door slam. That was the only noise I heard."

"Could you tell by the sound what kind of a door it was?"

"It sounded exactly like the door at my house, like a screen door slamming, metal against metal."

Nicolazzi asked if, at any point, she heard any arguments. She had not. Once in the kitchen that morning she called her little sister to come pick her up, but nobody answered the phone. There was no other movement in the house.

Mark Fisher was no longer on the couch, where she had last seen him. She decided to go out and find a cab. She made her way to Coney Island Avenue, where she found an ATM and took out $60 in cash. Next to the ATM, she testified, was a car service, where she got a car to Garden City.

Back at home in Garden City, she went back to sleep for a while; then she packed her car, picked up a friend of hers, who lived a couple of blocks away and also went to the same college, and they drove back to school together.

After she recharged her phone later that night, she discovered messages from her friends Maggie and Angel. Angel was the one who told her Mark was missing. Flannigan said, "They didn't know where Mark was and they couldn't find him, and everyone at school was getting really worried."

"What was the next thing you learned about that afterward?"

"Mark had been murdered."

"From whom did you learn that?"

"Not sure. Maggie or Angel."

"What if anything did you do after you got the news?"

"I called one of the Brooklyn Police Departments." That first call hadn't worked out. Meredith didn't know which precinct to call, or even the neighborhood she had been in. She had to call a friend, get some info, and then called the police back.

She was subsequently interviewed by the police. For the interview she flew home and was accompanied to the police station by a member of her family. That was the October 15 interview, the tape of which she had listened to just that morning.

"Jumping ahead a little over a year, were you back in the district attorney's office in November 2004, and did you testify in front of a grand jury?"

"Yes."

That concluded the day's session and everyone, except the defendants, was sent home until the next morning. Judge Marrus told Flannigan that they had hoped to finish her testimony in one sitting and apologized for making her come back an additional day. She said okay and agreed not to discuss the case or her testimony with anyone.

When court resumed the following morning, Nicolazzi took up her direct examination of Meredith Flannigan where she had left off. She showed the witness photos taken of Giuca's house and had Flannigan identify them as the location of the events she had previously described.

The photos were walked past the juries, so the panelists could better envision the witness's testimony. Each photo was marked with letters, placed by Flannigan, designating key locations: the railing Mark had leaned on, the couch he'd fallen asleep on, etc.

While they were doing this, Nicolazzi asked Flannigan to describe Mark's manner when he returned with Russo from the ATM machine. She said that he'd seemed quiet. How much distance separated the respective couches where Mark and the witness had fallen asleep? About twenty feet. She said she fell asleep at first, sitting up, but then later on her side, curled up. She described herself as a very light sleeper, which explained why she could hear a door slam even when she was asleep. She said that after she fell asleep in his living room, she never again had any contact with John Giuca. The same was true of Russo and Huggins. Never saw or heard from any of them again.

Going back to the tape of the witness's October 15,

2003, police interview, Nicolazzi asked Flannigan if it was true that she had said, "'John did not want Mark there anymore, and he said, "What are we going to do with him? Let's kick him out. He can't stay here anymore."'" She said it was, and then verified that she was being truthful when she originally recalled those words.

That concluded Nicolazzi's direct examination.

On cross-examination, Fink carefully went over her story. He asked approximately what time it was during the morning of the murder that she and the others had caught a cab from the Upper East Side of Manhattan to Brooklyn. She said, to the best of her recollection, it was somewhere between two and three o'clock in the morning.

When asked, she said that maybe fifteen or twenty minutes elapsed between the time she arrived at Giuca's house and when Russo arrived. Fink asked her if she recalled specifically anything Russo said at any time that night. She said she did not. She didn't, in fact, recall ever speaking with Russo.

Fink asked, "Is it fair to say that you and Mr. Giuca talked a lot that night?"

"Who is Mr. Giuca?" Meredith Flannigan asked.

"Sorry. I mean John."

"Yes, but not more than anyone else I was speaking to that night."

"I have no further questions, Your Honor," Fink said to Judge Marrus.

The judge turned his gaze to the other defense counsel and said, "Cross-examination, Mr. Gregory."

Under Gregory's cross the witness said that Mark did not buy her any drinks at Ships' Harbour the evening before the murder. She, on the other hand, bought several drinks for him.

Gregory led Flannigan through the times, both in Manhattan and in Brooklyn, when people had suggested to Mark Fisher that he should take a train back to New Jersey.

Each time this occurred, Meredith agreed, he refused to do so. At one point in Manhattan, she said, someone even stopped a cab and asked if it could take Mark to New Jersey, but the driver had refused.

Gregory asked if the primary reason for going to Giuca's house was to continue the party. She said it was. Drinking and smoking took place there. Yes, she had been among those smoking marijuana.

She said that John had promised to give Ecstasy to her friends if they came over, but, as far as she recalled, that was the only time the subject of Ecstasy came up. She herself took no Ecstasy, and although she heard John and Mark discussing a pill Mark had taken, no one said it was Ecstasy. In fact, Mark told her he believed the pill to be a painkiller.

Gregory pointed out that Angel DiGiovanni was Meredith's companion throughout the evening, the reason she found herself in Brooklyn in the first place. The witness agreed that this was true.

"And, at some point, you realize she is not there."

"That's right."

"She didn't tell you she was going to leave, is that correct?"

"She did not tell me, no."

Al hadn't said anything to her, either. Gregory quickly ran through the facts of her story, right up until the time she made a phone call from the kitchen, then left to find an ATM and a car service.

Gregory had no further questions. Nicolazzi had no questions on redirect. Meredith Flannigan was allowed to step down.

CHAPTER 32

Fairfield Witnesses

The next prosecution witness was Christopher James Peters, who was questioned by McNeill. He said he was a twenty-one-year-old student at Fairfield and one of Mark Fisher's buddies who had accompanied him on their Columbus Day weekend outing.

He'd known Mark for fourteen months as they played together on the Fairfield football team. They were good friends. McNeill asked him to recall for the juries where he was on October 11, 2003. Peters said that they had driven from school to Saddle River, New Jersey, on Friday night. On Saturday they visited Mark's parents, friends and family.

With them were Peter's friend from school Jackie Conway, and two other friends, Janet and Mark. Different Mark. Before leaving for New York that night, they were joined by two other friends, Kate and Caitlin, all Fairfield students.

They went to the Ships' Harbour, on the Upper East Side, and met Angel and her friend Meredith. Peters said he knew Angel previously because they went to the same school, but that he hadn't previously talked to her, that he could recall.

He knew Angel because she was the roommate of a girl he knew named Kate. McNeill asked if Peters saw Mark talking with anyone at Ships' Harbour. He said he'd met Angel's friend Meri and they had gone off by themselves to talk.

McNeill asked Peters to describe the relationship between Mark and Meri and he said it "seemed pretty flirty." After a while everyone went across the street to get pizza. After they finished eating, they decided to go to another bar, a place called Martell's.

The group that had started out in New Jersey, with the exception of Mark Fisher, all went to the new bar. Mark and Meri had said they would follow soon in a cab, but they never showed.

They stayed at the second bar for somewhere between a half hour and an hour, then returned to Saddle River, New Jersey, where Jackie lived.

"And did you ever speak with Mark Fisher after leaving the pizza parlor?"

"No."

"Did you ever see Mark Fisher again after leaving the pizza parlor?"

"No."

Peters testified that he slept at Jackie's house, and when he woke up, he had a message on his voice mail.

"It was from Mark. He said it was between four and four-thirty in the morning. I returned his call, but I didn't get a response. Then we decided to go back to Fairfield. You know, we figured he was either in his room, took a train to school or something, so we drove back to Fairfield, checked his room, went to Security. We eventually reached Angel, who said she thought Mark had gone home."

Mark Fisher, an honors student and star athlete, seemingly without enemies, was found murdered far from home, beside a street in Brooklyn during the early morning hours of October 12, 2003.

Mark Fisher's college football jersey has been memorialized in his old room in his parents' Jersey home.

The Lenape Valley Regional High School football field, which was the site of countless Saturday afternoon heroics by the school's star quarterback, Mark Fisher. *(Photo by Jules Mladinich)*

In close proximity to Lenape High School's baseball and football fields, administrators planted a tree in Mark Fisher's memory. *(Photo by Jules Mladinich)*

Not a minute goes by when Nancy Fisher doesn't think of her son. She says Mark was destined to do great things with his life.

The younger Michael Fisher recalls fond memories of his younger brother.

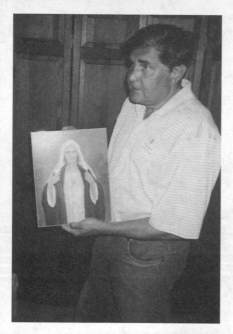

The elder Michael Fisher holds a drawing of the Blessed Mother that was sent to him by a perfect stranger, a retired NYPD detective who had also lost a son.

John Giuca, age ten. Are those the eyes of a killer?
(Doreen Giuliano)

Giuca graduated from Bishop Ford High School not far from his home and was attending John Jay College at the time of Mark Fisher's murder. *(Doreen Giuliano)*

John Giuca

718-469-7792
SAG

Anyone with show-business aspirations needs an eight-by-ten glossy, and this was Giuca's. He got some work as an extra, but now his mom uses the photo only to promote him on a prisoners-seeking-love Web site. *(Doreen Giuliano)*

Support for John Giuca, especially among his young female friends and acquaintances, grew steadily as the trial went on. By the time of sentencing, Giuca's followers were out in force at the courthouse, some wearing "FREE JOHN GIUCA" T-shirts. *(Doreen Giuliano)*

One of the things John Giuca and his friends had in common was that many had attended Bishop Ford High School seventeen city blocks away from the edge of Ditmas Park where Giuca and Russo lived. *(Photo by Nathan A. Versace)*

John Giuca first met Mark Fisher outside of this bar on Second Avenue.

Now under new ownership and bearing a new name, this is the bar on First Ave. where Mark Fisher's urban adventure began.

Hollywood film crews frequently used the Ditmas Park neighborhood as a setting for period pieces, because the streets of the neighborhood had such a "land-that-time-forgot" ambiance.

The original street sign at the corner of Albemarle and Beverley roads, carved in stone atop a pedestal of bricks. The stone had worn over the years and the signs were difficult to read, adding to the timelessness of the neighborhood.

The Victorian home where John Giuca lived and Mark Fisher attended his last party. Unlike the manicured perfection of the houses around it, the house was in need of a paint job and the front steps were broken. *(Photo by Nathan A. Versace)*

Antonio Russo lived in an apartment in this large building behind Giuca's home. Realizing he was under police surveillance, Russo took to sneaking out of his building using the back fire escape. *(Photo by Nathan A. Versace)*

The twenty-four-hour convenience store on Coney Island Ave.
where Mark Fisher made his last beer run.
(Photo by Nathan A. Versace)

One of Mark Fisher's last actions was using his bank card to
withdraw $20 from this ATM, just inside the front entrance of the
market. Police initially thought the motive for Fisher's killing was
robbery. *(Photo by Nathan A. Versace)*

Mark Fisher's body was found in front of this house on Argyle Road, around the corner from the Giuca house and only a few houses down from Albert Huggins' home. *(Photo by Nathan A. Versace)*

Mark Fisher's wallet was found at the bottom of this sewer opening at the corner of Stratford Road and Turner Place, near the Giuca and Russo homes. There was no money in the wallet. Police theorized that it had been discarded in hopes of delaying the identification of Mark Fisher's body.
(Photo by Nathan A. Versace)

Assistant District Attorney Josh Hanshaft, originally from Staten Island, loved nothing better than prosecuting cases. He thought John Giuca looked "slight and weak."

Deputy chief of the district attorney's rackets bureau Patricia McNeil.

The State Supreme and Family Court at 320 Jay Street in Brooklyn, where John Giuca and Antonio Russo were tried together (with separate juries) for the murder of Mark Fisher.

John Giuca's defense attorney Sam Gregory in his office above Gleason's Boxing Gym in Brooklyn.

It was just a coincidence that Jonathan Fink became Antonio Russo's defense attorney, but Fink nonetheless fought tooth and nail for his client's freedom.

James Petrillo saw himself as a soldier in the cause to free his friend John Giuca. He believed that Antonio Russo alone was behind the death of Mark Fisher.

Giuca's friend Jennifer Baker models the "FREE JOHN GIUCA" T-shirt she wore at Giuca's sentencing hearing.
(Photos by Robert Ecksel)

Jennifer Baker runs a group called the Brooklyn Calendar Girls. For a fee they'll liven up your party or bar.

John Giuca's mom Doreen Giuliano never stopped believing in her son's innocence.

Mark Fisher is buried in the Gate of Heaven Catholic Cemetery in East Hanover, New Jersey.

They eventually spoke to a friend who said she had heard about a murder in Brooklyn. Peters didn't know anyone in Brooklyn, but he had a friend in Queens, whom he called.

He learned on the morning of October 13—from two detectives, and from Fairfield Security—that Mark had been murdered. That concluded McNeill's direct. Neither defense attorney had any cross, so the witness was allowed to step down.

Angel DiGiovanni was the prosecution's next witness. McNeill did the questioning. The witness stated that her full name was Angel Frances DiGiovanni, that she lived in Nassau County and attended Fairfield University in Connecticut.

Angel recalled that during the Columbus Day weekend in 2003 she was also a Fairfield student, but was home in Garden City, Long Island, for the long holiday weekend.

She and a group of girlfriends from high school, including Meredith Flannigan, made plans to go into Manhattan that Saturday night. They had no set plans. They were going to take a train into the city and "kind of like plan it out when we got there."

McNeill asked if they had plans to meet anyone there, and Angel said yes, they intended to meet Albert "Al" Huggins. Al was her boyfriend Dan's friend, and he was interested in meeting some of her girlfriends.

He knew the city well, so he could help them navigate and go to the best places. They ended up at Ships' Harbour and, by coincidence, ran into some Fairfield students she knew.

These included her own roommate, Kate, a couple of guys from the football team, Mark and Chris, and some female friends of theirs, Jackie and Janet.

She thought that it was kind of funny that Mark and Meri were talking. She knew one of them from high school and the other from college and here they were hitting it off.

Mark, she said, came over at one point and told her how pretty he thought Meri was. Meri also came over and remarked how much she liked Mark. At one point Angel realized that many of her Garden City friends had moved on to another bar called Model T's.

So she and Al, who had showed up just as planned, and their friend Maggie Albanese started walking to the other bar. When she left, she said, Mark and Meri were still at the bar at Ships' Harbour.

Things didn't go well at Model T's. Neither she nor Al were allowed into Model T's because they were underage. After a few minutes Mark and Meri arrived at the scene outside Model T's.

Angel testified, "I kind of went up to her and asked her why she was still with him, because I was concerned that he wasn't with his friends. I didn't know what her plan was and what she was doing."

At about that time a few of Al's friends from high school arrived and she was introduced. The only one of them she remembered by name was John.

At the prosecutor's request, the witness identified John as the guy sitting in the front row of the courtroom wearing glasses and a gray suit.

Things were complicated by the fact that it was 3:30 A.M. They had missed the train back to Garden City and the next one didn't leave until 5:00 A.M. Waiting at the train station would have been too boring.

"At that time Al had asked me if I wanted to stay the night at his house. We had plans to watch the Yankee game the next day. I called my boyfriend to see if it was okay with him. It was.

"I asked Meri if she wanted to stay. She was going to come with me and spend the night and we were going to come and take the train home the next morning. Mark had also asked me what he should do. I gave him my cell phone, he didn't have his, to try and get in touch with the friends he'd been in the city with, but he couldn't get in touch with them.

"I was talking to a cabdriver to try and see if they would take him back to where he was staying, but he didn't know the address of the house. He also didn't have that much money on him, so he asked me if it would be okay if he could spend the night where we were staying."

"And what happened then?"

"We took a cab back to Brooklyn."

"Did you have a discussion with John Giuca about what you were going to do, your plans?"

"No."

She said the cab took them to John's house. No one appeared to be home when they arrived. They started out in the living room, but moved to the den. Angel was tired and fell asleep on a couch after about a half hour.

After a half hour of sleep, Al woke her up. Since she was asleep anyway, he said, it was probably time to go to his house. She put on her shoes. She didn't know what time it was, but when they walked the short distance between John's and Al's homes, it was still dark outside.

She testified it was approximately 6:00 A.M. when they arrived at Al's house. She had been there once before. She had picked up her boyfriend there before going to a family party. Once there, she went upstairs to a guest room. She called her boyfriend before going to bed. Al gave her some clothes to change into—fleece pants and a T-shirt.

She saw no one in John's house after waking up there, other than Al. She saw Mark in John's house soon after they arrived and he seemed quiet. She didn't see anyone at Al's house, either, although she heard a voice that she believed belonged to Al's mother, asking if he was home.

Al slept in his own room down the hall. Other than

Al's mom's voice, she heard nothing. She woke up at about 11:00 A.M. Moments after she awoke, Al came into her room.

Just then, he received a phone call from John asking if they knew where Meri was.

"He said she wasn't with us," Angel testified. "I asked Al to ask John where Mark was, if he was with Meri. I was told that John had given Mark directions to take a train and he took the train home the night before."

McNeill asked DiGiovanni what she did after that phone call. Angel said she tried to call Meri, but Meri didn't pick up her phone. Angel didn't get in touch with Meri until later that night, at which time Meri told her she wasn't with Mark.

Angel was asked what Al's demeanor was like that morning and she said it was normal.

After waking up, Al's mom made them breakfast. Mrs. Huggins said there had been a shooting nearby. But no one went outside to see what was going on. She helped Al clean out his garage; then they—she and Al—took a train to Garden City and went to Angel's house.

Once there, Angel showered while Al watched TV with Angel's dad. Plans were for Al, Angel and Angel's boyfriend to return to Al's house to watch the Yankee game on TV.

McNeill asked if, while she helped Al clean out the Huggins family's garage, if she noticed any police activity out on the street. She said she did not.

During the course of the day she received phone calls from Mark's friends, Chris and Jackie, asking again if she'd heard from Mark. She said no. They had her number because Mark had used her cell phone the night before to call them.

Angel testified that she didn't find out that something had happened to Mark until Monday morning, when her roommate, Kate, gave her the bad news.

Soon thereafter, she was taken to the Fairfield University Security Department and was interviewed by two detectives, although she did not remember their names.

That concluded McNeill's direct examination. Fink had no cross. Gregory said he did want to speak with the witness, but "briefly."

Gregory wanted Angel to describe the state of Mark's sobriety during the course of the evening. "He'd had too much to drink, correct?" Gregory asked.

"He'd been drinking. I couldn't know if he'd had too much to drink."

"At any time during the evening, did you become frustrated by his behavior?"

"No."

Angel told him that most of her interaction with Mark that night involved Meri. He felt that he wasn't getting anywhere with her. I explained to him that Meri liked men who were hard to get. Maybe if he cooled it when it came to hitting on her, he might do better.

"Would it be fair to say that he was a little drunk or very drunk, and he was coming on a little heavy?"

"Correct."

"Were you frustrated with him as anyone might be toward someone they were close to who'd had a bit too much?"

"Correct."

Gregory took the witness through the various attempts to get Mark to go home, none of which worked out. Moving to the point at which Al woke her up and said it was time to go to his house, Gregory asked, "Did you notice who was out on the porch at that time?"

"No, I did not."

Regarding Al's mother mentioning the next morning a shooting on the block, Gregory asked, "Would it be fair to say that the body may have been dumped there and not shot there, correct?"

"Correct."

That concluded the questioning of Angel DiGiovanni, and court was recessed for the day, to resume at 10:00 A.M. on September 16, 2005.

On the morning of September 16, the prosecution's first witness was Christopher Deneen, who was questioned by Trish McNeill. Deneen said he was twenty-one years old, and attended Fordham University. Back in October 2003, however, he'd been a student at Fairfield and a friend of Mark Fisher's.

On October 11, 2003, the Saturday of Columbus Day weekend, Deneen testified that Mark Fisher had called him. Fisher said he and a group of Fairfield kids were going to Ships' Harbour in the city, and did he want to go along?

Deneen had other plans and declined. The following day, Deneen said, Chris Peters called him twice asking if he'd spoken to Mark. Deneen said no.

"And then Chris Peters called me a few hours later, about ten o'clock at night, and he heard that there was a murder in the area of Brooklyn where they'd been and asked me to call up the precinct to see if it was Mark."

"Did you make that call?"

"Yes. They told me that there had been a murder in the area, but the officer I spoke to said it was not Mark."

"When did you learn that Mark Fisher had been killed?"

"The next Monday when I got back to school, Chris Peters met me at my car and told me the news."

"Were you interviewed by the police at that time?"

"Yes, I gave them a description of Mark, his name and the area he was in. That's about it, really."

That *was* about it. McNeill had no further questions. Fink and Gregory had no questions, so Deneen's brief time on the stand was over.

CHAPTER 33

Al Huggins

Next up was Albert Huggins, with Nicolazzi doing the questioning. Huggins said he was twenty-one years old and a junior at Penn State University. He'd only been going to Penn State for a year. Before that, he'd attended Fordham University in the Bronx and St. Francis College in Brooklyn.

He said he'd been a close friend of John Giuca's since second grade. At Nicolazzi's request, Huggins identified Giuca as the man in the front row wearing the pink shirt and jacket.

Huggins said that Giuca was one of his best friends and that the two spoke to one another, on the average, about once every other day. He and Giuca lived two blocks apart in what he referred to as the "Flatbush section" of Brooklyn.

Then Huggins told his version of that night's events, how he went to the city, met up with Angel DiGiovanni, the girlfriend of one of his good friends from Fordham.

Angel was in a bar called Ships' Harbour with a couple of her friends from Long Island, and there they bumped into some friends of hers from Fairfield. They got pizza, then went to Model T's. It was when he got to Model T's that he called John Giuca.

"I told him where we were," Huggins testified. "I made plans with him earlier in the night to meet up later, if they didn't get into the club they were trying to get into downtown." Huggins's group tried and failed to get into Model T's.

Soon thereafter, John showed up with his friend Tommy Hassan, who hadn't had any better luck with their fake IDs downtown. With John and Tommy were James Petrillo, James Mamorsky and some girls he didn't know.

Petrillo, Mamorsky and the girls got into the bar, but Giuca did not, leaving him out on the sidewalk with Al and Angel. Angel kept getting calls from Meri, asking how to get to Model T's.

"We were just hanging out," Huggins said. "We didn't know what to do." Eventually Mark and Meri joined the group on foot. "Mark looked really trashed."

Huggins's cell phone rang. It was his mom. She was ticked off because he wasn't home yet. "I got to go," Huggins told the others. Angel said she'd missed her train. Huggins said she could stay at his place. She called her boyfriend, who said it was okay.

While Huggins was trying to hail a cab, Meri said there was a problem. What were they to do with Mark? He had no money. No cell. He wasn't sure where he had to go.

John spoke up. He was sick of just standing there and suggested they go to his place. So they all got in a cab. John and Al split the fare.

Huggins's version of what happened at John's house synched up nicely with Meri's at first. They started in the living room, but moved into the den because John's mom wanted to keep the living room neat. They drank beer and wine.

"The doorbell rang," Huggins testified, "and John got worried that it was going to be Lauren, his girlfriend." No one answered the door. Then Huggins's phone rang. "Hey, we're outside, let us in," the caller said. But it wasn't Lauren. It was Tommy Hassan, who was with James Mamorsky, the friend everyone called Jimmy. Someone let Tommy and Jimmy in.

Nicolazzi asked if there was anyone else in the house at that time. Huggins said he later learned that John's brother, Matt, had been asleep in the house when they got there, but he didn't know that at the time.

Matt didn't wake up and make an appearance until about a half hour after Tommy and Jimmy arrived.

Huggins related the now-familiar story of Mark sitting on a table, only in Huggins's version John made one brief comment about not sitting on a table and it was Tommy, not John, who told Mark in no uncertain terms that in Brooklyn they used chairs.

Tommy started to roll a joint. Mark said he wouldn't mind getting high, to which John said, "You want to smoke, go get some money." Mark said okay, he had an ATM card, all he needed was a machine.

John started to give Mark directions as to how to get to an ATM machine, could see it wasn't registering, and told Tony to take him there.

"Who is Tony?" Nicolazzi asked.

"Antonio Russo," Huggins said, and then identified the defendant as the one sitting in the front row of the courtroom with the gray jacket and green shirt.

"When did Mr. Russo arrive?"

"Shortly after Tommy and Jimmy."

After Tony and Mark left, some people went outside to smoke. Al and Angel stayed inside. After a few minutes Mark and Tony returned and went out onto the porch.

Angel fell asleep on a couch and Huggins was close to falling asleep next to her. Al went outside and announced that he was leaving. Meri asked him if Angel was going with him. Al said yes.

Angel and Al walked the short blocks to Huggins's home. He gave her clothes to sleep in and led her to a guest room. His mom said, "Oh, you're home." He said, "Yeah."

Then he went to bed in his own room. He woke up at about 11:00 A.M. His mom was already up and told him that there had been a shooting nearby and a body had been discovered "in a driveway somewhere."

Nicolazzi asked what the relationship was between Tommy Hassan and John Giuca. Huggins said they were good friends. What about James Mamorsky? Huggins said he was also a good friend of John's, maybe not as close as Tommy, but still good friends.

"And what about the defendant Antonio Russo?"

"They were friends, but I felt that John was more of the boss and Tony would do whatever he said."

"How long had you known Antonio Russo?"

"Probably almost as long as I know John."

"How did you meet him?"

"Through John."

"You mentioned someone named James Petrillo earlier. What was his relationship with John?"

"I didn't see him as much, so I don't know. They were friends. I don't know how close."

"Do you know a person by the name of Anthony Palumbo?"

"Yes, he also lived in the neighborhood, on Beverley Road." Huggins said Palumbo wasn't around as much, so he didn't know how close Palumbo's relationship was with Giuca.

"How would you describe the relationship between John Giuca and Antonio Russo, based on your observations?"

"Tony always wanted to impress John. He would do anything to impress him."

"Do the initials GM mean anything to you, Mr. Huggins?"

"Yes." He knew about GM through John, he said. The initials stood for "Ghetto Mafia."

"What did John tell you about the Ghetto Mafia?"

"It was like part of Crip, except that Crip started earlier and it evolved into that. I know that their colors were orange and blue. I knew that Rob Lancaster (pseudonym) started it and was the head of it, and John was one of the capos. Gregg was one of the capos. I know they had meetings. I wasn't allowed to be at them."

"How did you know that they had meetings?"

"Because I would be on the block hanging out with John and he would tell me, 'Listen, we're going to have a meeting in a few minutes, so you have to go.'"

"Where would those meetings take place?"

Huggins said meetings took place at John's house, the Wenningers' house in Bensonhurst and sometimes outdoors on Turner Place, next to the big apartment building where Antonio Russo lived.

"Are you saying that the Crips evolved into the Ghetto Mafia?"

"Yes."

"What did you mean when you said their colors were orange and blue?"

"That's what they wore. They had orange flags, they had orange beads that they wore around their neck."

"Who do you recall specifically wearing those beads, based on your observations?"

"John, Tony, Tommy."

"Do you know two individuals by the name of Billy and Jesse Wenninger?"

Huggins said he did, he'd met them through John. They were part of GM. Meetings sometimes took place at their house. Huggins was never at the meetings, however, because he was not a part of GM. He was, however, friends with members.

"I'm going to direct your attention to approximately a week or two before Mark Fisher was killed. Did you have a conversation with John Giuca about GM?"

"Yes."

"What, if anything, did he tell you?"

"He said GM was getting soft, and that John and Rob were talking about having to get a body before they got into GM."

"Are you familiar with the term to 'get a body'?"

"Yeah, it means to kill someone," Huggins testified.

"Did you ever hear any music with respect to GM?"

"Yeah, it was a rap song CD they remixed over some rap song and changed the words to GM stuff."

"Within GM, what was the relationship between John Giuca and Antonio Russo?"

"Tony wasn't a capo and John was higher than him."

"About a week before Mark Fisher was killed, did you have occasion to be in John Giuca's home, in his room?"

"Yes."

"What did you see when you were up there?"

"A gun."

"What, if anything, happened?"

"John was going over the bullets and the gun he had. He was showing me how this gun worked. He shot it into a closet filled with phone books, and took the bullets out and showed me what they looked like after they got shot."

According to Huggins's testimony, John said the gun was a .22-caliber Ruger.

"You say he took the bullets out. Where did he take the bullets out from?"

"The phone books. He showed me how a .22 goes further through something and he showed me a slug of a different bullet and how it's fatter and wouldn't go as far."

"On the night you went into the city, October eleventh,

or the previous night, did you have occasion at that time
to be in John's room?"

"Yes."

"What, if anything, did you see up there then?"

"He showed me a gun he bought, he said from
Harlem. It was a three-eighty he said, and it was in a
black case. There was a gun, clip and bullets."

"Was there a difference between the bullets for this
gun and those he'd shown you a week earlier?"

"They were fatter."

"Now, Mr. Huggins, I'm going to ask you a few questions about your own background. You say you are not a
member of the GM. Have you ever had contact with the
criminal justice system?"

"Yes, I have."

"How many times have you been arrested?"

Huggins said he'd been arrested once near Fordham
in the Bronx. He'd been out celebrating a friend's birthday, got drunk and got into a fight outside a bar. "I got
in a lot of trouble for it," the witness said. Two kids had
to be hospitalized they were beaten up so bad, but
they were out the next day. "It was a stupid thing and
I regret it," Huggins added. Huggins took a youthful-
offender adjudication and was given five years' probation for the incident.

Huggins identified photos of Ships' Harbour, Model
T's, and John Giuca's house, which were then offered
into evidence.

"After you woke up on the morning of October 12,
2003, and your mother told you there was a body found on
the block, did you receive a phone call?" Nicolazzi asked.
Huggins said he had. The call was from John Giuca.

That concluded Nicolazzi's direct examination. It was
Fink's turn to cross-examine. Huggins told Fink that,
during the early morning in question, the group had
arrived at John's house at about five o'clock. Fink then

established that, according to this witness, the incident involving Mark Fisher sitting on a table instead of a chair occurred before Antonio Russo arrived at the party. Huggins said he remembered Russo wearing GM colors on other occasions, but did not recall what Russo was wearing that night. He didn't remember if anyone at the party was wearing GM colors or beads, for that matter.

Bringing up the GM members, the Wenninger brothers, Fink asked where they lived. Huggins said they lived in Bensonhurst. Fink asked how far that was from his house. Huggins said it was a twenty-minute car ride.

Fink asked about the time Giuca told the witness that GM members would have to "get a body." Huggins reiterated that Russo was not in the room when John made that comment, that Giuca and Huggins were alone at the time. That concluded Fink's cross-examination.

Gregory began his cross with a transcript of Huggins's grand jury testimony in his hand. He pointed out that in the version of the sitting-on-a-table story that he'd told on December 16 he said that it was Tommy who'd scolded Fisher for not using a chair. In today's testimony he'd said that both John and Tommy spoke to Fisher about the infraction of household rules.

"It was only after your preparation with the DA yesterday that you changed your testimony, correct?" Gregory asked. Huggins agreed that it was.

Gregory noted that in Meredith Flannigan's version of the evening, she had been in the bathroom making phone calls when Angel and Al left the party. But in Al's version, Al had announced he was leaving and, after Meri asked, had added that he was taking Angel with him.

"It's not that you slipped out while Meri was on the porch without saying good-bye so you could take Angel back to your house? Didn't happen that way."

"No."

"So you're positive you said good-bye to Meri, correct?"

"Yes, I am." Huggins said he was not with Angel later that morning when Meri called her cell phone asking where they were.

After establishing that Huggins met Fisher for the first time that night, he asked if it was clear to him that Mark Fisher was not from Brooklyn.

"That's fair to say," Huggins replied.

Gregory made it clear that he thought Huggins's version of the story was odd. Angel was his friend's girlfriend. She was supposed to introduce him to her girlfriends. Instead, though, Al and Angel were attached at the hip all night. Huggins stuck with his version of the story.

Gregory wanted to know, when the group was still in Manhattan and there was talk of how to get Mark back to New Jersey, if it wasn't in his mind that, with Mark gone, he and John could go back to Brooklyn with Angel and Meri?

"I didn't really care," Huggins said.

Under Gregory's cross-examination, the atmosphere at the early-morning party was revealed to be edgier than it had seemed during earlier testimony. Gregory drew Huggins's attention to a time after the group arrived at John's house and the doorbell rang.

"Would it be fair to say at that time you say to Mark, 'This may be a problem, we have a problem with people in the neighborhood, we may have a problem.'"

"Yes," the witness said, smiling at the memory.

"It would be fair to say that you said this because you were playing the Brooklyn-tough-guy routine, that you hang with tough guys and you're a tough guy, too?"

"Okay. Yes."

"And would it be fair to say that Fisher says something that displays what kind of person he is?"

"Yes."

"He says, 'Even though I never met you before, even though I don't know you, I got your back,' correct?"

"Yes."

"When Tony Russo came to the party, did he look at Fisher and say, 'Hey, Yarmulke'?"

"Yeah."

"You start laughing, correct?"

"I didn't laugh."

"When Tommy Hassan told Mark Fisher to get off the table, he was nasty, correct?"

"Yeah."

"Did you stand up and say, 'Hey, wait a second, Tommy, the kid's with me, he came with Angel and Meri, take it easy on the kid.' Did you stand up for him?"

"No."

"Was your demeanor that night the same as it is now talking in front of these people?"

"No, it wasn't."

Gregory then returned to later on during the morning of October 12, 2003, after Huggins's mom told him there had been a body found on the block and he received a phone call from John Giuca.

"Did you tell John what your mother had said about there having been a shooting?"

"Yes."

"And he said, 'We may have had something to do with that,' correct?"

"Yes."

"Did you think at that time that you should go find out if this person who's shot and body is in the driveway is alive or dead?"

"No."

"You are telling the jury that John told you that 'we might have something to do with that' and you didn't seek to find out if the victim was alive or dead?"

"I couldn't find out if he was alive or dead. I went outside and looked for a body or something and there was nothing."

"Did you go and ask a neighbor what was going on?"

"No."

"After what John said to you on the phone, were you concerned?"

"Yes."

"Did you express your concern to Angel DiGiovanni?"

"No."

"In fact, what you did is, rather than investigate, you carried on with the day as though nothing had happened, correct?"

"Yeah."

Gregory pointed out that Al and Angel went to her house, watched TV with Angel's dad and had dinner with the DiGiovanni family. "At that time, did you know Mark Fisher was dead?"

"I didn't know for sure."

"Did you know Mark Fisher had been shot?"

"I suspected it, but I didn't hear from John."

"Isn't the reason you went on with your day as though you knew nothing about what had happened [was] because you were trying to hide what you knew about this incident?"

"I didn't know exactly what happened."

To emphasize the proximity between the location where Mark Fisher's body was found and Huggins's home, Gregory showed the witness a crime scene photo that showed Fisher's body, and Huggins's house in the background.

Gregory asked if Huggins had received a phone call at five fifty-seven A.M. on the morning in question.

"That's what the records say," the witness replied. The records, in fact, indicated that the call came from John Giuca, and a sixty-four-second conversation had taken place. But the witness had insisted all along that he did not remember this call, a forgetfulness he testified to here as well.

Gregory's cross was halted at this point by an objection. Since this phone call had not come up on direct examination, it was deemed outside the scope of cross-examination.

Gregory shifted gears and began to ask about Huggins's room in his house, which, at the time of the murder, was on the side of the house facing Argyle Road, with windows that looked down over the street. In other words, all Huggins had to do to see the crime scene was look out his bedroom window. Huggins admitted that in the past he had heard sounds coming from Argyle Road when he was in his bedroom; yet he had not heard any shots or any of the police activity that followed.

Gregory had no further questions, but Nicolazzi said she had a few on redirect. She asked questions about the appearance of some of the individuals who had been at the party at John Giuca's house. It was established that Tommy Hassan was white, and James Mamorsky was black.

Under redirect Huggins said that, while it was true he hadn't mentioned John talking to Mark about sitting on a table, he did mention that John, at another point during the party, mentioned that Mark was "disrespecting" his house.

Nicolazzi asked if he had overheard Meredith and John have a conversation regarding the drug Ecstasy. Huggins said he had. Asked for details, the witness replied he'd heard Meri say she wanted some Ecstasy and John say that he had some. That concluded Nicolazzi's redirect.

The attorneys then met with the judge in a sidebar session and it was decided that, for Gregory's recross of the witness, the Green Jury would be in the courtroom, but the Red Jury would be excluded. The court then recessed for lunch.

That afternoon, before the Giuca jury came back into court, there was discussion among the attorneys and Judge Marrus regarding the 5:57 A.M. phone call. Gre-

gory said in open court that his client, John Giuca, remembered making the phone call very well, and that he
had said to Huggins, "This kid can't stay here. You left
him behind, Huggins. He's coming to your house."

Judge Marrus ruled that since the witness had testified
he didn't recall the phone call, it would be improper for
Gregory to refresh his memory by quoting a statement
made by the defendant. At that point the Green Jury was
allowed back in the courtroom and the questioning of
Albert Huggins continued.

Nicolazzi asked Huggins to describe the phone call
he'd received from John Giuca later in the morning in
question. Huggins said he was alone in the dining room
of his house when he received the call.

"John asked me if Meri was at my house," Huggins said.
"I said, 'No, why would she be here? I left with Angel.
Meri doesn't even know where my house is.' I told him my
mom had said there'd been a shooting on the block and
he said, 'Oh, well, we might have had something to do with
that.' I said, 'What do you mean?' He said, 'Don't worry
about it. Just find out where Meri is and get back to me.'
So I went to Angel and asked her to call Meri and find out
where she was. Angel called a bunch of times, but Meri
didn't pick up the phone. I called John back and told him
Meri wasn't answering her phone. John said to keep trying.
He needed to know where she was. So, Angel called one
of Meri's friends and found out that Meri had taken a cab
and was at home sleeping. I called John back and told him.
He said, 'How could that be? She didn't know where she
was. How could she take a cab home?' John wanted Angel
to keep calling Meri until she spoke to her in person. I asked
him where was Mark. He said, 'Don't worry about it. He left.
He took a train home. He's fine.' And I don't know if it was
that call or another one when I asked him what he meant
by 'we might have had something to do with that.' John said,
'Tony left with him, if you know what I mean.'"

The witness said he next spoke to John on the phone after he had taken the Long Island Railroad to Garden City as he was accompanying Angel back home. At that point John asked again if anyone had spoken to Meri, and Huggins said no.

"John said, 'Listen, the cops are going to come and question you, just don't say anything, just keep asking for your attorney, just keep asking for your attorney.' He said it like three, four times," Huggins testified. "I was right in front of Angel when he said it and I was trying to keep calm. I hurried him off the phone. I said, 'Yeah, yeah, cool, whatever.' I knew there was something wrong at the time, but I tried to keep it together in front of Angel because I didn't want to worry her."

Huggins spent time at Angel's house and then returned to Brooklyn with Angel and her boyfriend. They were supposed to watch the Yankees–Red Sox baseball game on TV, but it was rained out, so they watched movies instead. During that time Huggins sneaked out of the house and went over to John's house to find out more about what had gone on.

"John's girlfriend, Lauren, was there and right away they got into an argument. John still couldn't figure out how Meri got a cab. 'You probably called for it while she was laying in bed with you,' Lauren said. We went up to John's room and he said he hoped Mark was alive. He said, 'I told Tony do one thing, he does another. I really hope he didn't do something stupid here.' He was regretting that he gave Tony the gun after he got upset about Mark disrespecting the house. He wanted Mark to be alive to clear his name, to be able to say, 'It was Tony, and not John, who shot me.'"

"Was John specific about why he'd been upset with Mark the night before?"

"Yeah, Mark had been a drunk fool all night and John was pretty much fed up with him. He told Tony to show him what's up. Tony asked for the gun and John gave it to him. Tony went outside and waited on Turner Place for Mark. John walked Mark to the door and sent Mark out. John said that once Mark was outside, Tony jumped out and started beating Mark. Mark fought back. Tony shot him and then beat him some more, and then came back to John's house. He gave the gun back to John. He told him it was done."

During their conversation during the evening of October 12, Giuca asked Huggins how Mark had gotten connected to the group the previous night. Huggins told him that Angel and Mark went to school together.

"That really surprised John. I don't think he knew that," Huggins testified.

Huggins subsequently returned to his home, where Angel and her boyfriend, Dan, were eating pizza and watching movies. Angel's friends called looking for Mark and Huggins gave them the precinct number to call. Angel and Dan left and Huggins went to sleep.

The next day, that Monday, Giuca called Huggins and told him to come over. Huggins did and they went through the newspapers to see if there was anything about the shooting. John again said he wished Mark were alive, that he didn't kill him, and that responsibility was not going to fall on him. Huggins asked Giuca if the house was clean, meaning were there guns or drugs about, in case police searched. Giuca said yes, but then remembered he kept a box of bullets in the roof gutter outside his bedroom window, which was on the third flood of the Stratford Road house. Huggins wasn't sure what Giuca did with the bullets, but he thought Giuca might have flushed them down the toilet. Huggins told Giuca that an attorney named Phil Slocum (pseudonym) was a friend of the Huggins family and that Giuca should call him.

Nicolazzi returned to the gun Giuca showed to Huggins

the week before, the one he had fired into the phone books in his bedroom closet. She asked the witness what type of gun it was and he said it was a semi-automatic. When Giuca fired the gun, a shell popped out. Huggins remembered that specifically because he'd been the one to pick the shell up off the floor.

Nicolazzi returned to the Monday following the murder, when Huggins visited Giuca at his house. She asked about any further conversations Giuca and Huggins might have had. Huggins said that Giuca again said that the police were going to have questions, and when they did, it was important that they had their story down. Giuca told Huggins to say that Giuca had fallen asleep on the back porch, that Fisher woke him up and said he wanted to go home, so Giuca walked Fisher to the front door and pointed the way to Church Avenue, where Fisher could catch the Q train (subway). Finally he closed the door, saw Meri asleep on the couch and went to bed.

The witness said that the police did come the next day to speak to him and he had answered just as Giuca had instructed him to do.

Regarding the attorney Phil Slocum, Huggins didn't want his parents to know what was going on, so he called Slocum himself and went with John when they met the attorney on Monday night, outside, at a location on Beverley Road.

Nicolazzi said, "I'm going to direct your attention to November 2004 when you were reinterviewed by different detectives." The witness said that he recalled those interviews, and agreed that he had his own lawyer present, and that members of the DA's office were also there. At that time he made a sworn, audiotaped statement. After that, he had testified before a grand jury. Nicolazzi had no further questions.

* * *

Gregory was now free to cross-examine without Russo's jury in the room.

"Mr. Huggins, did you ever see Lauren Conigliaro remove evidence from John Giuca's house?"

"I saw her remove a gun bag that I had seen before."

Gregory had Huggins verify that he had known Russo for years, that Russo lived on Turner Place, and there was a spot in front of Russo's apartment building that was one of their group's favorite places to hang out. By the group, he meant Russo and Jimmy and Tommy and John. Gregory clicked off the names and Huggins agreed to them all. The witness agreed that this was a group that he wanted to be a part of, and that, when hanging with that group, he affected a certain persona.

"You wanted to be a tough guy, right?"

"Yes."

"You wanted to impress these guys with how tough you are, right?"

"Yes."

Gregory then led the witness through the three phone conversations Huggins had had with Giuca during the hours after Mark Fisher's murder.

"John Giuca came to you as a friend and said, 'I need help,' right?"

"Yeah."

"'Please don't tell the police that I set up this terrible homicide,' right?"

"Yeah."

"'All I want you to do is, just keep your mouth shut,' right?"

"Pretty much, yeah."

Huggins verified for Gregory that he'd known he was in trouble. He learned Fisher was dead and he knew he'd been among the last to see Fisher alive—irrespective of anything John Giuca had told him. He knew all of this before he spoke to the police for the first time on Tuesday,

October 14. At that time he had lied to the police. He lied to protect Giuca. It didn't take the lies long to break down, however.

Only two days after that first interview, he was asked a second time if he'd ever seen anyone at the party with a gun, and he said, yeah, John Giuca. Although Huggins admitted that he stopped lying about that point, he did not concede that he had done so to deflect blame away from himself and toward Giuca.

Gregory, using his questioning, reminded the jury that Huggins was not an altar boy by any means. He was serving a five-year probation sentence. Any involvement in Mark Fisher's murder, any at all, would have been a violation of his probation and would have meant jail time.

"You may be a tough guy out on Turner Place or in this courtroom, but you don't want to be upstate, correct?" Gregory asked, referring to prison.

"No, sir."

"They were squeezing you, correct?"

"Eventually they did."

"In June, did you come up with an idea of how to get the heat away from you?"

"Excuse me—"

"You said, 'If I take a lie detector test, they'll leave me alone,' right?"

"Yes." Huggins testified that he took such a test. And after the test the police left him alone—for a short while. Then they were back. The pressure mounted again.

Gregory spoke of the time when Huggins and Dan and Angel watched movies at the Huggins house, the Yankees–Red Sox game having been rained out, and Al had sneaked out to have a conversation with Giuca. Huggins said he only left the house that one time.

Referring to a girl Huggins liked, Gregory asked, "Do you recognize the name Rema Ibrahim?"

Huggins said he did. Gregory asked if he didn't visit

Rema that night as well. Didn't they meet and walk the dog? Huggins responded that he did visit Rema, but that was "much later," after Dan and Angel left his house.

Gregory covered, step by step, the way in which the witness had initially lied to the police, but then changed his story to the one he was telling now. Then he asked: "Did it come to your attention between October 14, 2003, and today that there is a reward in this case? One hundred thousand dollars?"

Huggins responded that he did know there was a reward, but he "didn't want a penny of that money."

"Did your statement about this Ghetto Mafia come after you knew about the reward?" Gregory asked. Huggins admitted that it had.

Gregory returned to the subject of Tony Russo. He asked if Russo was a fun guy to hang around with. Huggins said no. Did Huggins hang out with Russo anyway? Yeah, he did. Huggins wouldn't say that he'd had a good time with Russo.

Sure, he always had marijuana, and he was "kind of comical at times," but he was "nuts." He had a temper, the kind of guy who could snap.

Still, it wasn't like Huggins thought about leaving Ginca's house on the morning of the murder because crazy Russo showed up. Huggins was busy being a tough guy, trying to impress the suburban kids from Jersey and the Island.

Gregory then focused on the time Huggins got in trouble outside a bar up in the Bronx. Gregory asked if the version Huggins had offered the court during direct examination had been "sanitized," made vague so as to seem less horrible than it really was.

Huggins agreed that was true. A few important details had been left out. He'd left out the fact that he'd been in the bar, drinking and acting tough with a bunch of other tough guys. Gregory asked if a friend of his had clocked a couple guys over the head with a hard object and then, while they were down, if Huggins hadn't kicked the guys in the head with his boots on. Huggins said that wasn't what happened.

Gregory was frustrated by this and began referring to paperwork that had been done at the time Huggins was released. He'd been held in booking for two days.

It was revealed at this point that Phil Slocum, the lawyer that Huggins had called because of Giuca's trouble, had been Huggins's lawyer when he got in trouble in the Bronx.

Huggins agreed that the paperwork said he'd kicked the guys in the head with his boots on. Yeah, he also beat them with his fists. A police officer had rolled up on the scene and witnessed it. Was Huggins telling the jury the cop was lying? No, he said.

At this point Nicolazzi interrupted the intense cross-examination to complain that Gregory was standing too close to the witness, that they'd agreed to stay back and Gregory was bearing down on Huggins as he spoke.

Gregory apologized and said that he wouldn't cross that line again. Judge Marrus said that he understood that Gregory liked to move around when he asked questions, and that was fine, as long as none of the movements were aggressive in any way toward the witness.

Gregory's momentum had been interrupted and it took him a moment to get back in the flow, but when he did, he found that Huggins, unwilling to say the arresting officer was lying, did indeed get drunk and, while trying to impress his tough-guy friends, used his boots to "step on the defenseless."

The jury got the analogy. If Huggins was willing to be vicious to impress his friends once, he might do it again. The body of Mark Fisher sure was found close to Huggins's house, and he certainly demonstrated a lack of curiosity about the incident when his mother first told him what happened.

Huggins agreed that at the time of the murder, he knew there was a gun in Giuca's room—but he denied that it was he who told Russo where the gun was. Huggins denied knowing ahead of time that "something was going to happen" to Mark Fisher. He denied leaving with Angel DiGiovanni when he did so that he would have an alibi when the violence came down. Gregory had no further questions.

On redirect Nicolazzi asked Huggins to characterize his relationship with Russo. The witness said he'd call it "friend of a friend." Huggins only hung out with Russo because he was a friend of Giuca's.

Huggins said that, while some of his observations about Russo—the ones that he had testified to—were based on personal observations, the majority of the information was secondhand, having come from Giuca.

Nicolazzi put a little chronology, a timeline, in the jury's collective mind when she asked when the witness learned there was a reward in this case and when Huggins first told the police about the Ghetto Mafia and the "get a body" rule. There was a year between the two events, making it seem less likely that Huggins told the story to the police in order to collect the reward.

On recross Gregory had the witness acknowledge the fact that, in order to collect the reward, there had to be a conviction. That concluded the questioning of Albert Huggins and court recessed for lunch.

CHAPTER 34

"He Wanted to Have a Family"

The afternoon session began with both the Red and Green Juries in the courtroom and Michael Fisher, the victim's father, on the stand. Fisher said he lived in Sussex County, New Jersey. He had a wife, Nancy.

They'd had three children: Michael Christopher, the oldest; then four years later, Mark Steven; and then three years after that, Alexis, who was now nineteen. He said they were a close family.

In October 2003, Mark was nineteen years old. He would have turned twenty on November 8. Since Mark was a student at Fairfield University, starting his second year there, Fisher only got to see his son about once a month, maybe once every two months.

Mark had been studying accounting and marketing. He played football at school; he played the guitar. He liked art. He was involved in numerous activities. He helped in the church, helped in the community.

Fisher saw his son Mark on the afternoon of October 11, 2003, when he and two or three other people stopped by the house. The visit was a surprise. Father and son had had a long talk that day, not knowing it would be their last.

"He told me he wanted to have a family. That was his biggest thing," Michael Fisher testified.

Mark told his father that he was going to a friend's house to watch a ball game, and was going to visit Jackie Conway. There was no mention of a trip into New York City.

"I am going to draw your attention to the morning of October 19, 2003. Did you learn that something happened to your son at that time?"

"My wife had gotten suspicious. Mark was supposed to call-in that day. At the time I was working nights. I was sleeping. She was trying to get in contact. My first awareness was at two A.M. when two detectives came to the house. They showed us a picture of Mark and asked us to identify him."

"The photo was of your son Mark?"

"Yes, it was."

"Later that same day, did you travel, together with your wife, into Brooklyn?"

"Yes, in the morning we had to go to Kings County Hospital morgue to identify his body."

"Did they ask you to make an identification at the morgue based on a photograph?"

"I wanted to believe it wasn't Mark—but it was Mark," the victim's father said.

Nicolazzi had no further questions. Neither defense attorney wanted to cross-examine.

Michael showed no emotion as he testified. He was stoic and efficient with his words, and he got through it without breaking down.

CHAPTER 35

Three Detectives

Detective James Gaynor, who had previously testified at preliminary hearings for both defendants, was next called to the stand, with both juries in the courtroom. After giving a brief recap of his history with the NYPD, he testified that, yes, he'd been working on October 12, 2003.

He was the assigned homicide detective in the murder of Mark Fisher and first responded to the crime scene on Argyle Road at 8:00 A.M. on Sunday. When he arrived, there were already other law enforcement personnel on the scene.

Gaynor described his observations at the crime scene, how evidence was gathered. He took the jury through the process, right up to the point at which the body was removed from the spot where it had fallen and taken to the medical examiner's office at Kings County Hospital. The clothing and the blanket had been sent with the body to the medical examiner's office there.

Gaynor said that the first order of business after

the crime scene was completely processed was to identify the body. According to Detective Gaynor, various computer checks were made under the name that was on the ATM receipt. Gaynor went to the morgue and fingerprinted the corpse. Those prints were delivered to the Latent Prints Unit of the NYPD to see if they could identify them.

But the break that led to an identification came when a young person named Chris Deneen called the NYPD. Deneen, a Fairfield student, said his friend Mark Fisher had gone into the city and he hadn't heard from him. Chris said he was afraid that something might have happened to Mark.

Gaynor then got in touch with the Fairfield Security Department, and got contact information for Mark Fisher's parents. Gaynor went to New Jersey to talk to Mark's parents at their home in Andover, New Jersey. During that visit Gaynor, through Michael and Nancy Fisher, was able to ascertain that the body found on Argyle Road was that of Mark Fisher.

The next morning, after making one last visit to the crime scene to make sure nothing had been overlooked, Gaynor went up to Fairfield University to talk to the people who had accompanied Mark Fisher into Manhattan on the previous Saturday night.

The day after that, he interviewed Meredith Flannigan, Angel DiGiovanni and Albert Huggins. These interviews took place at the Seventieth Precinct. He also interviewed Russo and Giuca.

James Mamorsky and Tommy Hassan were interviewed after that. Then came Gregg Cunningham, the Wenninger brothers, Anthony Palumbo and James Petrillo. He talked to Russo and Giuca's respective girlfriends, Crystal Guerrero and Lauren Conigliaro.

NYPD interviews took place in Connecticut, New

York, New Jersey and California. Gaynor ordered phone records on anybody who might have attended the party at Giuca's house.

During the course of his investigation Gaynor learned that the blanket found around the feet of Mark Fisher's body had come from John Giuca's house. The blanket had been shown to Giuca's mom and she identified it as one that came from her home.

Then he checked the status of all the evidence gathered at the crime scene. A gunpowder residue test was made on Mark Fisher's clothes in an attempt to determine how far the shooter had been from his victim when he or she pulled the trigger.

Hairs and fibers found at the scene were tested. Fingernail clippings were taken from Mark Fisher's body. DNA testing was done to see if he picked up any skin from his killer during his apparent struggle before he was shot, skin that might have been used to positively identify the murderer.

The effort was futile. No DNA material was found on Mark Fisher's fingernail clippings, except his own.

While looking for the missing murder weapon, the sewers in the vicinity of Argyle and Stratford Roads were searched. These searches were conducted on October 24, 2003, and were done with the assistance of the Department of Environmental Protection (DEP), otherwise known as the New York City Water Board.

In order to conduct the searches, the DEP used a basket truck with a claw on it, going though the sewer traps, the claw removed the sludge from the bottom of the sewer.

While investigating a sewer opening at the corner of Turner Place and Stratford Road, a man's black wallet was discovered. A DEP employee opened the wallet and said that identification with the name Mark Fisher was in it; at this point Detective Gaynor ordered him to immediately put the wallet down.

That wallet, Gaynor noted, was subsequently checked for fingerprints, but none were found.

Gregory tried in cross-examination to get Gaynor to admit that he had used legal leverage—such as putting pressure on Albert Huggins, who could have been cited as having been in violation of his probation by lying to police, or on Lauren Conigliaro, who had hopes of one day being a U.S. Marshal—to get witnesses to play ball.

Gaynor admitted that background checks were done on many of the witnesses, but that was because he thought it might be helpful to know more about them, not because he was looking for witnesses who would be most vulnerable to being leaned upon.

Gaynor finally conceded that it was possible that police sometimes use the fact that witnesses are facing possible jail time, or might be fired from their jobs, to get them to cooperate.

The court was recessed for lunch at that point. The Giuca jury was told that they could go home until the following Monday morning.

After the noon recess the questioning of Detective Gaynor continued, but this time with only the Red Jury in the courtroom.

Nicolazzi asked Gaynor many of the same questions that she had asked him during Russo's preliminary hearing. Gaynor said Russo was questioned at the Seventieth Precinct on October 14, 2003, but he was not a suspect at the time.

Russo, the detective said, was being questioned solely because he was on the list of people who had attended the early-morning party at Giuca's house and therefore had been among the last to see the victim alive.

Russo told Gaynor that at 4:00 A.M., October 12, he'd

gotten a call from Giuca saying he was having a party at his house. Russo gave a list of those at the party that jibed with the recollection of the others. John and his brother, Matt, were there. Jimmy, Tommy, Al and a girl Al knew, and another girl and another guy, whom Russo didn't know. Soon after he got to the party, Russo decided he wanted a beer, so he took a walk to a nearby convenience store. As he was leaving, the kid he didn't know indicated that he needed an ATM, so they walked to the store together. He was back at the party for about twenty minutes when he fell asleep. When he awoke, it was about 6:00 A.M. He and the kid he didn't know were the only two left in the house. He didn't know if there were others upstairs or not, but he didn't want to risk leaving the stranger alone in the house, so he woke him up and told him it was time to leave. The kid asked where the girls went and Russo told him he didn't know. Maybe Al's house. Russo said he walked the stranger to the door, gave him directions on how to get to Al's house and never saw him again. Then, he said, Russo went home.

"Did you ask him any questions about his hair?" Nicolazzi asked Gaynor.

"I asked him if he'd cut his hair. He said he had and wanted to know if that made him guilty of anything."

"Did you ask him about the blanket that was discovered under Mark Fisher's body?"

"I asked him if the kid walked out of John's house with a blanket. He said no, he thought he would have remembered that."

That was the substance of Gaynor's first interview with Russo. Nicolazzi had no further questions.

Under Fink's cross-examination Gaynor said he was only one of several detectives to question Russo at the Seventieth Precinct. Detectives Byrne and McMahon carried on after he went home. He'd been up for two straight nights working and needed rest. Although he was extremely tired while questioning Russo, he hadn't called Russo a liar. He did, however, mention that there were elements of his story that didn't make sense.

Gaynor was asked how long Russo was at the police station and replied that he was there until 9:00 A.M., October 15. The next day Gaynor spoke to McMahon about Russo. McMahon told Gaynor at that time that Russo had talked about the Ghetto Mafia, and had said that John Giuca was a member. Russo, however, never said that he himself was part of the GM.

With that, Detective Gaynor was allowed to leave the witness stand.

The prosecution called Detective Samuel Ortiz, who had also testified at Russo's preliminary hearing. Ortiz told Trish McNeill that he, too, had interviewed Russo at the Seventieth Precinct.

His interview took place in the middle of the afternoon on October 15. Russo had told him that on "Monday afternoon, between four and five o'clock, he had received a telephone call on his cell phone from John Giuca telling him to come up to Gregg Cunningham's apartment. Once he got to Gregg's apartment, Gregg asked John, 'Did you take care of the burners?' John said he took care of it. John told Gregg that something happened and he killed a guy. Russo said he left Gregg's apartment during this conversation."

McNeill had no further questions.

Fink established in cross that no one had assigned Ortiz to question Russo, that he'd had the conversation with the defendant on his own volition, and that when he did so, he was unaware that Russo had already been helpful with the investigation, assisting police, for example, in recovering illegal guns.

* * *

Detective Ortiz was excused and Detective Peter Mc-Mahon, another detective who had previously testified at Russo's preliminary hearing, was called. McMahon testified that he had interviewed Russo at the Seventieth Precinct on October 14, 2003. Russo told him that he'd gotten a call during the early-morning hours of October 12 from his friend Shady who said there was a party going on at his house.

When Russo got there, he found there was a guy at the party he didn't know. At the end of the night, Russo said, he was the last person left in the house, he and the guy he didn't know, who was passed out on a couch. Russo woke the stranger up and told him he had to leave.

Earlier in the evening, Russo said, he noticed there was "something going on" with John Giuca and Albert Huggins, that it seemed to him like they were plotting something. Russo heard John asking the stranger's girlfriend what she was doing with a guy like that.

After Russo had gone home that morning, Russo told McMahon, he got a call from Giuca saying, "I have some work to take care of." McMahon asked Russo what that meant to him. Russo said it meant Giuca planned to shoot the kid.

The next day, according to Russo, Giuca said to him, "I banged the guy, I took care of him."

McMahon said that Russo originally told the story about him and the stranger being the last ones in the house, but he later changed his story. In the new version Russo went home while the party was still going on, so he was home when Giuca told him he had "work to do."

Then later John said he'd shot the guy and told Russo what to say in case police asked him questions. Mc-Mahon asked Russo where was the gun that had killed

Fisher. Russo said he figured it was still in the closet of Giuca's room. Or else maybe Giuca got rid of it.

Russo told McMahon about the house in Bensonhurst, where a person could take a gun that was hot. A search warrant was acquired and Russo took police to the Wenninger brothers' house. A gun or guns were confiscated. There was an arrest at that location as well.

Russo brought up GM with McMahon and this time admitted that he was part of it. Russo talked about some other shootings he thought Giuca might have been involved in. Russo said that, with the exception of the victim, the guys at Giuca's party were GM.

He even mentioned Giuca's little brother, Matt Federicci, as being a member. McMahon confirmed that at least one gun was confiscated at the Wenninger house—he couldn't be certain because he had not entered the home, but had rather stayed outside in the squad car with Russo. He didn't believe the gun had anything to do with Mark Fisher's death.

McMahon admitted under Fink's cross that he wasn't sure if a search warrant had been acquired before the first visit to the Wenninger house, that there was a chance that police had been given consent to search the premises at the door.

McMahon admitted that he was not the first to interview Russo at the Seventieth Precinct. He said he'd been told by the previous interrogators that the witness was holding out. He had *not* been told that Russo was lying.

McMahon also admitted that he took notes during and after his questioning of Russo, but he had misplaced those notes, which were never found.

That concluded the questioning of Detective McMahon, as well as the day's proceedings. Judge Marrus banged his gavel and wished everyone a pleasant weekend. Court was recessed until the following Monday morning.

CHAPTER 36

A Long Trip to Brooklyn

When court was called to order on Monday morning, September 19, 2005, a couple loose ends needed to be tied. An alternate on the Russo jury had been taken to the hospital over the weekend with vision problems. There wasn't time in the schedule to wait, so the alternate was officially dismissed.

Fink moved for a mistrial on the grounds that Al Huggins had testified that John Giuca had said, "We might have had something to do with that" in front of both juries. Fink felt the statement should not have been made in front of his client's jury, the Red Jury.

Judge Marrus denied the application for a mistrial, noting that there was no inference in the witness's statement that the "we" referred to Giuca and Russo.

And, because the prosecution had forgotten to ask a series of questions to Al Huggins, Huggins had been summoned again from Penn State University, and, since the defenses had no objection, he was again put on the witness stand.

Nicolazzi drew Huggins's attention to the time he was in Giuca's room and Giuca was cleaning some bullets. She asked if at that time the witness and Giuca had had a conversation about a gun. Huggins said that they had. Nicolazzi asked what was said.

"I asked them if they are still in the house and he said no, Anthony took them," Huggins replied.

"Who is Anthony?"

"Anthony Palumbo." Huggins explained that Palumbo was a longtime friend of Giuca's, who lived a block away on Beverley Road.

"No further questions, Your Honor," Nicolazzi said.

Fink said he had no cross involving this point. Gregory had one question. He wanted to fix the date of the conversation, which the witness said was Monday, October 13, 2003.

Huggins was dismissed and allowed to return to Penn State. It had been a long trip to Brooklyn for a questioning that lasted less than five minutes.

CHAPTER 37

The Law's Murphy

Loose ends officially tied, the prosecution continued their case by calling Detective Dennis Murphy, who'd been with the NYPD for more than twenty years, and had been assigned to the Seventieth Precinct Detective Squad at the time of the murder. McNeill asked the questions.

During the evening of October 14, 2003, Murphy was one of the officers who picked up Russo at his apartment building and brought him to the police station for questioning. Later that day he saw Giuca at the station as well. In the police station that night with Giuca was his stepfather, Frank Federicci.

Murphy testified that as Giuca and his stepfather sat in a waiting area, he overheard their conversation. Federicci asked Giuca what had happened over the weekend while he was away.

Giuca, according to the witness, replied, "Let's see what they have and see what they offer me."

McNeill had no further questions.

In cross-examination Fink asked if a fellow named Lew Askins had been with Russo at the time he was picked up. Murphy said yes, Askins was a police detective and a Jennings-Russo family friend.

Fink elicited from Murphy the fact that Russo did not resist when he was brought in for questioning and that both Russo and his friend Detective Askins were frisked. Murphy said that as far as he knew, Russo had not been read his Miranda rights before or during his questioning at the Seven-Oh.

"Do you recall if you were present when a person named Crystal Guerrero was questioned on October fourteenth and fifteenth?"

"No, I don't know who that person is," Murphy said.

"I have nothing further."

In redirect, McNeill asked Murphy what happened in the elevator at the time Russo and his cop friend were picked up. Askins, Murphy testified, was carrying a black leather pouch. He asked what was in the pouch and Askins said a gun.

"Then what happened?" McNeill asked.

"I grabbed Mr. Askins, grabbed the leather pouch out of his hands, pushed him into a corner and began to frisk him."

"Did you know that he was a police officer at that time?"

"No, I did not. But he started yelling, 'I'm a cop! I'm a cop. I'm on the job.'" Askins then produced identification to prove who he was.

The Red Jury was then asked to leave the courtroom. Gregory's cross-examination of Murphy would be given in front of the Green Jury only as it pertained solely to the guilt or innocence of Giuca.

Murphy said that Frank Federicci had come to the precinct by himself, had talked with police and, when informed that the police wanted to speak with Giuca, called John on his cell phone.

Giuca arrived at the Seven-Oh a few minutes later. He was on foot and alone. (The Seventieth Precinct headquarters was about thirteen blocks from Giuca's home.)

At the time there was a lot of activity at the station. Newspaper reporters, TV reporters and policemen mingled outside the building. Gregory asked what Murphy did next.

Murphy replied, "I informed Mr. Giuca and Mr. Federicci that there was a lot of press outside, that I was going to walk inside and that it was in their best interest to walk in, because they didn't want to be seen outside."

Giuca and Federicci followed Murphy, who led them to a second-floor waiting area. Federicci told Murphy he wanted a few minutes to talk with his son. Murphy agreed, but stayed within hearing distance, although he maintained that he did not purposefully listen in.

After establishing that Federicci could have been worried just because Giuca had an unregistered gun in the house, Gregory asked, "You testified that Mr. Federicci asked John Giuca, 'What did you do?' Correct?"

"Yes."

"And Giuca did not say, 'I'm responsible for Mark Fisher's death,' correct?"

"No, those were not the words I heard."

Detective Murphy was dismissed.

CHAPTER 38

Russo's Ex-Girlfriend

It was still Monday morning when eighteen-year-old Crystal Guerrero, Russo's ex-girlfriend, was called to the stand, with both juries in the courtroom and McNeill doing the questioning.

Guerrero told McNeill that she was a student, that Antonio Russo was her ex-boyfriend, and she knew him to go by the nicknames Tony and Tweed. They were boyfriend and girlfriend at the time of the murder.

McNeill asked if Guerrero still remembered Russo's phone number. She did. She remembered all of them, the number for the phone in his apartment—where he lived with his grandmother, mother and brother—and the numbers for both of his cell phones. She recited the numbers to prove her point.

Guerrero told McNeill that she also knew Giuca, who was a friend of Russo's. She knew Giuca by his nickname Slim. She knew "Slim" lived around the corner from Tony, but didn't know the exact address. (Guica's nicknames included both "Slim" and "Shady," both of which came from the title of an Eminem CD.)

She knew Giuca's little brother, Matt Federicci, but she did not know Albert Huggins, Anthony Palumbo, Tommy Hassan, or Billy and Jesse Wenninger. She did know Gregg Cunningham, who was Russo's best friend.

"Do you know if Antonio Russo belonged to any particular group?"

"Yes."

"And what was the name of that group, if it had one?"

"OMC. Outlaw Mafia Crip."

"Is that a set of the Crips?"

"To my knowledge, yes."

She said she only knew this because Russo had told her. She was unaware of what position he held in the group, or where the group hung out. She did know that according to Russo, John Giuca was in OMC, too. Giuca was Russo's "head."

She knew that OMC's colors were blue and white. She had never seen Russo wearing beads of any color, she said, but she had seen friends of his wearing blue-and-white beads. She said the colors were like war colors, for when they were going to "fight somebody or something." The group, she knew, also "had their own little handshake."

Russo told her about the initiation to get into OMC. It was called getting "squared in." A member had to fight four people at once. McNeill had no further questions.

On cross-examination Fink asked, "Is it fair to say, Ms. Guerrero, that you deal crack cocaine?"

"No."

"Were you arrested in August of 2005?"

"Yes."

"And you were arrested for dealing crack cocaine, right?"

"I'm charged with that, but I did not do it."

"At the time of your arrest you were also endangering the welfare of a child, correct?"

"No. I am charged with that, but I was not doing what they're saying I was doing."

"Taking you back to August 17, 2005. You recall being on Sixty-fifth Street at nine in the evening."

"I was one block from Sixty-seventh Street."

"Was your baby in a backseat of a car?"

"Yes, my son was in the car. Yes."

"And you were dealing crack cocaine to an undercover police officer, correct?"

"No." She said her boyfriend was sitting in the front seat of the car, and he wasn't dealing crack, either.

As she said this, Russo began to react. Guerrero's appearance on the stand caused Russo to lose his composure. He had been slumped and subdued thus far during the trial, almost inanimate. He became animated as soon as Guerrero appeared, and not in a good way.

As she spoke, Russo mocked the woman with exaggerated facial expressions. When Guerrero got to the part about the baby, Russo let out an audible laugh. There was a cacophony of silence as all eyes turned to Russo.

"It's funny," he said.

The judge ordered Russo to stay quiet.

Fink said, "Do you claim to have never been involved in any drugs at all, that you've never smoked crack cocaine, never smoked marijuana?"

"I smoked marijuana. Never crack."

"Is it true that you've not only smoked marijuana, but you've dealt it as well?"

"No."

"You spoke about gang-related stuff. Have you had a lot of experience with gangs?"

"No."

"Are you familiar with the Latin Kings?"

"I know who they are."

"Aren't you a Latin Queen?"

"No, I'm not."

Fink then directed the witness's attention to the day of the murder. She said she was returning from a religious retreat that day, that she was trying to become more spiritual, closer to God.

"You say that Mr. Russo was your boyfriend at that time. Were the two of you having sexual relations?"

"Yes." Under further questioning, she said that there were a couple guys she was talking to at that time, but Russo was her only boyfriend.

She admitted that on October 15, 2003, the Wednesday following the murder, she was in the Seventieth Precinct. She spoke to detectives about Mark Fisher's murder, and she didn't tell the police the whole truth at that time.

Fink asked if Guerrero was aware that there was a reward in this case. She said that she was under the impression the reward had been "thrown out." She denied ever having any interest in the reward.

With that, it was Gregory's turn to cross-examine.

"Can you explain to the jury what the reasons were that you weren't truthful with the detectives about what you knew when you were originally interviewed back in 2003?" Gregory asked.

"I was pregnant with Antonio's child. I didn't want him going to jail and I was afraid of him," the witness replied.

That concluded the questioning of Guerrero with both juries in the room. The remainder of her testimony would be given with only the Red Jury present, as it did not pertain to the case against Giuca. Both juries exited so the court could take care of some business.

With the juries out of the room, Judge Marrus scolded Russo for his behavior during Guerrero's testimony.

"I want to warn you that if I see you making faces or mouthing anything while anyone is testifying, you're going to wind up being excluded from your trial. You have to sit there and listen like everyone else. If you have something to say, say it privately to your attorney. Do you understand that?"

No answer.

"Do you understand what I am saying?"

"Understood," Russo said.

With that, the Red Jury reentered the courtroom and the questioning of Guerrero resumed, once again with McNeill performing the direct examination.

"Did you talk to Antonio Russo during the early-morning hours of October 12, 2003?" McNeill asked.

Guerrero said she had. Russo had called her cell phone. She was at the retreat at the time.

"He was nervous," she said. "He was yelling at me, he was saying that it was all my fault because I wasn't with him, that I should never have gone to the retreat and that it was all my fault that he shot him. I tried to calm him down. I told him I'll speak with him when I get home because I had to go downstairs for breakfast."

"Did you speak to Russo later that day?" McNeill asked. Guerrero said that she had. He had called her repeatedly, begging her to come over and visit him at his apartment. She finally visited him that night, about eight-thirty. He was still nervous and agitated, but it seemed as though he calmed down a little bit when she arrived.

"What did he tell you at that time?"

"He told me the whole story of what happened."

"What specifically did he say to you?"

"He told me he was scared; he didn't want to go to jail; he didn't want to leave me and the baby; he shot some-body; he could be facing jail time, and he'd been seen with him while going to an ATM."

"He'd been seen with who?"

"The kid he shot. He was afraid they got him on camera at the store."

"Did he specify how the kid ended up getting shot that night?"

"He said all he meant to do was rob him, but it ended up being more than that."

"Did he tell you where the shooting took place?"

"Yeah. He said it happened on Argyle."

Guerrero said that she noticed as she spoke to Russo on the evening of October 12 that he'd cut his hair. She asked him why he'd done that and he said he needed a new look, in case they had him on the video camera at the store.

The next day, Guerrero testified, Russo showed her a *New York Post* article about a "bullet-riddled" body that had been found on Argyle. Russo said that was the kid he'd shot.

"He was still nervous," she said, "but he was kind of proving it to me. 'See? I did do it.'"

After his long interrogation at the Seventieth Precinct, Russo asked to be dropped off at Guerrero's house. When Guerrero's mother was in the room, he denied having anything to do with the murder and said that he was afraid he was going to end up going to jail for something he didn't do. He said his friends had done it and he was afraid to rat them out. But when Guerrero's mother was out of the room, he once again said that it was he who had shot Mark Fisher.

"He said, 'You know I did it. You know I shot him, right?'" Guerrero testified.

In future conversations on the subject Russo became increasingly agitated.

"He was becoming paranoid," she said. "He was scared and he was yelling at me and asking me if I was scared, telling me did I even care he was going to jail? That me and the baby would be left alone. Did I even care about him? Did I ever love him? Then he said he didn't do it. John did it. 'I didn't do nothing,' he said.

That if he went to the police and said that John did it, that something bad would happen to me or the baby."

"Did he ever say at any point that he spoke to John Giuca about the shooting?"

"Yes. He told me everything was going to be okay. He spoke to John and that John is not going to say nothing. He seemed a little more relaxed."

Russo later changed his story, yet again. This time, according to Guerrero, he said that both he and John had shot the kid. "John shot him and then he finished him off," she testified that Russo said.

On October 17, five days after the murder, Russo went to California to see a friend. He flew from New York to Los Angeles on Delta Airlines Flight 151. According to airline records, Russo returned from California on October 23, taking Delta Airlines Flight 150.

"He said everything was hot. He couldn't be in Brooklyn. He had to go to get away a little bit," Guerrero testified. "That the police were over his friends. He was scared of his friends. Everything was just crazy and he needed time away, time to calm down."

Guerrero said that she talked to Russo while he was in California, but he was still paranoid. He didn't want her mentioning the murder on the phone in case someone was listening in. He'd stayed in California for about a week and then returned to Brooklyn.

The subject then turned to Matthew Federicci. Guerrero said she knew him, that he was John's younger brother, and she had known Russo and Federicci to hang out together. One time after the murder she'd been in Russo's room and Federicci visited. They asked her to leave. She went into the living room and helped Russo's brother with his homework. She said Federicci seemed tense, but he was friendly to her. After Federicci left, Russo told Guerrero that everything was going to be okay.

McNeill had no further questions.

During cross-examination Fink established that even though Guerrero was questioned during the days and weeks following the murder, it wasn't until a year after Mark Fisher's death that she first told police that Russo had made incriminating remarks to her.

Fink went over her grand jury testimony and picked at discrepancies between what she had said then and what she said now. For example, she'd said earlier that Russo had cut his hair because a lot had happened and he needed a different look. Now she said that it was because he was afraid he'd been picked up on a convenience store video while accompanying the victim to an ATM. She'd previously said she couldn't recall where Russo said the shooting had taken place. Today she remembered he'd said it happened on Argyle Road. Fink's inference was that memories grew more vague with time, but in Guerrero's case, her memories grew sharper. He hoped this fact would make the jury skeptical as to her truthfulness.

About his cross-examination of Guerrero, Fink later recalled: "When I cross-examined her, that was one of the first things I hit her with that really brought her credibility to light. When she claimed to have spoken with Russo about admissions he made, I believe she said she had been on a religious retreat, almost as if she was this person coming across as someone who had gotten into religion, trying to find God. Here we are at the trial and she's in a car where crack is allegedly being dealt out of with a baby. There were also inconsistencies with what she said in the grand jury and to police and at the trial. I attacked those inconsistencies. She was trying to portray herself as a forthright and honest person and the evidence suggested that she wasn't such an honest person."

Guerrero's time on the stand was done. Judge Marrus recessed court for lunch.

CHAPTER 39

"The Kid Came from Money"

Both juries were present for the start of the afternoon session, and the prosecution called Lauren Conigliaro to the stand. Nicolazzi handled the questioning. Conigliaro said she was twenty-two years old, working full-time and starting law school in January. She had a bachelor's degree in criminal justice.

She acknowledged that she knew John Giuca and used to date him. They dated "on and off" for four years. During that time she became close with John's family as well. She knew most of John's friends, including Hassan, Mamorsky and Russo.

Nicolazzi asked Conigliaro if the initials GM meant anything to her. She said yes, that John and his friends used to call each other GM. She didn't know if there were colors associated with GM but had noticed that they all wore orange a lot. They wore orange beaded necklaces, she recalled.

She knew from talking to Giuca that these guys got together for meetings sometimes. She had no idea what happened at those meetings, but she knew sometimes they took place in the neighborhood and sometimes at the Wenninger house on Eighty-sixth Street in Bensonhurst.

"What was Russo's relationship with Al Huggins, if you know?"

"Not a close relationship. They lived in the same neighborhood, that's all." Both Russo and Huggins were closer to Giuca than to each other, she said. She said that Matt Federicci was a friend of Russo's.

Regarding Anthony Palumbo, she said that she was still a close friend of his. "He's a close friend of John's as well," she added. At the time of the murder Palumbo lived on Beverley Road, just off Coney Island Avenue.

Asked if she remembered phone numbers, she rattled off Palumbo's cell phone number with ease, but failed to remember Giuca's, only recalling that it had two 4's in it, and that John's phone number was similar to that of his brother Matt's.

At that point the Red Jury was excused. The Red Jury and Russo were told they would not be needed back in the courtroom until the following morning. The remainder of the questioning of Lauren Conigliaro would take place in front of the Green Jury only.

Once that movement of people was accomplished, Nicolazzi began her Giuca-specific direct examination of Conigliaro. She started by asking the witness to describe the relationship between the two defendants.

"They were close. I believe Antonio looked up to John," Conigliaro replied.

"Did you see John Giuca on the night of October 11, 2003, and the early-morning hours of the following day?"

"No, I did not."

"What, if anything, did you do that evening?"

"I went out with my friend Michele to the city." She said that she and her girlfriend had stayed at a "lounge" until it closed, had a meal at a fast-food place, then returned to their respective homes. Conigliaro said she got home about 5:00 or 6:00 A.M.

She went to bed and soon thereafter received a phone call from Giuca. He said he just called to make sure she was home and that she should come by and visit the next day because he needed to talk to her. So, on Sunday afternoon, she went to Giuca's house.

Albert Huggins was also there. She and Huggins sat in Giuca's bedroom on the third floor, while Giuca stood and talked. Giuca told her what happened the previous night: how he'd gone into the city, then returned to the house with a group of people because his parents were away.

Giuca told her that later on, Tony Russo had come up to him in the kitchen and had told him "he wanted to rob Al's friend." Nicolazzi asked if Giuca explained why Russo wanted to commit this robbery. Conigliaro said it was because Russo could tell the kid came from money, and besides he was "a cocky guy."

"And what, if anything, did John tell you he did after Tony said that to him?"

"He said that Tony asked him for a gun and that he took him upstairs and gave one to him."

Then, according to the story that Giuca reportedly told Conigliaro, Al's friend—Mark Fisher, that is—went to a closet and took out a jacket.

John said, "I don't know you. I'm not giving you a jacket. Take a blanket from the couch. I have a lot of them."

Nicolazzi asked why, according to what Giuca had told her, did Al's friend need a jacket? The witness said it was because he was heading out to an ATM. He had spent all of his money and needed money to get home.

"While John was saying this, what was Al's reaction, if you recall?" Nicolazzi asked.

"He was pretty wrecked about it. He looked upset, very upset," Conigliaro replied.

"What did John tell you happened after the boy left with the blanket?"

"He said he stayed home and then heard sirens going toward Argyle. Al added that the sirens were heading to a spot over near his house." The kid had been shot. Giuca and Huggins said they didn't know if he was alive or dead, and that the shooting was probably in the paper.

During the conversation John was acting pretty normal. He didn't seem nearly as nervous as Huggins. Conigliaro said she left after that. She had other plans for the day. Huggins remained at Giuca's house after she'd gone.

Conigliaro testified that she next spoke with Giuca the following day. She drove her car to his house. He climbed in and they drove together to the neighborhood McDonald's.

At that time Giuca told her he had a "funny feeling" that he and some of his friends were going to be called in for questioning by the police.

While they were still in the car, his phone rang and it was his mother saying there were five detectives at their house and to come home because some of them were leaving to get a search warrant.

"How did John respond to that?"

"At first, he just kept saying he wasn't coming home. Then he agreed to go to the precinct on his own." She drove him to the precinct so that he could be interviewed.

Nicolazzi then asked if Giuca had ever briefed her as to what to say if the police asked her questions. She said that he had, but that was later.

"He just said that it's possible that I might be called in as well, even though I was not there, and not to worry because I know Sam Gregory and Lance Lazzaro as well."

Nicolazzi made sure the jury realized that the two names mentioned were both attorneys.

Nicolazzi asked about the status of Giuca and Conigliaro's relationship at the time of the murder. Conigliaro said that "it was at kind of a point where you are making it or breaking it." Asked for a time frame, the witness said that her relationship with Giuca began to deteriorate the summer before the murder, and that they finally broke up the month after the murder.

Nicolazzi asked if Conigliaro continued to have contact with Giuca after they stopped being boyfriend and girlfriend. Conigliaro said she did. They had a lot of the same friends, so it was hard not to have contact.

Nicolazzi asked if it was true that Conigliaro was first interviewed by the police regarding Mark Fisher's death on October 15, 2003, and she said yes. The prosecutor asked if Conigliaro was wholly truthful during that first interview and the witness said no, she was not. In fact, she was interviewed by the police several times during the remainder of that year and didn't tell the complete truth on those occasions, either.

She first told the whole truth, she admitted, in November 2004 when she gave an audiotaped interview to the DA's office, and then again when she testified before the grand jury on December 2, 2004.

That concluded Nicolazzi's direct examination. Gregory came out firing on cross-examination.

"Did you remove a gun from [Giuca's home on] Stratford?"

"No, I did not."

"Are you sure about that?"

"Absolutely sure."

"Have you applied for a job with the U.S. Marshals?"

"I have."

"Would it be fair to say that a career in law enforcement

is something you've been looking forward to for many years?"

"Yes, of course."

It was Gregory's theory that the prosecution had some sort of leverage on all of their witnesses. Huggins was facing jail time. Guerrero was facing drug-dealing charges. Even the "good girl" Conigliaro needed to be cooperative or risk ruining her chances of a career in law enforcement.

Gregory then took Conigliaro down the rocky road of her relationship with Giuca. They'd met early in high school, dated for about four years, when, sometime before October 2003, she learned that Giuca was seeing another girl, a girl named Mercy. She admitted to being angered by this and agreed that this was one of the factors that was making her relationship with Giuca falter. Gregory asked if it wasn't true that, at that same time, Giuca began to suspect that Lauren was seeing someone else as well, a boy named Peter.

"If that's how he feels, that's how he feels," Conigliaro replied to that. The witness agreed that it was fair to characterize her relationship with Giuca as one of mistrust during October 2003. She agreed that she had caught him saying he was going to be one place when he really was at another.

Gregory asked if there weren't times when the police asked her questions about Giuca and she said that she knew nothing, that they did not trust one another—and if he had something to hide, he would not have mentioned it around her. She agreed that was true.

She also admitted that during subsequent interviews with the police, attempts were made to put words in her mouth, words she did not want to say, and that on at least one occasion a policeman reminded her during an interview that there was a reward for information leading to Mark Fisher's killer or killers.

During one interview the DA's office reminded her that they were aware of her aspirations to be a marshal, putting further pressure on her. Gregory got the witness to quantify her desire for a career in law or law enforcement, how she had worked hard in high school, studied for hours while attending John Jay College. And here the DA's office was telling her that all that work would be for naught unless she played ball. Then they would ask again if John had told her he was involved with the murder. With her future at stake and the suspect no longer her boyfriend, Gregory inferred, it would have been easier for her to lie about what had been said, to make John Giuca sound guilty.

"Before you came in today, were you asked by Ms. Nicolazzi whether or not you had removed any evidence from [Giuca's home on] Stratford?"

Conigliaro said that she had been asked that question, but that she denied it.

"And would it be fair to say that if you had removed that evidence, you would be guilty of a felony and you would have problems with your future career?"

Conigliaro said she hadn't thought of that, but her answer didn't matter to Gregory. It was the *question* he wanted the jury to hear.

Gregory then focused on the statement Giuca had reportedly made to Conigliaro regarding Tony wanting to rob the victim. Gregory asked if she had ever heard Giuca admit that he'd instructed Russo to show the victim "what's up." Conigliaro said she never heard him say anything like that.

To indicate that the witness was confused about the specifics of the conversations she testified to, Gregory pointed out that during a previously taped interview, she'd said that the conversation between John and her and Al in John's bedroom the day following the murder had been interrupted briefly when Giuca's brother,

Matt, came into Giuca's room. She had left Matt out of her trial testimony.

Gregory asked, "Isn't it true that you subsequently learned that Matt had spent the night in the Bronx at Yankee Stadium waiting in line for tickets, and so couldn't have interrupted your conversation?"

"This is the first I'm hearing of that," Conigliaro replied.

Then Gregory pointed out that some of the things she said happened on October 13 must have happened on October 14, again to indicate that the witness's memories were muddled—and with that, he concluded his cross-examination.

In recross Nicolazzi asked the witness point-blank if the police or the DA's office had ever told her what to say. She said no. Nicolazzi asked point-blank why Conigliaro had finally decided to tell the truth after holding back for so long.

Conigliaro said that her coming clean regarding what she knew occurred not because of threats by the police or the prosecution but because she was told she was going to be put under oath before the grand jury. She did not want to commit perjury.

Gregory objected, saying that, to his knowledge, Conigliaro had not testified before the grand jury. Judge Marrus noted that she had not said she had. She changed her story when she believed she *would* be put under oath.

The truth was that Conigliaro had testified for the grand jury, but the prosecution had not provided Gregory with a copy of the transcripts of her testimony. Gregory didn't know it existed.

Nicolazzi's questioning reinforced for the jury that if the witness began telling the truth because she thought she would soon be put under oath, she must certainly be telling the truth now, when she *was* under oath.

Nicolazzi painted a picture of the frenzy of activity the witness underwent during the days immediately following Mark Fisher's murder, indicating how easy it would be to think something happened on October 13 when it really happened on October 14.

True, the witness might be unclear as to what interview she had made statements for the first time, or during which conversation Giuca's little brother had walked in unexpectedly. However, that didn't reflect on the accuracy of her memories of the key conversations she had testified to—and that was what really mattered.

Gregory asked on recross if Conigliaro had ever been with Huggins again after they were together with John Giuca in Giuca's room on October 14. The witness said no, that was the last time she had seen Huggins. So, it was impossible for her, at a later date, to have sneaked a gun pouch out of Giuca's house while Huggins observed? Conigliaro agreed. That would have been impossible.

"Can you think of any reason why Albert Huggins would want to make up a lie about you?" Gregory asked.

"Objection," Nicolazzi said.

"I have no idea," the witness blurted out.

"Sustained," Judge Marrus said, a nanosecond late.

Gregory asked if she ever had any trouble with the DA's office because of her problems remembering who said what, when. She said no, she had just explained that she wasn't good with dates.

That completed the questioning of Lauren Conigliaro, and the day's proceedings. Judge Marrus ordered everyone to be back at 10:00 A.M. the next day.

With neither jury present, the next morning's proceedings began with an angry Sam Gregory moving for a mistrial because he had not been given the transcripts of Lauren Conigliaro's grand jury testimony before he cross-examined her.

Judge Marrus said that declaring a mistrial was not necessary. The error could be corrected. Gregory would be supplied with the necessary transcripts. Conigliaro would then be put back on the stand and Gregory could cross-examine.

Gregory had a problem with his jury sitting through Fink's cross-examination of witnesses to whom Gregory planned to ask no questions. If Gregory was to cross-examine first and said he had no questions, it was a routine matter to dismiss the Giuca jury. But if Fink cross-examined first, the Giuca jury sat through a cross-examination that didn't pertain to the case they were hearing. Judge Marrus noted that the defendants were accused of acting in concert, but granted there was much merit in Gregory's argument. The judge said that in the future, if Fink was scheduled to cross-examine first, and Gregory planned no questions of that witness, he should tell Judge Marrus beforehand so that Giuca's jury wouldn't have to listen to Fink's cross-examination. This would help lessen any future criticism of the dual-jury system, which, if unguarded, could turn into an unfair two-on-one situation.

Nicolazzi said that the prosecution's first witness of the morning was to be Anthony Palumbo. She wanted the court to know that Palumbo, in exchange for his honest testimony, had been granted immunity. The immunity, Nicolazzi explained, was limited to "crimes of criminal possession of a weapon, hindering prosecution and tampering with evidence." Whereupon Judge Marrus called for the Red and Green Juries to be brought into the courtroom, and the morning's first witness was called to the stand.

CHAPTER 40

A Black Gun

Prosecutors hate not having the murder weapon. In cases where the murder weapon is located and identified, they enjoy holding it up, showing the court, letting the jury examine it. Feel it. Feel its deadly power.

But in this case they had no murder weapon to hold up, to allow the jury to touch. So, they did the next best thing. They provided the jury with testimony that put the assumed murder weapon in John Giuca's hands only a short time after Mark Fisher's murder.

Anthony Palumbo took the stand. He was a twenty-three-year-old plumber, a good friend of Giuca's. At the moment, though, he was going to school and not doing any plumbing. He was the father of a two-year-old girl.

Palumbo had known Giuca since he was eight or nine years old. He said that he had known Russo for just as long, because they all grew up in the same neighborhood together. He said he was also friends with Hassan, Mamorsky, Cunningham and the Wenninger brothers.

On the night before the murder, Palumbo said, he'd been out with his family in Queens. Because of this, he did not go into the city with Giuca and the others. He did get invited. John had called him, but he said he had other stuff to do.

He testified that sometime, not long after Mark Fisher's murder, John Giuca called him on the phone.

"What did Giuca say to you?" the prosecutor asked.

"He said, 'I need you to do me a favor. I need you to give something to somebody for me.'"

"What did you do?"

"I said okay. I went to John Giuca's house, and while I was there, he put a bag in the trunk of my car."

"When you got back in your car, did you look in the bag?"

"Not then. I didn't look in the bag until I got all the way home."

"And when you looked, what did you see in the bag?"

"It was a gun. A black gun."

"Was it a revolver or some other type of gun? Was it a semiautomatic?"

"I don't think it was a—it's not a revolver."

"What did you do with it?"

"I picked it up and looked at it; then I figured I got my fingerprints on it, so I wiped it clean with a T-shirt."

"Had you been given instructions by John Giuca as to what to do with the bag and its contents?"

"Yes. He told me to take the package to the corner of Stratford and Beverley Roads, and to leave it on the sidewalk. Then I was to wait. A man was supposed to come and take the bag and leave money."

The location of the drop was just around the corner from Giuca's house. Palumbo testified that he did as he was told. He put the bag on the ground and then used something to cover it up. The man—a guy the witness had never seen before—did show up, just as Giuca had said he would, to exchange the bag for another bag. The second bag contained money.

"I called John. I told him I had the money for him. He said, 'Just hold on to it. I'll see you tomorrow and get it from you,'" Palumbo testified. The witness said he didn't count the money. He saw Giuca the next day. Palumbo called Giuca on his way home from work.

He pulled up in front of Giuca's house. Giuca ran out and Palumbo gave him the bag with the money in it. Yes, he was subsequently interviewed by the police, first in a precinct house down in Coney Island.

No, he didn't tell the truth right away. It was only after a couple hours of questioning that he finally told the cops about the gun. He later gave a sworn statement to the DA's office after being read his Miranda rights, and agreed to testify at this trial in exchange for limited immunity.

Nicolazzi asked if the witness had a criminal record. He said that a few years before, he had been arrested for drunk driving, but that was it.

"At some point during the winter of 2004, did you go to Rikers Island and visit with Antonio Russo?"

Palumbo had, for an hour-long visit during which Russo asked him for many things.

"He was asking me for a favor, but I didn't understand him at first. He said, 'Did you do that?'" As Russo asked the question, he had made his hand into the shape of a gun so Palumbo could see.

In cross-examination Gregory wanted to talk about Giuca's ex-girlfriend, Lauren Conigliaro. Palumbo said they were close friends.

"Would you say that you were close with Lauren Conigliaro in a way that was independent of John Giuca?"

"Yes. We talked a lot. She and John had a problem.

Their relationship was rocky. She came to me for advice. She would always call me."

"After the incident in which you removed the gun, did you see Lauren again?" Gregory inquired.

The witness said he had, maybe once a month after that. She told him things that were confidential. She discussed John cheating on her.

"Did she ever tell you in confidence that John had told her he gave Antonio Russo his gun?"

"Objection," Nicolazzi said.

"Sustained," Judge Marrus ruled.

"Did she ever tell you that the police had told her that if she didn't do what they wanted her to do, she'd never become a U.S. Marshal?"

"Yes."

"No further questions," Gregory said.

Fink asked Palumbo if he knew Gregg Cunningham. Palumbo did. In fact, Palumbo, along with Mamorsky, Giuca and a relative of Palumbo's, went to visit Cunningham at the Greene Correctional Facility, in Coxsackie, New York, where he currently resided.

Fink then asked Palumbo if he remembered specifically when he went to Rikers Island to visit Russo. The witness said that it was in January or February 2005. The visit lasted about an hour.

"During that hour you couldn't understand what he was saying to you, correct?"

"Correct."

"He was babbling, right?"

"Correct."

The witness reiterated that one of the things he did understand was when Russo said, "Did you take care of that?" while making a gesture with his hand that suggested a gun.

"He never used the word 'gun,' correct?"

"Correct."

In redirect Nicolazzi asked Palumbo if, with respect to the confidential conversations he had testified to having with Lauren Conigliaro, if he ever told anyone other than the police what he had done with the gun in the bag that Giuca had given him. Palumbo said no, he told no one other than the police.

The testimony had helped the prosecution a lot. It established that the murder weapon had been in the hands of one of the defendants a short time after the murder, and it had provided a viable reason why police had never found the weapon.

CHAPTER 41

"John Called
the Meetings"

Gregg Cunningham was next on the stand. Cunningham testified that he lived in Upstate New York as a resident of the Greene Correctional Facility serving a seven-year sentence for attempted murder.

He'd shot somebody during the summer of 2002. He'd gotten into a fight behind his building, which was also Russo's building, after attending a party at Anthony Palumbo's house. After a couple of skirmishes with one guy, the witness had returned home, gotten his gun and returned, at which time he shot the guy, with whom he'd been fighting, once in the back.

He pleaded guilty to the charge of attempted murder and was one year into his seven-year sentence.

He'd grown up in Park Slope, a neighborhood west of Prospect Park, but had been neighbors with Russo and

Giuca for about six years. He had gone to Bishop Ford High School with Giuca.

He admitted to being "close friends" with Giuca, Russo, Mamorsky, Palumbo, Hassan and Lancaster. He knew Albert Huggins, but only as an acquaintance.

He said, yes, he was a member of the Ghetto Mafia, as were all of those Nicolazzi had just mentioned—with the exception of Huggins. He said GM's color was orange. Before joining GM, he said, he'd been a Crip.

He testified that Russo, Giuca and Hassan were also former members of the Crips. The Crips' colors were blue and gray. The GM either held their meeting in his neighborhood or sometimes on Eighty-sixth Street in Bensonhurst.

"Who were the leaders of the Ghetto Mafia?" Nicolazzi asked.

"John Giuca and Tommy Hassan," Cunningham replied. "Most of the time John called the meetings."

Nicolazzi asked Cunningham what he'd been doing on the night Mark Fisher was murdered. Cunningham said he had been instructed to watch a film by his social worker, and that was what he was doing. He did not see Giuca or any other of his friends that night.

At about seven or eight o'clock on the morning of October 12, he went to the store and on his way out he saw Russo. Russo was with a guy he knew only as "Crazy." Nicolazzi asked if the guy's name was Crayson. Cunningham said he didn't know.

When he saw Russo and Crazy, they were smoking by the building's parking lot. When he saw Russo, he started laughing. "Antonio didn't have any hair," the witness said.

At that point the Green Jury was dismissed. The remainder of Cunningham's testimony did not concern Giuca and would be heard by the Red Jury only.

Cunningham said he next saw Russo later that day,

Sunday, when he went to Russo's apartment and into Russo's room. Nicolazzi asked what, if anything, Russo had told him at that time.

"Told me he shot somebody," Cunningham said. "He was nervous. I asked him who he shot. He said it was someone I didn't know. A big dude. He said he shot and robbed a kid. The kid charged him and he shot him. He aimed low and that was it. The kid fell.

"He said that he and the kid had been to the store before that, the store at Beverley and Coney Island. They went to an ATM. After he shot the kid, he said, he ran off with his wallet and threw the wallet in the sewer."

"Did he tell you which sewer?"

"No."

"Did he tell you what he did after he threw the wallet into the sewer?"

"He went to cut his hair."

"During this conversation, did he say he was going to go anywhere?"

"Going to California."

Nicolazzi established that, at first, Russo told Cunningham he'd gotten the gun, which he used to shoot the kid, from Giuca, but later he changed his story and said he'd gotten it from the Wenninger brothers.

Cunningham testified that he and Russo discussed the shooting more after Russo returned from California. At that time Russo mentioned, for the first time, that the "big dude" he had shot had died.

Cunningham admitted to Nicolazzi that he did not tell police what he knew the first time they interviewed him, or the second, or the third. Only after he was in prison and police brought him back to Brooklyn did he tell the story he was telling now. He gave a sworn statement to the DA's office that had been audiotaped and he subsequently testified before the grand jury.

During cross-examination Fink made Cunningham go through the number of times he had discussed his testimony with the DA's office, implying for the jury that this was a well-rehearsed witness. He asked Cunningham how nicely had the prosecution been treating him during his brief vacation from prison, and the witness admitted that he had been treated very nicely. He'd been fed well.

Fink asked if Cunningham was aware that Fink had written a letter to his social worker at prison requesting an interview, and that a message had come back to Fink that Cunningham refused to cooperate with Russo's defense. Cunningham said yes, he was aware of that.

Fink established that Cunningham was a guy who drank a lot and smoked a lot, that the primary reason he was currently in prison for shooting someone was that he had had too much to drink that night. Cunningham agreed with that. He tended to become violent when he drank.

Fink noted that during his grand jury testimony, Cunningham had claimed Russo had said he threw the big dude's wallet into the sewer at the corner of Stratford Road and Turner Place, but during his trial testimony he'd said Russo never told him which sewer it was.

Fink pointed out another discrepancy in Cunningham's statements. During his trial testimony he'd said Russo told him the story of the shooting on the afternoon of October 12. For the grand jury he'd said that same conversation took place a couple days after he saw Russo with the bald head, which would have made it October 14.

Cunningham admitted that he had read all of the newspaper articles about the shooting. He knew from reading those articles that a wallet had been found in the sewer at the corner of Turner and Stratford.

Fink noted that although Giuca, Mamorsky and Palumbo had all visited Cunningham while he was in prison, Russo had not.

On redirect Nicolazzi asked Cunningham again if he remembered if Russo had told him the location of the sewer he threw the wallet into. Cunningham said he did remember and that Russo said it was the sewer at Turner and Stratford.

Nicolazzi then had the witness state that his testimony was based solely on what Russo had told him and not on any newspaper reports he had read. That concluded the questioning of Gregg Cunningham.

The Green Jury was allowed back into the courtroom and the next witness was called.

CHAPTER 42

The Man Who Cut Russo's Hair

The next witness was Alfredo Bishop, and he was questioned by Trish McNeill. Bishop testified that he lived in the same apartment building as Russo and worked for a financial company. He and Russo's mother had grown up together, so he had known Russo all his life.

Bishop testified that at about seven o'clock on the morning of October 12, 2003, he'd gotten a call from his ex-mother-in-law, who also lived in the same building, asking him to come down to her apartment for a moment.

He did this. In her apartment was his ex-mother-in-law, whose name was Marie, her kids, and Russo, who seemed nervous. They were all in the kitchen and Russo asked Bishop to cut his hair.

Russo said he was going to California and he wanted his braids cut off, so Bishop did that for him. Bishop was in Marie's apartment for less than one hour, and left immediately after giving Russo his haircut. McNeill had no further questions.

Gregory announced that he had no cross-examination for this witness, so the Green Jury was allowed to start their lunch break early, while the Red Jury remained to hear the remainder of the questioning of the witness.

"At the time you cut his hair, did Antonio Russo tell you what happened the prior night?" McNeill asked.

"He told me he got off the subway at Eighteenth Street and Church Avenue and somebody tried to rob him. They got into a scuffle. The person had a gun. It was going to be either him or the other person. Eventually he said he shot him. Then he ran. That's it."

"While you were cutting his hair, did you notice anything outside the apartment building?"

"Police car. There were sirens going back and forth, passing."

"How did Russo act as a result of seeing the police car?"

"Basically, he thinks he fucked up," the witness said.

"Did Antonio Russo ask you to do anything other than cut his hair?"

"Yeah, he asked me not to say anything, to say he was at Linda's apartment all night."

"And by Linda's, you are referring to—"

"Maria, my ex-mother-in-law."

(It was not explained why the woman had alternate first names.)

"And what did you say?" McNeill asked.

"Well, we both said we wasn't going to get involved with it," the witness said, referring to himself and Maria.

Fink then cross-examined. He asked if Russo was "bald" when the witness was through cutting his hair. Bishop said he was not. Fink wanted to know when the witness first heard about Fisher's death. Bishop said it was probably a month later.

"Were you following the news?" Fink asked.

"None of my business. I wasn't following no news about nothing."

Fink asked if the witness had noticed the reward posters that had been pasted up by the police around his apartment building, and Bellamy acknowledged that he had. He said he first noted the posters a couple months after the murder.

"And you never told the police anything with regard to what Mr. Russo said to you?"

"No."

Through Fink's cross-examination the jury learned that Bishop first spoke to the police about Russo's statements on November 29, 2004, more than thirteen months following the murder. In fact, by the time Bishop first gave the police this information, Russo was already under arrest.

"At the time you cut Mr. Russo's hair, did you notice any bruises or marks on him?"

"No."

"Do you recall what he was wearing on that particular day?"

"A white sweater."

"No further questions."

"Any redirect?" Judge Marrus said, turning his gaze to Trish McNeill.

"Just two questions, Your Honor," she said. "Mr. Bishop, did you volunteer the information you knew when the police came to see you?"

"Yes, I did."

"And did you ever apply for the reward in this case?"

"No, I didn't."

That concluded the questioning of the man who'd cut Russo's hair, and the court recessed for lunch.

Fink later said that cross-examining Bishop required all his skills. "He was the most difficult person to cross-examine," Fink said. "He testified that he had cut Mr. Russo's hair and he also testified to statements that Mr. Russo allegedly made to him that morning. In terms of attacking him, I approached it simply in terms that he had waited months before actually going forward."

CHAPTER 43

"Skulls"

The first prosecution witness of the afternoon session was Ramdial Sikhial, questioned by Trish McNeill. Sikhail said he was a friend of Russo's. He had known Russo for about a year and a half. He'd first learned of Mark Fisher's death in the newspaper. There was a picture of the victim and another picture of Russo, whom the press had picked up on as one of the last to see the victim alive. After seeing the photo, he had gone to Russo and asked him point-blank if he was the one who "did it."

"And what did he say to you?" McNeill asked.

"He didn't give me no answer."

"Did you give him the article?"

"He had the article. He put it on his wall next to his bed."

The witness said that two weeks later he had another conversation. At that time Russo told him he had a beef with the kid, but that "he and his friends took care of it."

Under cross-examination by Fink, Sikhial said his

nickname was Skulls, and that he drank every day. He used to smoke a lot of marijuana, but he stopped that. He stopped because he was on probation—for two robberies committed in 2002—and it would be a parole violation to smoke.

He also admitted to choking one guy during one of the robberies, but insisted that he only stole because he needed money for alcohol, and those were the only two robberies he ever committed.

On redirect, McNeill had one question: "Why did you keep asking Russo if he was the one who did it?"

The witness replied, "Because people in the street, everybody was talking about it."

Jonathan Fink later recalled that "Skulls" wasn't the sort of witness that he stayed up nights worrying about. He simply didn't think the jury would take him seriously, since he was so obviously a mess.

"He was an individual who said he drank every single day," Fink said. "He was not a witness I was overly concerned with, based upon who he was. If you saw this guy, it looked as if he was brought in off the street to testify."

The final prosecution witness of the day was Police Officer Dillon Stewart, with McNeill questioning. Officer Stewart said he was employed by the NYPD. During the early-morning hours of October 12, 2003, he was in his patrol car, cruising the streets of the Seventieth Precinct.

At six-thirty that morning he responded to a radio call backing another unit to Argyle Road. Shots fired. When he got there, they spoke first to the individual who had made the call. He and several other officers began canvassing the area. They found an individual lying on the sidewalk facedown. The body was lying on top of a blanket and in a pool of blood. He was not moving and he did not appear to be breathing. He appeared to be dead.

An ambulance was immediately called. Then a crime scene was made up, and efforts were made to keep other people away from the immediate location. This was done to keep evidence from being inadvertently contaminated. The area was isolated. The street was closed off and the sidewalk was blocked off to prevent pedestrians from approaching.

Later in the day the officer reported to the medical examiner's office. There he identified the body that was in the morgue as the same one he'd found on the sidewalk.

That concluded McNeill's direct examination. Neither defense attorney had any questions of this witness. By establishing that the body in the morgue, the one identified as Mark Fisher, was the same as the one at the crime scene, the prosecution had established a chain of evidence, so it was no longer necessary to introduce into evidence the crime scene photo that showed Mark Fisher's face.

CHAPTER 44

"Why So Stressed?"

The first prosecution witness of the next court session was Alejandro Romero, questioned by Trish McNeill. Only the Red Jury was in the courtroom. McNeill began her questioning by establishing that Romero was not testifying by his own free will. He was testifying because he had been compelled to testify, and for no other reason.

"Do you know an individual named Antonio Russo?" McNeill asked.

"Yes, I do."

"And how do you know him?"

"Off of the neighborhood."

"And what is your relationship, if any, with him?"

"Really, no relation," Romero replied.

Romero said that he had no contact with Russo during the night of October 11, 2003, or the morning of October 12, but sometime after that he was walking down the street and he noticed that the sewer opening at the corner of Stratford and Beverley was being searched.

That location was one block to the north of the sewer opening in which Mark Fisher's wallet was found, at the corner of Stratford and Turner. Romero said he saw two police officers searching the sewer, two detectives, a woman and a man.

A few days after seeing the sewer searched, Romero testified, he'd had a conversation with Russo on the topic.

"I was just hanging out and he approached us, kind of, you know, stressed out. I asked him, 'Why are you acting so funny? Why are you acting so stressed?' He said, 'If someone was never in this predicament, this would never have happened.'"

"Did you notice anything different about his appearance at that time?"

"He had cut his hair."

"Did you ask him why he'd gotten a haircut?"

"Yeah, he said he just had to do it."

"Did you tell him about seeing the sewer being searched?"

"Yes. He said, 'They're searching the wrong sewer.' He said, 'I would never put two things in the same sewer.'"

McNeill asked if the witness and Russo, as they discussed the sewer, also discussed a kid with the nickname of Crip.

"There was something about a kid named 'Crip,' but I really can't remember much about it, to be honest with you."

McNeill asked him if he had testified before a grand jury in this case. Romero admitted that he had, but he had been forced to do so on that occasion as well. McNeill showed him a transcript of the comments Romero had made to the grand jury regarding the kid named Crip.

"Does that refresh your memory?" McNeill asked.

"It was just a conversation about a kid named Crip

who lived a couple of blocks away. I know him as Crip. I don't know any of his other aliases or nothing."

"Did you ask Russo at some point if he left something near Crip's house?"

"He said he never leaves things in the neighborhood like that. I don't remember."

McNeill asked the witness where Crip lived and Romero said on Beverley Road.

"How far is Beverley from Stratford and Turner?"

"Like a block," the witness said. McNeill had no further questions.

On cross-examination Fink asked Romero if it was true that he'd first talked to the police in March 2004 about the conversation he'd had with Russo, which was about five months after the conversation had taken place. The witness said it was true.

Fink asked if, at the time of his conversation with Russo about the sewer, Romero was with a friend named Damien. The witness said he was. Fink asked if Romero was aware that Damien was "in Brooklyn right now?"

"Actually, Damien wasn't present at the moment," Romero said, meaning that Damien did not hear the conversation about the sewer. "He was there for a moment and then he went back upstairs. That's all that happened."

Fink asked if Romero had been lying when he told police that Damien had been there when he and Russo talked of the sewer.

"No, because he was there for most of the conversation. He just wasn't paying attention, like I was."

Prompted by Fink's questions, Romero said that his conversation with Russo about the sewer had occurred after police found a wallet in the sewer at the corner of Stratford and Turner, and that he had been following reports of the murder and the subsequent investigation "every day" in the newspaper.

"Do you recall telling the police that when you discussed the sewer with Mr. Russo that he wasn't making any sense?"

"Yeah, he was just speaking off the top of his head, and it was just piece by piece by piece—"

"And he wasn't making any sense, right?"

"Yeah, I told them that."

That concluded the questioning of Alejandro Romero. Because the court had other business to attend to, Romero would be the only witness of the day. The Red Jury was told they could take the rest of the day off and return the following day, September 22, 2005, at 11:00 A.M.

Jonathan Fink later remembered Romero this way: "He was very reluctant to be in the courtroom. He said Russo seemed nervous and agitated while talking about the police looking in sewers. The police at that point had already recovered Mr. Fisher's wallet, I believe from a sewer. My recollection of cross-examining him was that I nullified him."

CHAPTER 45

The Snitch

The prosecution's first witness on Thursday, September 22, was thirty-five-year-old John Avitto. Avitto was what the defense attorneys would call a "jailhouse snitch." He said he knew Giuca from their time together in the city jail on Rikers Island.

Since his testimony had nothing to do with the case against Antonio Russo, it was given with the Green Jury only in the courtroom.

Sam Gregory was pleasantly surprised when Avitto was called. Using a jailhouse snitch in a trial is usually considered a sign of desperation. Gregory saw no reason why this witness could be trusted, and he didn't think the jury would see any reason, either.

The witness told Nicolazzi that he'd been in jail on a burglary charge at the time he met Giuca. He was asked the status of that charge and answered that he'd pleaded guilty to burglary in the third degree and was sentenced to an eighteen- to twenty-four-month drug program.

The witness admitted to having been a cocaine and heroin addict and, as a result of his addictions, had a lengthy criminal history dating back to 1989. Among other things, he had been arrested in separate incidents for driving a stolen car, for stealing power tools and for attempting to steal laptop computers.

He'd also been arrested for selling a drug called PCP. He said that during his most recent drug program, he'd relapsed once, sniffing coke, and had immediately called his caseworker explaining what had happened and asking for further help.

He explained that he'd had plenty of time to talk to Giuca when they were both at Rikers, as they were in the "same dorm." They were together twenty-four, seven. They became friends and passed the time playing cards. Sometimes chess.

He'd first discussed Giuca's case with him in the bull pen, the holding area for before a court appearance. Giuca told him that he'd been arrested one year before, but they didn't have enough evidence against him so they released him. Then they arrested him again more recently on the same charge.

"He told me there was a party. They ran out of alcohol and he never left the party. By the way he was saying it to me, I knew that he was lying," the witness testified.

That brought an objection from Gregory. Judge Marrus sustained the objection. The judge warned the witness to stick to the facts and leave his opinions out of it.

The next conversation the witness claimed to have had with Giuca occurred in February 2005. Giuca and Avitto were together in the Rikers visiting area. Giuca was receiving a visit from his stepfather, aunt and cousin, while Avitto was being visited by his mother, brother, girlfriend and daughter. It was very friendly and the two families were introduced to one another.

Avitto said that Giuca's dad was skinny just like him,

his aunt was dressed really well and his cousin was young and cute—although Giuca later told him that she wasn't as young as she looked. She was actually twenty-two.

Avitto said that he overheard part of the conversation that Giuca had with his father. His father asked him why he had had a gun with him, and Giuca had replied that he "just had it." After that, father and son discussed Giuca's mom and other family stuff.

The next purported conversation between the witness and the defendant occurred the following day in the dorm.

"We were playing cards," Avitto recalled. "He told me he was at the party, they ran out of alcohol, they needed money, the deceased person offered to go to the ATM and get some money. The guy only got twenty dollars out. John got mad. He pulled out a gun. He hit him on the side of the head. The kid went down. They started punching and kicking him. Then one of his other friends pulled the gun off him and shot the kid."

Doreen Federicci, sitting in the spectator section of the courtroom, looked at the jury, then looked at Avitto testifying, and then looked back at the jury. They knew, she thought. The jury could tell that this guy was making things up. Surely, the jury was hip to that bullshit. She thought it was a very good sign, that the prosecution was getting desperate. By Doreen's way of thinking, the prosecution had made its case against Tony Russo, but they were going to have more trouble convicting her John. That was why they threw in the snitch, but the jury could tell it was bullshit, so it was a good thing. Doreen may have fidgeted a little when she had these thoughts, but she was convinced.

"Did the defendant tell you, other than the victim, who else it was that went with him, with the victim, when they went to get the money?" Nicolazzi asked.

The witness replied that Giuca had told him two other people went along, but he didn't use any names. He didn't say where the shooting took place, although he did say that the punching and kicking began after the victim handed over the $20 he'd gotten from the ATM. Giuca didn't say what anyone did after the shooting.

At some point after that conversation the witness remembered Giuca getting angry because his picture was in the paper. He was afraid that someone had ratted him out.

Nicolazzi concluded her direct examination by asking if the prosecution had promised him anything in return for his testimony at this trial. The witness replied that it had not.

During his cross-examination Gregory made sure the jury understood that the witness was a "career criminal," and that although the prosecution might not have overtly promised him anything in exchange for his testimony, the truth was that he was in a drug program when he could have been sentenced to seven years in prison.

Gregory tried to establish, with some success, that the witness's criminal career was more than just a matter of stealing to support his drug habit. He asked the witness if it was not true that he'd been charged at one point with "using a kid for sexual performances." The witness denied it. He had been charged with endangering the welfare of a child, but that was because he'd gotten in a fight with a guy when the guy had his kid in the backseat of his car.

Gregory asked what medication Avitto was on at that moment and Avitto said he was taking a medication called Seroquel, which is normally prescribed for schizophrenia, but he used it as a sleep aid.

"You can ask John," Avitto said. "I gave him a few because he couldn't sleep. You didn't know about that, did you?"

"Can I have a few? I couldn't sleep last night, either. Give me a couple, would you?" Gregory replied.

That cracked up Giuca, the first time he had smiled during the trial. The gallery and both juries laughed as well. Judge Marrus acknowledged that this was all very entertaining, but warned Gregory and the witness to get back to business.

"Inmates are nervous about who's a rat and who isn't a rat, correct?" Gregory asked.

"Correct."

"And it would be fair to say that when you come in there, you got 'I'm a rat' written all over you by the way you talk and the way you act, correct?"

"No."

"Is it fair to say that John Giuca wouldn't talk to you or associate with you while he was in there because you were an outcast?"

Avitto said, "John Giuca was scared to death that he played his bunk like a punk. I took him under the wing, and that's why he opened up to me and talked to me."

Gregory asked if Avitto was a Muslim. The witness said he was.

"Did you become a Muslim to get along better in jail?" Gregory asked.

"That had nothing to do with it. I've been a Muslim for eight years."

Gregory turned the topic back to the witness's meds.

"Could you give the court a complete rundown of the pills you take?"

"I take one pill for anxiety, Zantac for gastritis, Zoloft for depression and Seroquel to sleep. I have trouble sleeping because I have nightmares about something that happened to me. I was molested when I was younger."

That completed the questioning of the witness. Judge Marrus called for a short recess. When court resumed, both juries would be present.

CHAPTER 46

Autopsy Report

Thursday, September 22, was a tough day in court for the victim's dad. Michael Fisher was forced to abruptly get up and leave during a forensic pathologist's testimony describing his son's wounds. The show of emotion was a rarity from Michael Fisher, who had remained stoic and quiet during the trial. The victim's mother, Nancy, and younger sister, Alexis, had calmly left the courtroom before the pathologist began his testimony.

The medical examiner testifying in regard to Mark Fisher's death was Dr. Joachim Guitierrez, who lived on Staten Island. Dr. Guitierrez was questioned by Anna-Sigga Nicolazzi. His official position was that of a medical examiner two. He was employed by the New York City Office of the Chief Medical Examiner.

He was a forensic pathologist, specializing in a branch of medicine that deals with the study of diseases and injuries and applies this knowledge in the courts of law and in determining the cause of death.

Dr. Guitierrez had been a forensic pathologist for about twenty years. His duties included investigating all unexpected and unnatural deaths—unnatural deaths being homicides, suicides, accidents and those caused by drugs.

During those twenty years on the job, he had performed approximately seven thousand autopsies, an autopsy being the dissection of a body and its organs to determine the manner and cause of death.

Dr. Guitierrez testified that on October 13, 2003, Dr. Charles Cantanese performed an autopsy on the body that would subsequently be identified as that of Mark Fisher. Each autopsy he performed was given a number, to help distinguish it from all the other autopsies. Fisher's autopsy would be known as K03-4880.

Dr. Cantanese soon thereafter left the New York City Office of the Chief Medical Examiner and was not available to testify. Dr. Guitierrez had read the written autopsy report and had viewed the photos taken during the autopsy, and would testify on Dr. Cantanese's behalf.

He went through the results of the external examination of the body, that there was bruising consistent with a beating. He described, one by one, the bullet wounds in Mark Fisher's body.

He discussed the results of the toxicology report on fluid and tissue samples taken from Fisher's body. Although drugs and alcohol were found, the quantities of those substances were not high enough to be a contributing factor to Mark Fisher's death. The cause of death had been the gunshots.

Nicolazzi produced a diagram of a human body and asked Dr. Guitierrez to mark on the diagram the locations of the abrasions and contusions that had been observed during the external examination of the body, as well as the location and paths of the gunshot wounds that had been observed during both the external and internal examinations of the body.

Dr. Guitierrez testified that the cause of death had been gunshot wounds. The manner of death had been a homicide.

During cross-examination Fink got the pathologist to admit that he couldn't be sure if Mark Fisher had been hit by five or six bullets. (There was a chance that the in-and-out wound of the elbow had been caused by the same bullet that had caused one of the other wounds to Fisher's torso.)

The doctor also admitted that he only knew that the abrasions to Fisher's face had been caused by blunt impact, and could not determine if they had been caused by the victim being struck, or by his falling on his face after he was shot.

Gregory began his cross-examination by focusing on the toxicology report: "If you would, could you tell the jury the level of alcohol or ethanol found in the blood and urine makeup of Mr. Fisher?"

The witness said that the alcohol level in the victim's blood was .21 grams percent and in the urine it was .27 grams percent.

Gregory asked about the stimulant that had been found in Fisher's system: "Would that be methamphetamine and amphetamine?"

"Yes."

Gregory asked his final question of the witness: "Would that commonly be known as Ecstasy?"

"Yes."

In redirect Nicolazzi asked the pathologist if the abrasions and contusions found on the victim's body would be consistent with his being beaten, kicked and punched. The doctor said they would. She asked if the blunt-impact wounds would have been consistent with the victim having been struck by an object, such as a gun. The witness said they would.

Dr. Guitierrez was allowed to step down from the witness stand.

CHAPTER 47

The Firearms
Examiner

Detective Mark Basoa, of the NYPD's Firearms Analysis Section, sat upon the witness stand and stated that he had been a cop for almost eighteen years. For the last nine of those years, he'd worked as a firearms analyst.

Trish McNeill asked the witness to explain what the Firearms Analysis Section of the police department did.

"We test any firearms that come into the police department for operability and ammunition. We do serial number restoration of defaced firearms, distance determinations, computerized ballistics and microscopic comparison of ballistics evidence."

"What are your duties as a firearms examiner?"

"I do just about all the tests I just described. I primarily do microscopic comparison."

"How many firearms have you examined and tested?"

"About twenty-four hundred."

"What is a microscopic comparison?"

"When a firearm is discharged, when a live cartridge of ammunition is discharged, what's left over is the bullet or projectile that comes out, and the discharged cartridge casing. Using a comparison microscope— which is basically two microscopes that are optically bridged, so I can look in one set of optics and see two images at the same time—I can make comparisons of the discharged cartridge casings to each other and bullets or pieces of bullets to each. In this way I can determine how many guns were used at a shooting scene. Or, if guns were submitted to us, I can determine if those guns were actually used."

"How many microscopic comparisons have you done during your time with the Firearms Analysis Section?"

"I've handled eighteen hundred cases—but that would represent thousands of pieces of evidence."

"Have you received any special training in the area of ballistics and microscopic comparison?"

"Yes, when I was first assigned to the office, I worked in an apprentice relationship with senior detectives in the offices, working on firearms operability cases. Then I was sent to what are called armor schools, which are schools certified by firearms manufacturers so you can work on their firearms mechanically. I've had training separate from that with gunshot residue and distance determinations. After a period of time you do supervised casework with a senior detective, who oversees your work. And then you're allowed to do your own work. That was for firearms operability. For microscopic comparison I had ten months of full-time training by a forensic consultant and subsequently passed some principal and academic tests."

The witness said this was his 155th time testifying in a court of law as a ballistic expert.

"Detective, can you explain to the jury the difference between a revolver and a semiautomatic pistol?"

"Both are handheld firearms," the witness replied. "A semiautomatic pistol has a solid frame and what we call a movable slide on top that is spring-loaded. The ammunition is fed into it by a magazine, which is a metal or plastic spring-loaded box that can hold a number of live cartridges of ammunition. You place that in the grip area, pull the spring-loaded slide to the rear and let it go. As it goes forward, it's going to strip off a cartridge of live ammunition, putting it in the chamber. When you discharge the firearm, the bullet will come out of the barrel. And the same energy that was used to get the bullet out of the barrel will also be used to extract and eject the cartridge casing from the firearm. So, each time I fire, not only does a bullet come out of the firearm, but a casing will actually come out of the firearm as well.

"In a revolver it's a solid frame with a revolving cylinder. The live cartridges go in chambers of that revolving cylinder. Each time I pull the trigger, the cylinder revolves, the next live cartridge of ammunition is discharged. The cartridge casings themselves stay inside that cylinder until you manually open it and take them out."

The witness testified that he'd received various pieces of ballistic evidence with respect to this case. He'd received two spent shell casings recovered at the crime scene and concluded that they were two .22-caliber discharged cartridge casings that were fired by one and the same firearm.

Detective Basoa said that he'd also received five bullets taken from the body of Mark Fisher. He was able to determine that four of them were .22-caliber. He could not determine the caliber of the fifth piece of evidence, which was a small lead fragment.

"What condition were those bullets in?"

"All of them were deformed."

"Did you perform a microscopic examination on these bullets?"

"Yes. I did a microscopic analysis of the individual characteristics within the tool mark from the firearm that discharged them, which is left behind on the bullets after they travel down the barrel. The four bullets that could be determined to be twenty-two caliber were all consistent and similar in their rifling and had consistent and similar tool marks on them. However, because of their deformity I was unable to positively conclude that they were all fired by the same gun. I could, however, conclude that they were all positively fired from the same type of firearm. The casings were all fired from a semiautomatic pistol, and the bullets were of the same caliber."

"Could those bullets have been fired from a twenty-two-caliber Ruger?"

"Yes. The firing pin and impression on the casings would be the type of firing pin that a Ruger is manufactured with."

"No further questions," McNeill said.

"Cross-examination, Mr. Fink," Judge Marrus said.

Fink elicited from the witness on cross that, given the evidence, he could tell that the cases had been ejected from a semiautomatic weapon, but he could not determine for certain if the bullets had been fired from a semiautomatic or a revolver.

Fink pointed out that if the prosecution's theory of the case was correct, five shots were fired from the same gun, a semiautomatic, which meant that five shell casings would have been ejected. They would have all been ejected in the same direction and approximately the same distance. The witness stated that since no murder weapon had been recovered in this case, it was impossible to test the gun for an "ejection pattern."

Nonetheless, Fink asked, wouldn't any .22-caliber semiautomatic eject each shell in the same direction and approximately the same distance? The witness said that this was true.

Could he approximate the direction and distance that such a firearm would eject its casings?

"As a broad approximation, I would say that there's a range of anywhere from five to thirteen feet to the right and to the rear of the shooter, if the gun was held in the manner it was designed to be held, which often isn't the case."

Fink had no further questions of the witness.

On redirect McNeill asked, "Because you don't have five shell casings, does that in any way tell you that there were not five shots?"

"No," Detective Basoa replied.

CHAPTER 48

Last Two Witnesses

The last testimony came from two NYPD detectives who were on the Fisher case, traveling as far as Florida and California to talk to anyone connected with the murder suspects.

Detective James McCafferty was the first to take the stand. He stated his name, his badge number and the fact that he was assigned to the Brooklyn South Homicide Squad.

The witness told Nicolazzi that he had been a member of the NYPD for twenty-one years, the last fifteen of those as a detective, the last ten of those on his precinct's Homicide Task Force.

The witness stated that he first became involved with the investigation into Mark Fisher's murder in May 2004, about seven months after the crime. He was assigned to the case at the same time as two other detectives, Steven Grafakos and Thomas Burns.

Nicolazzi asked why he had been assigned to the case

so long after the crime. McCafferty said the feeling was that it was time for a "fresh look at the case." He said the three new detectives on the case, including himself, worked in conjunction with prosecutors, even though there had yet to be any arrests, and this was because there were plans under way to convene a grand jury.

The first steps he took after his new assignment, Mc-Cafferty testified, were to review the case, reinterview witnesses and analyze telephone records. Those records included those that the police already had when he came aboard and those that were subsequently subpoenaed and received.

During the course of the investigation, he said, "approximately one hundred to one hundred fifty witnesses" were interviewed, many more than once.

He testified that while many of the interviews took place within the five boroughs of New York City, some took place in other areas of New York State, and in other states as well.

"Did you travel to California with respect to this investigation?" Nicolazzi asked.

"Yes, I did, " Detective McCafferty replied. The trip, he explained, was to interview people who were in contact with Russo, during the time the defendant was on the West Coast immediately following the murder.

The detective stated that he also traveled to Georgia to interview a person named Rob Lancaster, who had received phone calls from people connected with the case. He had first searched for Lancaster in Brooklyn, but discovered that he was away at school, making the trip necessary.

Nicolazzi's questioning then focused on interviews McCafferty conducted on July 3, 2004, in Palm Harbor, Florida. He was with Detectives Grafakos and Burns, as well as members of local law enforcement from the

Pinellas County Sheriff's Department, when they encountered John Giuca.

Giuca had been picked up by a local sheriff's car and then taken to the sheriff's office. According to the witness, while in the car, Giuca had asked, "Is there a warrant for my brother also?"

Later that day, during a break in the questioning, Giuca made a phone call. That call was to his mother. Asked if he overheard any part of that conversation, the witness said he had.

"I heard Giuca say, 'Call Tommy and Lauren. Make sure that you call Tommy and Lauren.'"

Nicolazzi then shifted her questioning to the time, during autumn 2004, when an investigative grand jury was impaneled in Brooklyn. McCafferty stated that the grand jury heard testimony from a number of subpoenaed witnesses and eventually handed down an indictment with respect to Antonio Russo.

From that indictment, an arrest warrant was generated and, on November 23, 2004, McCafferty was at the huge apartment building on Turner Place for the purpose of apprehending Russo.

The witness testified that he went to the fifth-floor apartment in that building and knocked on the door. The knock was answered by Russo's grandmother. McCafferty said that he was there to talk to Russo.

"She said that they had an attorney and wouldn't permit us in," the witness said.

"What was done at that point?" Nicolazzi asked.

McCafferty said that he gave the grandmother his business card, told her to call her attorney and have him get in touch. He then backed down the hallway, verified the arrest warrant was in place and, later that morning, when Russo stepped outside the apartment, the arrest was made.

Nicolazzi asked McCafferty if he knew to whom Giuca had been referring when he said Lauren and Tommy. He said he did. Giuca had been talking about his girlfriend, Lauren Conigliaro, and his friend Tommy Hassan.

Returning to the phone records, Nicolazzi asked how the records were used in the investigation. In some cases, McCafferty explained, witnesses were asked about phone calls the records said they had made. In other cases the records were compared to statements that witnesses had made, to see who was lying about to whom they had talked and when.

McCafferty admitted that, among those whose records had been examined were Anthony Palumbo, Albert Huggins, Matt Federicci, John Giuca and Antonio Russo. Most of the examined phone records involved calls that were made between October 12 and 14, 2003, during the forty-eight hours after Mark Fisher's murder. When asked, McCafferty said that there had been no call between Huggins and Russo during that time, but there had been calls, during that same time period, between Giuca and Palumbo and also between Russo and Giuca.

Nicolazzi introduced the phone records into evidence, with phone calls from Russo to Giuca marked in blue and those from Giuca to Russo marked in green. There was also one call marked in black that was from Matt Federicci to his brother, John Giuca, at 6:42 A.M. on the day of the murder.

McCafferty noted that during the two days before the murder, Giuca and Russo had spoken on the phone four times, each having dialed the phone twice. During the two days following the murder, the pair had talked to one another twenty-six times. That concluded Nicolazzi's direct examination.

During a short cross-examination Fink asked if, while in California investigating the case, McCafferty had had occasion to speak with Antonio Russo's uncle, a man named Nathaniel Bellamy. The detective said that he had.

Fink asked, at the time of Russo's arrest, if his client had resisted arrest in any way? McCafferty said that he had not. Fink asked if a search warrant had been executed regarding Russo's apartment. It had. Was anything pertinent to the case found during that search? The detective said there was not.

Gregory began his cross on behalf of Giuca by asking if, at the time the witness saw Giuca in Florida, he knew that Giuca's mom owned a condominium in that state? McCafferty did know that.

Did the witness know that Giuca had been in Florida with his mother and Scott Powers and Jennifer Baker and his brother, Matt? The detective said that he knew Giuca was in Florida, but he didn't know with whom.

Gregory asked if, during the many interviews he'd done during his investigation, he'd ever spoken to a young man by the name of John Avitto. McCafferty said that he had. Gregory then established that even though it was common practice for detectives to take notes during interviews and even record interviews to create a permanent record of what was said, there were no notes or recordings of his interview with Avitto. Gregory further established that before asking Avitto any questions, McCafferty had read the autopsy report and knew the location of Mark Fisher's wounds—implying that this knowledge would have allowed the detective to ask leading questions.

That ended Gregory's cross. Nicolazzi said she had a few questions in redirect. She had the witness point out that even though a search warrant was executed for Antonio Russo's apartment at the time of his arrest, the arrest took place a year following the murder, so the fact that the search bore no fruit was not terribly surprising.

Russo had had, after all, twelve long months to dispose of any evidence he might have had in that apartment.

McCafferty told her that although it was common to take notes during interviews with witnesses, and also common to tape-record interviews, it was just as common to interview witnesses with no tape rolling and no notes being taken.

Regarding the questions Gregory had asked about the witness's knowledge of Mark Fisher's autopsy at the time he interviewed John Avitto, Nicolazzi asked, "When you or other individuals in your presence were interviewing John Avitto, was any information at all given to him with regard to this investigation?"

"No. Absolutely not," Detective McCafferty stated firmly.

The prosecution's final witness, testifying for the Red Jury only, was Detective Thomas Burns, who had helped arrest Russo on November 23, 2004. He said Russo spoke to him later in the police station.

"He said to me, 'When are you going to arrest the other guys?'" Burns testified.

Following the testimony of the two police detectives, the prosecution rested its case.

CHAPTER 49

Hearing Motions

Judge Marrus said to the juries, "Ladies and gentlemen, what that means is that the prosecution has completed presenting their evidence in each of these two cases. I am now going to give each of these two defendants a chance to decide if they want to present any additional evidence to you. As I told you at the beginning of the trial, that is completely optional for them."

The judge then dismissed the juries until the following morning, again warning them not to discuss the case with anyone. With the jurors out of the room, the judge announced he would hear any motions.

Fink said, "Your Honor, at this time I'd ask that you dismiss all the counts against Mr. Russo. The main basis for doing so, I would argue—as I've continually done so during this case—is the allowing of the people to introduce gang-related evidence in this case, which, obviously, Mr. Russo's jury heard.

"It's always been my position that that evidence was

prejudicial, but, more so, I just don't see the basis for it coming in, particularly what Mr. Huggins testified to about the conversation he had with Mr. Giuca in regard to Mr. Giuca saying that the gang needed to be more tough and that violence would have to be, I guess, committed by someone or some people.

"In essence, Mr. Russo's jury heard that evidence and the people are arguing that that is the motive in this case for the murder of Mr. Fisher, and I don't believe that a connection has been made. Certainly, I would ask that they not even be allowed to make that argument in their summation. So, for those reasons, I'd ask that the counts against Mr. Russo be dismissed."

Judge Marrus said, "Mr. Gregory, do you want to make a motion at the close of the case?"

Gregory replied, "Judge, I do. I think, with respect to the intentional murder count, there's a problem. You have three witnesses who testified for the prosecution that make this case. Huggins's testimony is the only testimony that could arguably make out intentional murder. According to Mr. Huggins, Mr. Giuca gives Mr. Russo the gun and says, 'Go show this guy what's up.'

"Of course, we deny and dispute he ever said that, but even if it were said, 'show him what's up' in any parlance does not equate murder.

"Lauren Conigliaro doesn't mention anything except the robbery and Avitto says it's a robbery gone bad. So I do think, Judge, there's a problem with respect to the intentional murder.

"Also I think, Judge, the way I see this case proceeding, the DA is going to have to make two different arguments to two different juries based on the evidence here. They are going to argue in front of my jury that Mr. Giuca, acting in concert with Mr. Russo and another, and I'm not sure if he said Matthew Federicci, but another, assaulted and acting together caused the death during a robbery of Mark Fisher. To Mr. Russo's jury they are going to have to argue that he acted alone. So I think there are some real difficulties with respect to where this case is going."

The judge then ruled, "There are two theories of murder. I'll make a decision as to what I submit to the jury. At this time I am denying the motions."

And that was the last word of the day and the week.

Outside the courtroom Fisher's aunt Ruby Bonanno commented on the prosecution's performance: "They've done the best with what they had," she said. She noted the lack of physical evidence and eyewitnesses, but reiterated her opinion that she thought both of the defendants were guilty.

"They're as guilty as they come," she said.

Neither defense attorney planned on putting their clients on the stand. For that matter, they didn't present any witness testimony whatsoever. Jonathan Fink had let everyone know in advance that he didn't plan to call any witnesses. He was going to say that the prosecution had failed to make a case.

Sam Gregory said earlier that he might call one witness, but he'd yet to make up his mind. In the end he decided not to present any witnesses, agreeing with Fink that his best bet was to sit back, fold his arms and claim confidently that the prosecution had failed to prove his client guilty beyond a reasonable doubt.

With the Green Jury only in the courtroom, Gregory's case consisted of five exhibits. They were telephone records: Giuca's cell on October 11 and 12, Huggins's cell for the morning of Octoner 12, Russo's cell for October 10 and 11, Russo's cell for October 12, the landline at Giuca's home for the morning of October 12.

Judge Marrus said, "For the record, Mr. Giuca has decided that he does not wish to testify?"

"Correct," Gregory said.

"You've discussed that it is his right to testify?" the judge asked.

"Yes," Gregory replied.

Judge Marrus turned his attention to the defendant. "Is that correct, Mr. Giuca?"

"Correct," Giuca said.

CHAPTER 50

Closing Arguments

On Tuesday, Assistant District Attorney Anna-Sigga Nicolazzi addressed the Giuca jury. She had specifically requested that she be allowed to sum up her case for the Giuca jury first, and since she was the one who had to do two summations, Judge Marrus accommodated her.

She told the Green Jury that she believed, despite the fact that there were only two defendants being tried at these proceedings, that at least three people were involved in the killing. She said that the victim had been defenseless against the group he'd been thrust into, a group of young men who saw him as an "outsider" and wanted to "humiliate him."

She said, "Mark Fisher was ultimately a lamb surrounded by wolves."

Nicolazzi told the jury that it was the prosecution's theory that John Giuca had orchestrated the killing, but it was Antonio Russo who pulled the trigger, using the .22 Ruger that Giuca had given him.

Just days before the murder, she reminded the jury, that gun had been Giuca's pride and joy. He'd been showing it off to his friends. After the murder it was never seen again. It had been left on a street corner, then taken away in a clandestine operation worthy of international espionage.

She discussed the uncanny twists of fate involved in Mark Fisher being led to the time and place of his death. She said that it was when Meredith Flannigan decided she couldn't leave Mark Fisher alone in the city—that he was too drunk and lost, and so he had to come along with them in the cab from the Upper East Side to Ditmas Park—that it happened.

"That's when the worlds very slowly began to collide and fate began to play its unfortunate hand," Nicolazzi said.

Nicolazzi called Giuca's group "gangsta wannabes" and a "pathetic fledgling gang" with a depraved "get a body" rule. To stay in the group, one needed to take a human life. It didn't get any more depraved than that.

There were other gangs with violent initiation rites, of course. Some gangs made neophytes "draw innocent blood" before they could be a member. This fact, police believed, often explained otherwise unexplainable subway slashings.

Other groups required that new members take a woman against her will, and that was truly depraved. But the Ghetto Mafia wanted to up the ante.

Drawing innocent blood and raping frightened girls and young women wasn't enough. In order to be a member of the Ghetto Mafia, one had to kill. Blood wasn't enough. The life itself had to be taken, Nicolazzi told the jury.

Giuca believed that the killing would help boost the Ghetto Mafia's reputation and get them some respect. He was a young man who needed to be feared.

She told the jury once again about how Giuca's wrath had been raised first by the fact that Fisher was with a girl Giuca liked and further when Fisher drunkenly sat on his mom's table.

For those jurors who might have been inclined to believe Russo committed the crime by himself, she reminded them all that Fisher was nearly six-five and weighed two hundred pounds. He was a football player, and he'd been beaten before he was shot. Drunk or not, she said, the victim was not subdued by Antonio Russo alone.

"This case begins, continues and ends with John Giuca," she said. "All roads in this case lead back to this defendant. If it were not for this defendant, Mark Fisher would still be alive today. Instead, Mark Fisher was left lying in the street, lifeless, a nameless John Doe."

As she said this, she showed crime scene photos to the jury. The photos showed Fisher's body, in a pool of blood, lying in the street.

She said that it was not necessary for the prosecution to show that Giuca was at the scene of the murder when Fisher was killed for Giuca to be guilty of second-degree murder. The prosecution merely had to show that the murder had been Giuca's idea and he had set the events in motion that led to Fisher's death.

Nonetheless, the ADA said, they did believe that Giuca was there when Fisher was shot, and the evidence pointing to this came from the statements of John Avitto, to whom Giuca had spoken while in jail. Avitto said that Giuca had told him that he and two others had beaten Fisher because he'd skimped on the money he'd gotten out of an ATM to buy more alcohol after they ran out. Giuca said someone else pulled the gun away from him and shot Fisher five times.

Nicolazzi told the jury that using telephone records

and the statements of eyewitnesses, investigators had come up with a strong theory as to how the murder had gone down. She said that Fisher had passed out on Giuca's couch. They may have gotten Fisher off the couch and out of the house by telling him that Meri Flannigan had left the party and had gone to Al Huggins's house a few blocks away. This would have been a lie because Meri was asleep on another couch in the house in another room. Meri had not abandoned him. In fact, she would have snuggled up with him on the same couch if he'd fallen asleep in a position that would have allowed her to do so.

According to Nicolazzi's theory, Russo was lying in wait on Argyle Road, which was on the way to Huggins's house. Giuca participated in the beating and robbing.

Nicolazzi admitted that she didn't know if Russo had fired all the shots, or if Russo had fired some and Giuca had fired some. She didn't know. She didn't care. However it went down, they were *both* guilty of murder.

One strong indication that Giuca was not in his house at the time of Fisher's murder, said the prosecutor, was a four-second call to Giuca's cell phone from his brother, Matt Federicci, at 6:42 A.M. That was two minutes after the shooting. Matt was in the house and wouldn't have needed to call his brother if he had been home as well.

She reminded the Giuca jury of the testimony of Edward Feldman, a Ditmas Park resident who had heard the shots and called 911. According to the witness, there had been three shots, then a pause, then two more shots. She suggested that during that pause one defendant may have handed the gun to the other so he could finish the victim off.

So Giuca may have pulled the trigger, but again that made no difference. The prosecution merely had to show that Giuca gave a gun to Russo and sent him out to commit a crime with it. They had accomplished this, she noted, through the testimony of Giuca's ex-girlfriend, Lauren Conigliaro, and Huggins, his childhood friend.

Both Conigliaro and Huggins had said that Giuca had repeatedly admitted those facts to them in the days following the murder. Both Huggins and Conigliaro had testified to the fact that, by Giuca's own admission, Giuca had not only supplied the murder weapon—Giuca's own .22-caliber pistol—but had instructed Russo to teach Fisher "what's up."

She pointed out that earlier in the evening Russo had gone with Fisher to an ATM to get money, for beer or drugs or whatever, and this trip to the bank in the middle of the night had been orchestrated to give Russo a chance to kill Fisher.

But it hadn't happened. Fisher had gotten $20 out of his account at the ATM and had returned safely to the party. Was this, perhaps, because Russo felt outsized by his football-playing prey, and had decided that he couldn't take on the challenge of killing the college athlete on his own? Was that why there was a second run later that night, this time with Russo and Giuca, and perhaps others, escorting Fisher to his fate? This time, not only were there more bodies to carry out the attack, but Fisher was more inebriated.

She reminded the jury about the story Albert Huggins had told while he was testifying, how Huggins had tried to warn Mark Fisher that there might be trouble. Fisher, not getting it, had told Huggins not to worry. "I've got your back," Fisher said.

"It is more than a tragic shame that in the final moments of Mark Fisher's life, no one, nobody, had his back," Nicolazzi said.

* * *

Samuel Gregory, speaking on behalf of John Giuca, noted that there were inconsistencies between the stories that were told by the varying eyewitnesses, and many of the most damaging witnesses against his client were in trouble themselves and had cut deals with the prosecution.

They were people who were looking out after their own best interests and were telling the prosecution what they wanted to hear in exchange for some sort of preferable treatment.

As Gregory warmed up, he actually pushed his theory further, saying that witnesses had been coerced by the police to give statements against his client. That, in response to threats hurled their way by law enforcement, these witnesses had given false testimony.

"There's no consistency in this case because these people aren't being honest with you," Gregory said. "She (Nicolazzi) doesn't have a case, ladies and gentlemen."

The Green Jury was excused and the Red Jury brought into the courtroom.

Speaking to Russo's jury, the prosecutor said that Russo had, of everybody who was at Giuca's party that night, acted the most guilty following the crime. He had cut off his braids and split for California.

Change of appearance and flight had long been accepted as legal evidence of guilt.

She reminded the jury that Russo's girlfriend at the time of the murder, Crystal Guerrero, said that he'd admitted to shooting Fisher, and had even shown her an article in the paper about the case.

Why "get a body" unless you can impress your girlfriend with the accomplishment, right?

* * *

In his closing statement Fink pointed out the inconsistencies between the various witnesses' stories. None of the witnesses were trustworthy. They all had something to protect, something to gain. Fink's theory was that Russo had had nothing to do with the murder of Mark Fisher. It had been John Giuca, and John Giuca alone, who had done the crime. It was Giuca who had felt dissed when Fisher sat on his mom's table. It was Giuca's gun.

"The person who had the problem with Mr. Fisher in this case was not Antonio Russo; it was John Giuca," Fink said. He then pointed a figurative finger directly at Russo's codefendant when he told the jury: "I suggest to you that Mark Fisher was killed and that John Giuca had something to do with it."

In his instructions to the juries Judge Marrus explained that it was okay for them to consider the motivation a witness may have for testifying in a case, and they may consider if a witness would get any benefit out of testifying.

The jurors were also told that they were allowed to disregard all of the testimony of a given witness if, in their opinion, that witness lied about a material fact. The trial was over. Jury deliberations began.

CHAPTER 51

First Verdict

Giuca's jury might have been methodical and made sure that nothing had been overlooked, but it was clear that they had a unanimous verdict on their first ballot. It took them only two hours—about the minimum if they went about the process properly—to come back with a guilty verdict on both the murder and the robbery counts. After the verdict was read, the judge polled the jurors, one by one, to make sure the decision was unanimous.

Giuca muttered obscenities as the jury announced the verdict, and he flashed that panel his most intimidating glare. Then his eyes welled up with tears. His mother, Doreen Federicci, sat behind him in the courtroom. She said repeatedly, "He was set up. He was set up."

She got up to leave, but then noisily changed her mind and made an effort to get closer to one of the detectives in the case.

"I want to spit on him," she said.

Fisher's parents stood with faces stony and expressionless as the jurors were polled. Whatever emotions they were feeling were not to be shared with the public. They were reserved for each other, later and in private.

Giuca's attorney, Sam Gregory, said months later that he had been extremely disappointed with the verdict. In many cases lawyers can read the writing on the wall when cases are not going their way, but Gregory had been under the impression that some of the breaks had fallen his, and his client's, way.

"I thought we had a great shot," Gregory said. "Everyone was telling me they thought we had a shot. I thought my summation was very strong. A couple of crosses could have been better in retrospect."

To use boxing terms, he thought the prosecution in the case lacked a strong plan of attack and was rather content to counterpunch.

"All the way through the case, I think the DA was responding to me rather than running her own case. At the end of the case my feeling was that I thought calling (jailhouse snitch) Avitto was a sign that they didn't think they had a case. They called him because they didn't have a case. He was unreliable and therefore Giuca should have been acquitted."

Giuca's mother and stepfather were particularly devastated by the verdict because they hadn't seen it coming. They believed right up until the moment the verdict was read that their son would be vindicated.

About the guilty verdict, Gregory said, "It was not so much direct evidence against Giuca that was the compelling evidence, it was the peripheral evidence, the fact that he was so close to the case. People would have had to assume from the evidence that he would have had to know the gang stuff. And I really think the phone calls to Russo were damaging. The press in this case was devastating because Russo had made statements to the police that Giuca had done this. It was never their (police) theory early on. [Although] that testimony was admitted out of the presence of Giuca's jury, there was no question in my mind that all jurors, or some of the jurors, knew what Russo had said because it was published in the newspapers. It is hard to expect twelve or fourteen people could resist looking at newspapers."

Among the issues that would be dealt with on appeal was the dual trial, with two separate juries for defendants who were being tried together. The big argument in favor of the "split courtroom" style of trial was that it saved time, and therefore money. Gregory wasn't certain that was the case.

"I think it's a bad way to go. It doesn't save that much time. I thought they should have gotten separate trials, but that's an issue for appeal. Because of spillover, there is a prejudicial effect [on both juries]. It gives them (prosecutors) more prestige, but I don't think it's the way to go. The courts have said it's preferable to what they call sequential trials— one after another," Gregory said.

Although Gregory did most of his investigation into Giuca's case himself, he did hire a private investigator to help him after the trial was over. Although Gregory refused to discuss the details, the PI's investigation dealt with alleged jury impropriety.

After the jury proclaimed John Giuca guilty, his mother went into a bewildered daze. She felt blindsided. She had thought all along that the jury would be able to tell what was true and what was a lie. *The lies have been so transparent,* Doreen thought, *how can the jury not see through them?*

After a few moments, when she had recovered sufficiently from the shock, Doreen called her other son, Matthew, to let him know the bad news about the verdict.

Matthew had not been able to make the hearing. He'd been working one of his part-time jobs.

"No, no, no" was all John's younger brother was able to say.

Doreen later recalled that her youngest son didn't come home for three days after hearing of John's verdict.

"He was so angry," Doreen recalled. "He couldn't believe John got convicted."

Only hours after his conviction, Giuca received a visit from his old friend James Petrillo.

"How do you feel?" Petrillo asked.

"At least I'm still alive," Giuca said.

Petrillo later said Giuca had been alluding to Mark Fisher when he said that.

CHAPTER 52

Red Jury Blues

Meanwhile, the Russo jury was struggling. The judge began to receive notes almost immediately. The first note was not alarming. It read, "We, as the jury, need to sleep on it because some are a little undecided."

There was another question on the note that *was* troubling, because it called into question just how much some of the jurors were paying attention.

The judge felt that he could not have been clearer in his instructions to the jury as to what they needed to accomplish in order to come up with a satisfactory verdict.

And yet, the note said that there was a disagreement in the deliberation room. Some of the jurors felt that there needed to be a unanimous vote in order to bring a guilty verdict. There were others who thought you only needed a majority of the votes to convict.

"Which is it?" the note read.

The judge quickly got back to the jurors to remind them, as he had explained clearly during his instructions, a unanimous vote needed to be made before there could be a conviction.

The next day the notes became increasingly troubling to the judge. More disagreements. There were a couple of different opinions about what second-degree murder meant exactly.

The forewoman wrote that she thought some jurors didn't understand the charges. "Please, because people are getting confused," the forewoman's note read. "Could we have a written copy of the charges to make sure [we] were all on the same page? Please, we beg you," she wrote, adding a note of exasperation. Judge Marrus told them that providing the jury with a written copy of the charges was against the rules. He could repeatedly read the charges to them, but they could receive nothing on paper.

The judge did read an explanation of the charges to the jury, but couldn't have liked what he saw when he looked at their faces. The stress was clearly etched on their faces. One juror shut her eyes and shook her head slowly from side to side as the judge read.

The jury announced that it found Russo guilty on the robbery charge, but could not come to an agreement on the second-degree murder charge. Judge Marrus told them to go back and try again.

When the jury announced the guilty-of-robbery verdict, Russo's grandmother Mary Jennings began to cry.

Russo turned around to look at her.

"Don't cry," he said.

But the woman's sobbing continued steadily as Russo's hands were handcuffed behind his back and he was led from the courtroom.

Jonathan Fink felt his heart drop when he heard his

client had been convicted on the robbery charge. He was later asked if he thought it was possible for Russo to be convicted of robbery yet beat the murder charge, and he said, "Given that the murder count was a felony murder count, once they came back with the robbery count, it didn't look particularly good in terms of acquittal for murder."

Unlike premeditated murder or murder caused by depraved indifference to human life, felony murder is committed during the commission of a felony, such as robbery. Even if it is unintentional, it is still felony murder and carries the same sentence as the other types of murders, like premeditated and through depraved indifference.

After the proceedings were through, the grandmother inadvertently got on the elevator with several members of the press, who immediately began to fire questions at her. The woman said nothing until the questions stopped and there was a moment of silence. Then she said, "Thank you." No further questions were asked.

By the next day, in the courthouse, Russo's jury appeared to be coming apart at the seams. Two jurors had asked the judge to let them go home. They were done. Finished. One of them complained that there had been "hollering and screaming" in the jury room.

"People were acting in an uncivilized manner," the complaining juror said.

One of the jurors who seemed most conflicted was juror #3, a designation based on the jury box chair he sat in. He was an African American in his early twenties. He told the judge that two jurors, he didn't specify which, were arguing so much that they had almost come to blows.

Judge Marrus announced in court that two jurors "were almost about to engage in a fight."

The judge called the jurors together and told them to respect one another. He reminded them that they had a job to do, and he was not going to be quick to relieve them of their responsibility. He sent them back into the jury room to deliberate some more, but after a couple hours they were back in front of the judge complaining that no progress had been made. They weren't getting along.

"I want you all to know that it is much too early to declare a mistrial," Judge Marrus said. "I can't tell anyone to change his or her mind or how to vote."

It seemed like years had passed since Russo laughed at his ex-girlfriend as she testified about child endangerment. As his jury deliberated, he sat in court thumbing white rosary beads in his lap.

As court let out for the day, a *New York Times* reporter asked Russo's aunt Ruby Bonanno how the family was holding up.

"We're drained. Mentally and emotionally, we're drained," Aunt Ruby replied.

CHAPTER 53

Final Verdict

Yes, Russo was gloomy indeed, right up until Friday, September 30, the day it was announced that his jury had reached a verdict on the second count. On that day Russo, in his crumpled gray suit, had a bounce in his step.

"Hey, how's everything?" he said, smiling at a woman he knew in the spectator section of the courtroom. He was so chatty that court officers had to hush him. While waiting for the jury to enter the courtroom, Russo sat in his chair as close to prone as humanly possible, boneless in the deepest of slouches.

He rapped his knuckles rhythmically on the table in front of him and sang to himself. His head swayed from side to side with feigned rapture. He kept a cocky smirk on his face even as everyone stood for the reading of the verdict.

The forewoman took forever to unfold the piece of paper she was to read from, her fingers fumbling again, and again. Nerves frayed, muscles tightened and knuckles whitened while the juror's fingers failed, again and again, to accomplish a simple task that would have taken less than a second under more relaxed circumstances. Finally the paper was unfolded.

Juror #1's lips quivered for an agonizingly long moment before speech could come out. She then said, "The jury finds the defendant guilty of second-degree murder."

Nancy Fisher let out an audible sigh at the word "guilty." The prosecution was ecstatic. They were two for two.

Juror #3, the young black man who had seemed so troubled during deliberation, kept his head down and seemed subdued. His voice lacked the firmness and conviction of the others' when the judge went through the formality of polling the jury, one by one, to make certain that the verdict was unanimous. In fact, he looked down at his feet when he said, "Yes."

A court officer gathered Russo's wrists behind his back and snapped them together with handcuffs. As Russo was led from the courtroom, he looked back and called out to his grandmother Mary Jennings. "Come visit me tomorrow," he said.

Tears streaming, she called back, "I love you. I love you."

Michael and Nancy Fisher were escorted out of the room by court officers. The officers used their bodies to screen the parents of the victim from press and photographers.

The Fishers were exhausted. To avoid the daily commute back to Sussex County, they had been staying at a hotel. Plus, there had been the daily grind of listening to painful testimony.

Had Huggins actually referred to their son as a drunken fool? Plus, there was the daily cat-and-mouse game, trying to evade reporters. All in all, it had left the couple completely wrung out.

Outside, Michael did make one brief statement. "I'm

sure if these people had gotten to know Mark, they probably would have liked him," he said.

Asked about his feelings by a reporter from New Jersey, Michael said, "Nancy and I are just numb. We are in shock over both convictions. We just hope that whoever else is involved will be brought to justice eventually."

Nicolazzi said, "I'm pleased with the outcome, but, obviously, it doesn't bring back Mark Fisher."

Reporters spotted juror #3, the one who seemed least comfortable with the verdict, and began to shout questions at him.

"Why did you seem so tentative when the judge asked you if you agreed with the verdict?" asked one reporter.

"Do you believe the prosecution proved its case beyond a reasonable doubt?" called out a second.

"Were you the one who was holding out for a not guilty verdict?" shouted another.

Juror #3 grinned and ran down Jay Street. Several reporters thought about giving chase, but quickly dismissed the idea. As a pack they decided to stick near the courthouse, where more willing interview subjects were plentiful.

Juror #3 was not the only panelist who wasn't in a chatting mood. Most jurors declined to make a public statement about the case. All were content to go home without ever revealing their names.

One female juror was asked for a statement and agreed only on the guarantee of anonymity.

"Why don't you want to be identified?" the reporter asked.

"I fear reprisal," the juror said.

Asked if she was satisfied with the job the jury had done, the juror replied, "We went over every piece of evidence. We looked at the testimonies again and again to make sure we came to the right decision. We are just regular people, but we all gave our blood, sweat and tears—and, in the end, we think justice was served."

Fink was asked about his client's reaction. The defense attorney said, "He kind of expected that things were going to go the way they went yesterday," Fink said, meaning that once Russo was found guilty of robbery, he expected to be found guilty on the murder charge. According to Fink, Russo was more shocked by the first verdict than he had been by the second.

One of the interesting aspects of the dual-jury trial was that the Giuca jury was much quicker to convict than the Russo jury, despite the fact that, in most spectators' opinion, the prosecution's case against Russo was stronger.

Giuca's mom didn't blame the jury. The jury had been listening to lies in the courtroom, and before the trial started, they had spent many months reading lies about her son in the newspapers.

Doreen said that the jurors heard again and again, from the prosecution and from journalists, that her son was a gang leader and that the murder was a gang initiation.

Incredulous, Doreen would exclaim, "The gang leader stuff is so far-fetched!"

CHAPTER 54

Sentencing

The sentencing hearing was held three weeks later. Some spectators at the hearing, many of them female, were wearing T-shirts with an emblem on the front that read "Free John Giuca."

On the backs of the shirts it read, "To know him is to love him. The truth shall set him free!"

Spectators were fairly certain that Giuca's fan club had no intention of shaving their heads or carving swastikas in their foreheads or anything. The T-shirts, however, did show a level of organization.

When the supporters arrived in the shirts, part of an organized protest, there was a question among courthouse security personnel as to whether or not they should be allowed in the courtroom.

It was finally decided that there was a lesser chance of trouble if they were allowed in, and once inside the courtroom the wearers of the slogans behaved themselves.

When told by a reporter that the shirts had the defendant's name spelled incorrectly, Giuca's supporters claimed that they had spelled his name right. It was the newspapers that spelled it wrong.

The *New York Times* checked and, to their horror, discovered that they had been spelling Giuca's name incorrectly all along. They'd had it "Guica."

From that point on, the *Times* spelled Giuca's name correctly, and ended every story that included his name with an apology for misspelling the name so frequently during the years between Mark Fisher's murder and John Giuca's sentencing

An online petition was created on the Internet. Using a free service supplied by the Web site *petitiononline.com*, supporters could add their name to the list and leave comments and/or their address.

The petition was entitled "Free John Giuca." It was dated October 16, 2005, and addressed to the "Honorable Judge Marrus." There was a short preface that invited John's supporters to come to John's sentencing at 1:45 P.M. on the second floor of the Jay Street courthouse.

"At least say a prayer that the judge takes this into consideration," the petition read.

Composed by Giuca's attractive friend Jennifer Baker, the petition was well-written and tugged immediately at the heartstrings. It began by noting that John had recently had a birthday—on October 8, 2005, he had turned twenty-two years old. It should be a happy occasion, Baker wrote, except for the fact that he spent most of his twenty-second year on the planet behind bars for a crime he "did not commit."

The petition noted that he had been found guilty of second-degree murder in a court of law and could be sentenced to twenty-five years to life in prison. This despite the fact that there was "no evidence" supporting his guilt.

The petition said, "We (friends of John Giuca) are here today to tell a different story."

They would tell a story that wasn't available in the articles printed in the local newspapers, or in TV sound bites.

After noting briefly that the case involved the tragic death, on a Brooklyn sidewalk, of a nineteen-year-old college student named Mark Fisher, it went on to say that Giuca's conviction was the result of "corruption."

The petition noted that police and prosecutors took two years to accumulate the evidence necessary to indict John Giuca for murder. It said that the detectives in charge of the case referred to themselves as the "dirty tactics squad."

These detectives, it said, "took offense" to witnesses in the case getting representation from lawyers—as if it weren't the right of every citizen to get a lawyer anytime he or she wanted.

These detectives, it said, started a "campaign of highly unorthodox investigation." This campaign included threatening witnesses to say things that weren't true, and to create a "false story."

It noted that offers for $100,000 in exchange for information regarding the murder were placed in areas not far from where John Giuca lived, and many people were subpoenaed to testify before a grand jury.

Despite the fact that John's friends and acquaintances were blanketed with subpoenas, the person who knew John best—his brother, Matthew—was not asked to testify.

Although 150 subpoenas were handed out, and all of the potential witnesses were given preliminary interviews, "Prosecutor Nicolazzi" handpicked only a few to actually testify for the grand jury.

The prosecution said that they chose the "credible" witnesses, but it seemed more to the friends of John Giuca that they picked only the witnesses who were willing to say what prosecutors wanted to hear.

Those handpicked witnesses included "a college student on probation for assault, an ex-girlfriend who was threatened with losing her job, a self-admitted 'career criminal' who takes pills prescribed for schizophrenia, and a college student who had been under the influence of alcohol and drugs the night the murder occurred."

The petition said that this was proof that there was no real case against John Giuca and that everything the prosecution brought forth for the grand jury, and then at the trial, was either "pathetic speculation" or "false and rehearsed testimony."

It said that the Giuca jury took only two hours to find him guilty. It was as if they had made up their minds ahead of time. How could they be so quick when no murder weapon was found? How could the jury convict without any real deliberation when there was so much conflicting testimony and so many of the witnesses were "poorly chosen"?

The petition noted that John Giuca was convicted by the media even before proceedings against him had begun in court. Whatever happened to "innocent until proven guilty"? John Giuca's friends wanted to know.

"Only one man was responsible for Mark Fisher's death. That man is not John Giuca," the petition read, in an apparent reference to Antonio Russo. It complained that John was unfairly portrayed in public as a gang leader, rather than as what he truly was: "a brother, a son, and a loyal friend."

The petition concluded, "We are not asking you to agree with us that he is innocent; all we are asking is that you sign this petition showing that you agree that there needs to be a re-evaluation of the evidence and witnesses in this case. Please help this cause. This can happen to anyone; this time, it happened to be our brother. Help us show Judge Marrus, who has presided over this case, to re-evaluate the jury's decision. STOP THE CORRUPTION.

Our hearts and prayers go out to the Fisher family. May Mark Fisher rest in peace. Sincerely, The Undersigned. Send this to a friend."

Of the thirty-seven people who had, by the summer of 2006, put their names on the "Free John Giuca" list, twenty-six were female. Only one of the signatures came with a comment and an address. Supporter number thirty-four, a male, gave his street address in Brooklyn and, under comments, added: "innocent till proven guilty (with real evidence)." About forty more had signed by that autumn, although the list was now sprinkled with those who, in no uncertain terms, stated that they believed Giuca to be guilty.

Someone wrote, in all capital letters, "GIUCA IS A MURDERER! GIUCA BELONGS BEHIND BARS WITH OTHER MURDERERS!"

In response to that entry Frank Federicci came to his stepson's defense, writing, "I understand your pain. You are blinded by loss. I hurt too. Don't be fooled by our prosecutors' motives. Do they really care about Mark? Do you know John? What is your name? Why didn't you sign? Did you know that John was just as shocked finding out about Mark. I bet there is a lot you didn't know."

At the sentencing hearing Anna-Sigga Nicolazzi reiterated the cold-blooded nature of the crime. The prosecution had not put all of its eggs in a single basket when it came to a motive for Mark Fisher's murder.

Nicolazzi said, "Your Honor, the defendants are dangerous and the public should be protected from them for as long as possible. Besides being cowardly, their actions were utterly senseless. They had no qualms about taking advantage of this vulnerable young man. Antonio Russo is a vicious and dangerous individual. John Giuca is just as dangerous, but in a different way. He plays people like marionettes, using them for what he wants and protecting himself."

The prosecution may have had more than one theory as to how Mark Fisher died, but all of their theories had something in common. Whether it was a botched robbery or just something to toughen up the image of the so-called Ghetto Mafia, the crime represented the coldest type of murder, and because of that, she hoped the defendants would receive maximum sentences.

As was customary, the friends and family of the victim were allowed as well to have their say at the sentencing hearing. Mark's sister, twenty-year-old Alexis Fisher, spoke to the court about Mark's kindness, humbleness, excellence at sports and bright future.

Mark's sister said, "What happened to Mark should never happen to anyone, but, even so, I would have rather it been myself. Mark was my best friend. On the exterior, Mark could have been perceived as a standout athlete, a former prom king, an honor student, even just a tall and handsome guy. He had all the attributes that could have made him a cocky, arrogant, obnoxious jock, but Mark was anything but that. Mark was only nineteen years old, but he was special. He could have one day changed the world. I hope you will change the world today by ridding it of two murderers."

Judge Marrus noted that he had received several letters from friends of the defendant, and asked that these be read aloud in the courtroom. The first of the pro-Giuca statements came from Edward M. Frasier, a retired captain of the New York City Department of Corrections. Captain Frasier stated right off the bat that he was seeking leniency in the sentencing of "young Mr. John Giuca."

Frasier stated that he had known young John Giuca for most of his life and had always found him to be a good person. He noted that John was a student at John

Jay University and had showbiz aspirations, having appeared in TV commercials, movies and series.

This amounted to a very busy schedule, he noted, but nonetheless, from his observations, John was always able to find time to do everything, and to do everything with diligence.

"This is not the street thug the district attorney has portrayed," Frasier wrote.

He said Giuca was a young man from a stable home who just happened to get caught up with some childhood friends who had veered wide of the straight and narrow. Giuca had been trying hard to get away from his bad-egg friends, but he had not yet succeeded when tragedy struck.

The man noted that Giuca's parents—Frank and Doreen Federicci—had purchased a home in Florida and were determined to move John out of the neighborhood where he had entangled himself with the wrong crowd.

The move south hadn't come quickly enough, however, and before Giuca could pull free, he had become embroiled in the "terrible circumstances" that led to this trial.

Frasier wrote that he had attended every day of Giuca's trial, and never at any time had he heard anything that made him believe Giuca was guilty of the crimes with which he was charged.

Witness after witness lied, according to Frasier. He knew they were lying. They admitted to lying. When asked point-blank if they were pressured by investigators to testify in hopes of leniency when it came to their own crimes, they all admitted to that.

Those crimes had nothing to do with this trial, Frasier said, and all of those witnesses had made deals. Frasier noted that he was a veteran of law enforcement, and he knew how prosecutors made deals with witnesses in order to secure the evidence they needed to get a conviction.

And he knew how desperate the potential witnesses in trouble could be, and how they would say anything to get "out from under" the trouble they'd found.

He was sorry that the jury believed these witnesses in this case, because he did not. He said that at no time did he hear testimony that put a gun in John Giuca's hand or put John Giuca at the scene of the crime when the unfortunate young man was murdered.

Instead, Frasier noted, he heard much evidence that Antonio Russo had repeatedly admitted to committing the murder. In contrast, Giuca had always denied any involvement. There was only one witness that said Giuca did it and he repeatedly admitted to being a liar during his testimony.

He stated that "as a retired officer of the court" he was sad that Giuca had been found guilty and was sad that they were forced to abide by the jury's decision, "no matter what your opinion or mine might be."

Frazier offered Judge Marrus his résumé—twenty-one years in city corrections, thirteen years as an officer, seven as a captain—then stated that his opinion was that a long jail term would kill John Giuca. He stated that the goal of corrections was to rehabilitate people so that they could be returned to society.

A long term in Giuca's case, Frasier said, could only be detrimental to the young man. He suggested that Judge Marrus give Giuca a short prison term with an extensive period of probation attached. This, he said, would satisfy the unfortunate decision of the jury and justice as well.

It would also save the taxpayers money, he added.

He had no doubt that Giuca would do very well with a long probation period because he had strong family support. He was a college student and an actor, not a career criminal as his recent conviction might indicate. There was every indication that Giuca, if allowed to be free, would be a "peaceful productive member of society."

If Judge Marrus turned young Giuca free, Frasier all but promised, His Honor would never see Giuca's face in his courtroom again—ever.

The second statement in support of leniency for John Giuca came from Michael T. Dealy, Ph.D., who lived in the Bay Ridge section of Brooklyn.

Dated October 7, 2005, Dealy began by stating that he was writing with a heavy heart and that he had known John Giuca for many years.

Describing himself, Dealy said that he was a psychologist practicing in New York, was currently one of the headmasters at a private high school and was also an adjunct professor at several metropolitan colleges and universities.

However, he noted, it was his position as a director at a day camp years before that led to him meeting John Giuca. Dealy had been a director at several day camps and Giuca had been a camper under his supervision for many years.

"Year after year it was always remarked that he was the best camper in the program," Dealy wrote. He described Giuca as cooperative, well-behaved and noticeably kind to others.

Even when John was as young as ten years old, the former camp director said, he was always there when the counselors needed him—whether it was to run an errand or to help with a group activity.

When John's younger brother, Matthew, also attended the summer day camp, he was a supportive older brother. No one connected with that camping program, Dealy said, would have an unkind word to say about John Giuca.

Giuca became a member of the camp's junior leadership group and was known for his creative ideas designed to make the camping experience more fulfilling for everyone.

He was a well-organized lad who was not only punctual, but made sure that everyone else was punctual as well. He followed through on ideas and made sure that suggestions offered at meetings reached fruition.

Dealy noted that a change came over John when he reached adolescence, that with puberty came a new difficulty in completing his schoolwork. At the same time the positive self-image he had enjoyed during his younger years at camp "began to wane."

Dealy knew this because he had been Giuca's high-school math teacher. Though motivated to learn, John was sometimes slow to understand the concepts. Dealy believed that there were aspects of Giuca's educational experience that had taken their toll on the teenager's self-esteem.

Dealy recalled worrying at that time that the confidence and sense of self-efficacy that Giuca had enjoyed during his preadolescent years had been adversely affected by subsequent occurrences.

After being John's math teacher, Dealy noted, he continued to see John on a regular basis, and those meetings were always positive and pleasant. Dealy and Giuca had philosophical discussions "about life in general."

Oftentimes the conversations turned to John's younger brother, Matthew, and how John had been encouraging his sibling to fulfill his potential in school.

Dealy said that he mentioned these things because he wanted to dispel the notion presented by the prosecution in the murder trial that John Giuca was some sort of a "bad seed." Nothing could have been further from the truth, Dealy claimed. He wrote that Giuca was a "noticeably good seed.

"I know little of the current issues but it seems like a gruesome devastating affair for all involved," Dealy wrote. "I am very surprised and deeply saddened that John is in this position."

Dealy concluded his letter to Judge Marrus by offering sympathy to the judge. Dealy understood the difficult position the judge was in and had the writer's utmost professional respect.

"Thank you for considering this plea for leniency and a sincere prayer for the young lives and families destroyed by this experience," Dealy wrote.

The third letter asking for leniency for John Giuca was dated October 10, 2005, and came from New York police officer Edward Quinn, who began with a request that Judge Marrus "show compassion" when Giuca came before him.

Quinn then introduced himself to the judge as a forty-one-year-old law enforcement officer for the city of New York, a sixteen-year employee of the city, who'd known John Giuca "ever since he was born."

He stated that he had never known John to be impolite, dishonest, envious of others, perverse or malicious in any way. He only knew a John who was helpful and socially inclusive.

John was the kind of kid that would take time to talk to that other kid over in the corner, the one no one else would talk to. John embraced and comforted others. That was the John he knew.

Quinn noted that he had been among those who had encouraged Giuca to stay in college, and that Giuca had taken the advice and was trying to do that when "this all came about."

The police officer pointed out that Giuca had been a criminal justice major at John Jay College and had been succeeding. Giuca was employed at a restaurant, and had even been in a few movies as an extra.

"John is a very intelligent man who had a very bright future," Quinn wrote.

Quinn said that deep down in his heart he believed John Giuca when he said he had no knowledge of the crimes with which he had been charged. Giuca, Quinn noted, had prayed that Mark Fisher would live, because, if Fisher had lived, he would have been able to tell police that Giuca had nothing to do with it.

Quinn ended on an odd note, adding, "I plead with you and the Fishers for their son's life as well as John's." Quinn wrote "Sincerely yours," signed his name, then added his shield number.

The defendants were then allowed to offer last words, and both Russo and Giuca denied any role in Fisher's death.

"I send my deepest condolences to you all," Russo said to Fisher's family. "I am innocent and I remain innocent. Hopefully, justice will be served, and you will find the right person."

Giuca said, "My heart goes out to the Fisher family. I can't imagine the pain they feel. I didn't know any of them was going to hurt your son, and I didn't approve of it after. I'm being painted as an evil person, but none of that stuff is true."

A reporter from New Jersey sitting in the spectator section of the courtroom jotted down in his notebook that Giuca spoke with a "thick Brooklyn accent."

Then it was the judge's turn.

"These defendants were callous," Judge Marrus scolded. "This was a callous crime, and the defendants' reactions were callous—brutal, callous and shockingly senseless. So my sentence will be callous."

As the judge spoke, Russo sat slumped in his chair. He held his hands together, steeple-style, in front of his chest. He'd never grown his braids back. His hair was still cropped short, shaved really, with a little stubble showing. Some observers noticed that Russo was wearing his sweatshirt inside out. Did it mean something—or was he just careless about putting on his clothes?

Next to Russo, Giuca's narrow face was expressionless as the judge spoke. Giuca wore his hair longer and he wore it slicked back. Giuca wore small wire-rimmed glasses.

Both Russo and Giuca were sentenced to twenty-five years to life in prison for murder, the maximum. Both Russo and Giuca received additional, concurrent twenty-five-year sentences for robbing Fisher. Giuca received a fifteen-year concurrent term on a weapons charge. Both defendants officially noted that they would be appealing their convictions.

Giuca and Russo were handcuffed and led from the courtroom. Giuca went out first, and when Russo followed, his pretense of cool broke down for a moment as he walked right into a chair.

Outside the courtroom Michael Fisher made his first public statement in some time. He said that he was not moved by the defendants' apologies.

Mark's dad shook and held tightly to his wife as he said, "I feel these are cold-blooded murderers. Both got what they deserved."

Michael Fisher again pointed out that he did not find any closure and he felt that only an incomplete justice had been served. This time, however, Mr. Fisher was more specific.

"I feel that there is still a guy and a girl involved in this killing," he said.

Mark's sister, Alexis, had made copies of her written

statement, the one she had read in court, and made sure that interested members of the press got a copy.

Fisher's uncle Frank Pacheco said, "There are no winners here. We are not crying for blood, but we ask ourselves, why? They had no compassion for Mark. They just ambushed him."

The young people in the "Free John Giuca" T-shirts were hanging around outside the courthouse as well. They could be seen handing out pamphlets to passersby and other interested parties, but they refused to talk to reporters. One of them was Jennifer Baker, author of the online petition. Others were members of Jennifer's "Brooklyn Calendar Girls," an attractive group of young women who, for a fee, would liven up your bar or party. And, of course, there was a calendar for sale, with each of the girls gracing a different month.

Giuca's mom said, "Detectives will do anything for promotions. Of course we feel sorry for the Fishers, but they have revenge in their hearts."

Giuca's lawyer, Sam Gregory, said, "The stiff sentence was not unexpected. There's no winners in this case. After trying this case, I don't know if I want to return to the Sussex County area. This case is so sad and there are so many people there who knew and remember Mark Fisher."

CHAPTER 55

Sam Gregory
Looks Back

Months after Giuca and Russo were convicted, in his Brooklyn office over a boxing gym, Giuca's defense attorney, Sam Gregory, sat down with author Robert Mladinich to discuss the case.

What went wrong? Gregory was asked. He explained that the key factor was the way the jury perceived his client. Once they started thinking of Giuca as a bad boy, they needed less actual evidence to persuade them that he was guilty.

"The problem with this case was that the judge ruled that evidence of gang membership was permitted to be entered," he said. "There wasn't one speck of evidence that there was any gang motive in the death of Michael Fisher. Not one shred of evidence was presented that anybody talked about gangs or there was an initiation on the morning he was killed. The evidence was prejudicial that I had to deal with."

What was Gregory's theory of what happened that night?

"My theory in the case was this: that Russo had acted alone. There was an alternative theory presented by the prosecution. Theory A was that Giuca produced the gun and then he said 'Show him what's up.' He basically gave the gun to Russo so Russo could do something to Fisher. The nature of that something was not clear from the testimony. That was Theory A. Theory B was that Russo came to Giuca and said, 'I want to rob this kid, let me have a gun.' Albert Huggins had Theory A, that Giuca provided Russo with the gun. Lauren Conigliaro had Theory B, that Russo came to Giuca and asked Giuca for the gun. The third theory came from a jailhouse informant named John Avitto, which was Giuca left the house with Fisher and Russo and one other, and that all three of these guys attacked Fisher in the street. There were three theories put forward. My theory was that Russo had acted alone."

Gregory thinks Giuca got himself into trouble because he participated in the crime's cover-up—not because he was guilty of murder, but because he didn't want the crime traced back to his house and the illicit activities that had been taking place in his mother's home.

"The problem in the case was the phone records between Giuca and Russo that were close to or at the time of the Fisher shooting. There were numerous calls in the twenty-four-hour period after Fisher was shot. The problem was that Giuca was so close to this thing—even though I don't believe that he knew that this guy was going to die. He was afraid it would come back to his house. It's pretty obvious from the evidence that he tried to cover up what Russo had done. It looked as though it was a cover-up of his own culpability."

Why was Gregory convinced that Russo committed

the crime on his own? The answer had to do with the blanket in which Fisher was found wrapped.

"Fisher was found laying on the ground a couple of blocks from where Giuca lived. He had a very distinct blanket which was wrapped around him or on top of him. It had a picture of a lion on it. It came from Giuca's house. My feeling was there was no way Giuca would have planned to kill this guy, leave him on the ground two blocks away from his house with a blanket that basically had his family name on it. It just didn't make any sense to me, but he was so close to the case and I think the gang stuff put the jury over the top."

If Gregory was so convinced of Giuca's innocence, then why wasn't his client put on the stand at his trial so he could have an opportunity to defend himself?

Gregory said again it had to do with the judge's ruling that evidence regarding gang membership would be allowed as evidence.

"The ruling in my view opened up questions about a gang called GM—the Ghetto Mafia. A group of kids started it at thirteen or fourteen years old: neighborhood kids. I heard from various sources that to get into the gang, you had to chug three beers. They had witnesses saying the gang was looking to kill somebody. My feeling was that the entire cross-examination would have been about the gang. I didn't think Giuca would add much to the case, except denying he was involved, which is what he always said. There was nothing he could say to prove he didn't commit the crime, because he was so close to it."

Was there any truth to stories that Giuca had once been a member of the notorious gang known as the Crips? Gregory had his doubts.

"I heard that the Ghetto Mafia grew out of the Crips. A lot of stuff was talk," Gregory said, adding, "I've been doing this over twenty years and none of these kids came off as being particularly tough kids. I know tough kids. Many members of this so-called gang are in college or working at this time."

Although Giuca was floundering, would he have come into his own?

"I don't think there is any doubt about that. He used to get into trouble with his mother for stealing food out of the refrigerator and giving it to a couple of homeless guys on Church Avenue. He never came off to me as someone cruel, vicious or mean. Friends who knew him said that was the way he was. He was nice. The amount of support he got at the trial was shocking to me: people showing up every day, day after day after day. No one who knew him well ever thought he wanted this kid to die."

The number of supporters Giuca had in court was impressive. Why did Gregory think his client was so popular?

"One of the things you noticed in this business is when someone gets locked up or is in prison or jail awaiting trial, if they are lowlifes who hadn't done anything decent for another person, when they show up in court there is nobody there. Maybe the mother shows up, but that's it. They don't have the juice to bring someone to court when they're at Rikers Island. This guy always had a crowd of people waiting for his appearance, not because he was throwing money at people, not because he was a big shot in a gang, because people liked him, that's why."

Gregory conceded that Giuca and Fisher had not gotten along. Why should they? Fisher was drunk and was acting like a bit of a jerk.

The lawyer said, "There was never any doubt in my mind that there was no intent on Giuca's mind to kill anybody. Giuca didn't like the way the kid was acting in the house. One girl said that before he (Fisher) even got to the house, he was misbehaving at the bar. Giuca didn't appreciate the way the kid was acting in the house. The only thing

Giuca is guilty of is not being a little more understanding that the guy was drunk when disapproving of his behavior."

How did Gregory feel about his client's codefendant, Antonio Russo?

"Russo was a sad kid. They tried to say he would do anything Giuca said. I never saw it. He was a loose cannon. He showed the type of person he was in court, talking to himself, talking to witnesses. He lived around the corner from Giuca. I think they were friends by virtue of the proximity of where they lived.

"Russo decided he didn't like the kid [Fisher]. He was the kind of guy who was trying to make a name for himself. On his own he went out and killed this kid. Russo might have picked up on Giuca's dislike for this kid and taken it a step further," Gregory said.

The lawyer then added, "It was always my feeling that they didn't like Fisher, and Russo took it upon himself to take it twenty steps further than it would have been taken, had Giuca been present when this guy was shot. Giuca always maintained—and other people have told me—that Giuca had no problem with the kid. When Albert Huggins testified, he said it was Tommy Hassan who said stop sitting on the table and mind your manners. The kids should have been more understanding of Fisher and his condition. Russo picked up on other people's consternation and aggravation and took it on his own to a level he never should have taken it."

Gregory was then asked about John Avitto, the jailhouse snitch, who had testified that Giuca told him in detail, while they were together at Rikers Island, how Mark Fisher had been murdered.

"As a lawyer," Gregory said, "sometimes you run a case and get a witness list with maybe one hundred names on it. When Avitto appeared on their list, I asked who he was. They told me who he was and gave me a rap sheet; I said they are never going to call this guy. He's a career criminal, mostly burglary offenses and he's obviously a crack user. I said no way they're going to use this guy. Avitto served several stints in state prison for attempted burglary between 1989 and 1998.

"I thought I was hitting witnesses pretty good and we were winning the case—so did most people in the courtroom. Lo and behold, they come to me the day before the summation and say we are calling John Avitto. To me this was an indication they thought their case was falling apart. Here's a guy takes a statement from Giuca while both are in prison. He doesn't say anything to anybody. Only when he's out on a warrant on a case pending sentencing—and he's supposed to be in a treatment program—he allegedly calls the police to give this information. To me, that's enough. I wouldn't believe a word the guy said. He never came forward at the earliest opportunity. He didn't come forward to the police until he needed something from them."

Moreover, said Gregory, "they interviewed him on two or three different occasions. They did DD-fives, (follow-up reports) that contain an activity that took place. You do an interview, you write it up. You go to a scene, you write up what you saw at the scene. There were thousands of DD-fives. Every single witness that they interviewed, every single one had DD-fives, some of them numerous. Many of them were neutral, civilian witnesses with no criminal record, no ax to grind. They did DD-fives. Here they interview John Avitto on two to three occasions—not only no DD-five, there are no written notes. To me that was very disturbing that they didn't have some memorialization of what this guy had said to them. They didn't want notes. This guy said three or four different things to them before they got him ready to testify. They didn't want a record. I thought I hit the guy pretty well. My feeling subsequent to his testimony was that he had gotten all of his information from the

New York Post because he kind of tracked what was in the *Post* articles. That's the way the testimony sounded. I don't think the jurors were particularly impressed with his background, but that was something they could hang their hats on as icing on the cake."

Gregory admitted that the Avitto testimony was more harmful to his client than he believed it would be—but he didn't feel that Avitto's statements in court were the most damaging to John Giuca. That dubious honor, he believed, went to Albert Huggins.

"I don't think any particular witness was overwhelming," Gregory said. "What happened is they created an image of him that I could not dispel because I can't prove something didn't happen—can't prove a negative. They created an image through the introduction of the gang stuff that he was looking to kill somebody. That came from Albert Huggins, who—my theory was—knew more about this than he was willing to admit. He was the guy who brought Fisher to the party, this is the guy who leaves Fisher there with a stranger he never met before, leaves at around four-thirty or five o'clock. The next morning he's informed that somebody's been killed on the block, he denies that he knows the person who was shot, a guy who leaves Brooklyn immediately after finding out the guy is shot, goes out to Long Island and claims he still doesn't know it is Fisher. He was the source of Giuca saying 'We need a body to be taken seriously.' Here's a guy (Huggins) who always wanted to be part of the group, but never was permitted to be part of the group because people didn't like him. There was no other corroboration of that statement because the only one who can claim this was said was a detective."

Gregory said he never considered Giuca as being from a dysfunctional family. "Giuca and his mother had a great relationship," Gregory said. "He went through growing pains, going from being a kid to being a teenager to being a man, and some of the problems associated with that. But they had a wonderful relationship."

Gregory added that Giuca's relationship with his step-father, Frank Federicci, was also very strong. "He was a wonderful stepfather to him. He really, really loved him. They got along very well," Gregory said.

And, about Giuca's real father, the lawyer said, "He's a very nice man. He was the subject of testimony by an informant. John had warm feelings for him."

A close-lipped lawyer is not an unusual thing, especially when he's discussing a man, John Giuca's biological father, who, according to Doreen Federicci, was such a severe heroin addict that she was forced to end the relationship.

Giuca's mother and stepfather, according to Gregory, did not blame him for the trial's devastating conclusion. "They have been respectful of me and appreciated the work I did," Gregory said. "They took it real hard, but they've always been happy with the work I did. John's mother thought I gave it one hundred percent. She saw how I worked on the case. I stayed close to them, met with them on numerous occasions at their house. They got a bird's-eye view of how much heart and soul I put into the case."

Asked how it felt to lose, Gregory pulled out his grab bag of stock phrases and gave a general response, leaping away from specifics: "I always said in this work you lose more than you win if you're trying heavy cases. Lot of negative evidence, publicity hurts you, the newspapers are always against you. You just have to dust it off and go back for round two. The real nuts and bolts of this work is taking facts, analyzing facts and coming up with a theory of defense and implementing it. Unfortunately, most of the work we do is routine preparation. Most cases don't go to trial."

CHAPTER 56

Fink's Recollections

On July 7, 2006, Russo's attorney, Jonathan Fink, having been both a prosecutor and a defense attorney during his career—on both sides of the fence—was asked which job would have been easier in Russo's case: prosecution or defense?

"In some ways the case was easy to prosecute because the DA's office had every possible resource because of the nature of the case," Fink said. "It was such a high-profile case.

"My position in this case was that my client was innocent and my defense was that there was a lack of evidence. There were no eyewitnesses, no gun recovered, and in terms of Mark Fisher, he had bruises on his body that indicated he was in a struggle. With Mr. Russo, there was no testimony that he had anything on his body that would suggest that he was in a fight.

"The prosecution's case was that Mr. Russo had confessed to or made admissions to five different people," Fink continued. "When you consider the evidence in this case, the fact that there are no eyewitnesses, no DNA, a problem in terms of ballistic evidence, the case certainly was defensible. I think I put forth a good defense."

He answered the question from behind his desk in his office in Downtown Manhattan. On the wall was an artist's sketch drawn during Giuca and Russo's trial by artist Christine Cornell.

How does one deal with five admissions? That's a lot of admissions. According to Fink, one does it by attacking the credibility of the sources for those admissions. He said that the credibility of the prosecution's witnesses was the crux of his defense.

His favorite example was Crystal Guerrero, the woman who said she'd been on a religious retreat at the time of Mark Fisher's murder; yet Russo confessed to her only hours after it happened that the crime had started out as a robbery but had gotten out of hand, and she didn't go to the police.

He also mentioned Skulls, the prosecution witness who looked like he'd been brought in off the street to "recall" how Russo had bragged about taking part in a murder.

Gregg Cunningham was another one, a guy who was in prison for, as Fink put it, "putting a bullet in someone." In their back, no less. How can anyone believe such a person? Fink still wondered.

"That kind of thing is pretty powerful in discrediting somebody; the fact that he was brought down from living upstate in a correctional facility while he's testifying," Fink said.

His sentiments echoed those of Giuca's mom. How could you believe this ragtag cast of characters the prosecution had assembled? They were the jilted, the jealous and the jailed.

Fink also believed that he nullified the testimony

of Alejandro Romero, who acted like he'd rather be anyplace in the world than in the courtroom telling the jury that Russo had seemed excessively nervous when he saw that police were searching a sewer opening near his apartment building.

Fink went on: "There was testimony from a guy named Anthony Palumbo, who said Giuca had given him the gun that was used to kill Fisher. In terms of what he said, it didn't make sense that Russo would be concerned or nervous, because if the wallet had already been recovered and a person testified that he got the gun, why should he be scared?"

Fink recalled that Alfredo Bishop had been the toughest prosecution witness to discredit. He was the guy who had cut off Russo's braids following the murder and had testified that Russo had made damaging comments while receiving his haircut. Fink had to discredit him, not through his reputation or the bad acts he had committed but rather solely through the fact that he had waited a long time after the haircut to tell law enforcement what he'd heard Russo say.

Fink felt the time lag was a key factor in the case. It wasn't just Bishop. Many of the prosecution's witnesses had nothing to say about Mark Fisher's murder until many months after it happened.

"There was a huge delay by all of the witnesses to come forward. The police had this case for months and months before anyone came forth with these claims. This is something I tried to use to discredit all of these witnesses," Fink said.

Fink was asked if there were any of the prosecution witnesses who bolstered Antonio Russo's defense.

"In a sense they all did. My defense was, let's look at the murder of Mark Fisher and what the evidence is and then compare it with what the witnesses said. If he really murdered the kid, if it really happened the way the prosecution's theory was, what they were saying simply did not make sense. The fact is, there was not a single eyewitness and no marks on Russo."

What about Russo going to California?

"The prosecution made a big deal about that, but you know what? He went to California and he came back from California. It wasn't a situation where he was indicted by the grand jury and all of a sudden the police were flying out to California to get him. He came back within a week."

Fink added that although he wasn't sure, he didn't think the trip to California was Russo's first journey out there.

"I believe he'd been to California before," Fink said. "He had relatives there."

How was Russo as a client?

"In terms of my relationship with him, he was very respectful. As far as having him for a client, there were no problems whatsoever."

What about his flippant attitude in court, singing, whistling, smiling?

"He came to court, and sat in court. Like certain people accused of crimes, he didn't act out. Maybe the way he acted was a positive. I never got a sense that the way he presented himself in the courtroom was in any way a detriment to him."

What was his theory on how Fisher died?

"Other than the fact that John Gluca was responsible for his murder; if he wasn't solely responsible, it wasn't Mr. Russo that had anything to do with it. Honestly, I don't know. That's one of the weird, troubling things about this case. I don't think the prosecution really had a case, either. Just in terms of their theory, the way Ms. Nicolazzi summed up to separate juries. I think she presented two separate theories to the juries, which suggests the real lack of understanding of what happened in this case: if this had something to do with a gang situation, if this had something to do with jealousy about a girl, if this was simply him being robbed by somebody and not gang related. I really don't know."

Did he believe that the Ghetto Mafia existed?

"I really don't know," Fink said.

Was the purported gang affiliation detrimental to the case? That brought an enthusiastic response from the lawyer.

"Absolutely! I know that myself and Sam [Gregory] really tried hard to keep that part out of it. I don't think that the prosecution established a link in terms of making an argument that this was somehow gang related. Yet, once the jury heard about gang affiliations, that evidence was devastating to the defense."

In fact, Fink believed that if Russo was to be granted a new trial on appeal, it would be because Judge Marrus allowed the gang-related testimony to be heard by the jury.

When the judge allowed it, was Fink less confident of winning?

"I certainly wasn't happy about it. Anytime a judge makes a ruling that allows evidence in that's going to be prejudicial to someone you're representing, it's certainly going to cause you to think your chances of winning are limited. I definitely was not happy about it, but still confident and I expected to win."

Fink felt there was one decision by Judge Marrus in particular that affected his ability to exonerate his client: "I asked Judge Marrus for a circumstantial evidence charge, but he wouldn't give it. [Because of that], I wasn't able to make a legitimate, believable defense of this case.

"That's because once you have alleged statements, technically that makes evidence direct evidence. Even so, there were no eyewitnesses and I think that the lack-of-evidence argument in this case was something the jury bought into. One particular juror had some problems in terms of wanting to convict. I believe it was juror number three (the African-American male)."

Was Albert Huggins damaging to Russo?

"He was more damaging for Giuca than he was for me," Fink said. "Whatever he testified to regarding the thing that Giuca told him, my jury was not present for that. He did testify about gang-affiliation stuff—the Ghetto Mafia stuff came about from him. That was damaging."

Why did Fink and Sam Gregory want separate trials, not a dual-jury trial?

Fink said, "Because even though Judge Marrus ruled that each jury would only hear certain portions, given the strong amount of media attention, even if one particular jury wasn't supposed to hear things, they would hear it from the media. Of course, we lost that motion as well."

In addition to the gang-related testimony being allowed in by Judge Marrus, Fink believed the next best reason his client was deserving of another trial was the very fact that the first trial was a double-jury affair, a process of justice that makes it unusually difficult for a defense attorney.

Fink said, "The double-jury system makes the whole process more complicated. Using Albert Huggins as an example, he was a witness where some jurors were there for part of his testimony, but my jury was taken out. Just in terms of the cross-examination process, it makes it more complicated."

Did the prosecution have a winning case against Russo? Fink still didn't think so.

"Regardless of what the prosecution did have, there was a lot they didn't have. That's what I focused on in defending Mr. Russo. Without the things you might see in other cases, the jury really shouldn't have convicted him."

Fink had been around long enough to know that the press came flocking to murder cases that involved unlikely victims. The victim here was a guy who, like Fink himself, was clean-cut and went to college.

"That certainly was a tough thing," Fink said. "I truly felt horrible for this kid. I truly felt horrible for his family. But, although he was murdered, that doesn't mean Mr. Russo was the one who did it."

Fink explained that he was pleased with the familial support his client got. "Especially his grandmother (Mary Jennings). She was someone who I dealt with a lot. She was anxious and eager to know at all stages of the case what was going on. I believe she came to every single court appearance."

Did he believe that Russo was present when Fisher was killed?

"I did maintain that when Fisher was killed, Russo was not present at that time. He certainly didn't rob him; he certainly didn't shoot him; he certainly was not acting in concert with anyone to do either or both of those things."

Did he offer an alternative theory?

"It was pretty much that Giuca had an issue with Fisher in terms of Fisher sitting on a table in his parents' house. In terms of animosity toward Fisher, it was Giuca that had this animosity, not Russo. Lack of evidence. I didn't put forth any other theory than that."

Did Fink believe that Giuca had a Svengali effect on Russo?

"As far as Giuca, other than sitting at the same table that I was sitting at with my client, I never got any sense of him other than what witnesses testified to in the courtroom."

Did he have any information about Russo's youth or Russo's parents that he wanted to share? The answer was no. Fink refused to discuss Russo's upbringing or what he knew of his family dynamics.

CHAPTER 57

Giuca as a Child

Some insight into Giuca's character could be gleaned from comments made by one of his grade-school teachers. Robert Mladinich spoke to MaryAnne Greene (pseudonym) during May 2006.

Greene had Giuca in her classroom at St. Saviour Elementary School in the early 1990s. St. Saviour is in the Park Slope section of Brooklyn, immediately to the west of Prospect Park.

When she taught John, she had about six years' experience teaching first graders. There were at least thirty students, possibly more, in the class. She remembered him as being "very withdrawn and shy. He isolated himself from the other students."

Greene used to monitor the after-school program, where "kids whose parents worked" stayed until six o'clock in the evening. There were various activities for the kids. Mostly they played in the gym.

It was during the after-school program that the teacher

had the most contact with Giuca's mother. She used to pick him up from the after-school program.

Greene believed that Giuca's younger sister had either recently died or was dying from leukemia. She was not certain of this. She didn't believe that John's father was present in his life.

A coworker of Greene's was a neighbor of John's cousins, where he used to go after school on days when his mother was busy and he needed to be babysat. The cousins, she remembered, were a lovely family with three girls. Both parents were attorneys.

"It's funny, but John seemed fine with that," Greene said. "When I was visiting my friend, I'd see him playing outside next door, having fun. But in a large group, he couldn't seem to get his act together."

The teacher was under the impression that John's family was undergoing a lot of turmoil during the time John was in her charge, and she chalked that factor up as the most likely reason for his lack of interaction with the other students.

"He was not a troublemaker," she recalled. "But also not a participant."

She remembered him as a sweet boy: "When you did interact with him or got into a one-on-one in a small group, he was a very sincere little boy. But he had a lot of heavy weight on his shoulders, even at that early age. He stood out mainly because he was withdrawn; he had a blank stare. I think the family had just moved to the area, so that didn't help."

The teacher made attempts to get John to be more social. "At that age it is important that kids learn how to interact with others, and learn new things in a new school. Other students would reach out to him; they could see that he was withdrawn."

Not only was John oddly alone in social situations,

but his mother's reaction to his isolation, Greene felt, was downright peculiar.

"Little ones want other people to play with, but John didn't. His mother didn't find that alarming, which I found very odd."

Had she ever seen John laugh?

"A couple of times, most especially with cousins. I saw him outside playing kickball with those girls and everything seemed fine. This was very private. He knew these people. He felt very comfortable with them."

Was he smart?

"John was an average student," she said. "He kept up with the work. He didn't excel, but he wasn't behind, either. You would have thought he'd be way behind other students, but he wasn't. He absolutely held his own."

Greene said that she had last seen John when he was fourteen or fifteen. He was hanging out on Ninth Avenue in the Windsor Terrace section of Brooklyn, which was near Bishop Ford High School and Prospect Park. There used to be an arcade there, and she would see Giuca there hanging out with other boys, including Albert Huggins, who had also been a student of hers. Albert and others acknowledged her and were polite, but Giuca completely ignored her, as if he had no idea who she was.

She remembered that even as an adolescent, John wore ghetto regalia: baggy pants and shirts that were hanging out. She said that Antonio Russo was already among the crowd John hung out with at that time, although she admitted that she did not know Russo personally.

"I saw him on the avenue," she said of Russo. "He was a wannabe tough guy, really trying to impress people with a 'don't mess with me' attitude. They all looked like they thought they were somebody. They were nobodies wanting to be somebodies. They were just looking for somebody to pick on. They wanted to be known for something."

How did John look? "He looked very callous and cold," his former teacher opined. "He looked exactly the same, but older, even more distant and withdrawn."

She added, "By then, he was hanging out with a crowd a little bit older than him. It was definitely a crowd I never expected him to be with. I could see by then he was not on a good path. Neither were the boys he was hanging around with. They were looking for trouble. They were wannabes who definitely wanted to be thought of as thugs, gangsters.

"Now looking back, I guess the signs were there. But at the time this isn't where I thought he would be (where he ended up). [By the time he was a teenager], he was trying to put on the act that he had everything together. But you could tell that he didn't.

"How he made the decisions he did, I don't know, because I really thought he was a follower, not a leader. He was definitely not someone who was going to take any command by any stretch. He seemed to get into a crowd where he wanted to be a big shot. That's exactly what happened.

"They were walking around, trying to act tough, just looking for trouble, wanting maybe to fight with somebody."

Asked if she thought John recognized her, but pretended not to, she said: "No! John was distant. He didn't seem to have those kinds of feelings, which was kind of bizarre. His face was very blank."

If not for the murder, would she always have remembered John Giuca?

"Yes! Absolutely! Certain students I always have in here," she said, touching her heart. "You place some children in your mind. You always see their face at the end of the day."

In the small-world department, Greene noted that she had a friend from New Hampshire, whose daughter went to Fairfield University with Mark Fisher. The girl wanted to go to Fordham, but the parents were afraid to send her to New York because of the perception of crime. After Fisher was killed, they spoke.

"When I told her I knew the kid who did it—oh, my God—it was so bizarre," the teacher said.

The teacher remembered John's mother from the times she would pick him up at school, and from their ten-minute parent-teacher conferences. "Her jeans were a little tighter than I was used to and her tops a little more provocative than some of my other mothers."

Greene was somewhat ambiguous about her description of Giuca's mother. On one hand, she said she cared for her son, but she kept reiterating that something was wrong at home. In cases like John's, Greene knew, problems often do root back to the kid's family life.

CHAPTER 58

Doreen and James

During an interview with Doreen—and James Petrillo—on July 9, 2006, in the Americana Diner in the Dyker Heights section of Brooklyn, she was asked if she had seen John's friend Al Huggins since the trial.

"I saw him once and he threatened me," she replied. "I was in a rented car on Albemarle Road and I slowed down to watch a man cut down his tree. He was behind me and beeped to make me hurry up. I went through the stop sign and he made all kinds of motions with his hands. He knew it was me once he pulled up to my side and didn't stop. I've told some of John's friends about that, but [I] won't tell John. He wouldn't have done it if John was around. John would have punched him."

Petrillo noted that this entire ordeal had not changed Doreen Federicci's personality at all. She was still going out of her way to do favors for people.

"One time when we were at Rikers Island to visit John," Petrillo said, "she offered a ride to a complete stranger." Rikers Island would have been Giuca's home during the trial, before his conviction and subsequent move to the Upstate Correctional Facility.

The stranger, it was revealed, was a woman visiting her boyfriend at Rikers. She had been strung out and stranded, but Doreen offered her assistance. Some folks were always bringing stray dogs or stray cats home, but with John and his mom, it was stray people, Petrillo said, and that was a pretty good prescription for trouble.

According to Doreen's worldview, her son John was in prison because a series of witnesses were all willing to lie. They put an innocent man behind bars in order to save their own asses.

Huggins, of course, was the perfect example. According to Doreen, police had threatened Huggins with upgrading assault charges they had on him, stemming from the "kick 'em when they're down" incident in the Bronx.

The police had told Huggins some gobbledygook about it being a felony if an assailant kicked a person while they were already on the ground, and Huggins bought it. That, Doreen said, was the reason he was willing to lie in court.

Besides, Doreen added. Huggins had been the last person in her house on the night of the murder.

Petrillo added, "Huggins was there. He had threats over him (by detectives and DAs). [When cops would come to my house], I'd say talk to my lawyer. That's my lawyer's job. If I did have three detectives around me and I was the last person there, they (cops) would have leverage over me right there. He was in that house. They can throw at him a million different things. He was willing to talk to them."

Doreen was asked about Anthony Palumbo, the prosecution witness who said that he received a gun, presumably the murder weapon, from John Giuca, and left it on the corner of Albemarle and Beverley Roads, where it was picked up by a man who replaced it with cash.

"I think at one point Palumbo told cops that John gave him a three-eighty gun, but Palumbo really got rid of a twenty-two. For some reason Palumbo changed his story four times," Doreen said dismissively.

How did she feel regarding John Avitto, the jailhouse snitch who testified at the trial that John Giuca had described to him in detail how the murder of Mark Fisher had gone down?

"He got a 'get out of jail free' card. There were no notes (police notes) at all," Doreen said.

Petrillo added, "He claimed on a visit he heard John and his father talking about a gun. John's father was sick before John got arrested. He had a stroke and can't speak at all."

Doreen concluded, "No way the prosecutor knew John's father had taken a stroke about 2001 and can't speak. He couldn't talk, so how's he going to ask him, 'What did you do with the gun?' He's lying, and the prosecutors know he's lying."

Why wasn't John's father put on the stand?

"[Sam] Gregory said it would look bad because his father has a criminal record. But he (the father) had nothing to do with his upbringing."

Petrillo noted that despite all that had happened, no one in Petrillo's family had turned on John Giuca. Members of Petrillo's family, he noted, were still writing to Giuca in prison.

Petrillo remembered how proud Giuca was of his career in show business, particularly the fact that he had appeared in the movie *Spider-Man*, based on the Marvel comic-book character.

"He was always telling me to watch it," Petrillo remembered with a laugh. "I'd always get to the scene he told me to watch for, but I couldn't see him. Finally I get him to my house and he made me rewind to the scene and you could see him one thousand feet back."

In *School of Rock*, a comedy starring Jack Black, Giuca's appearance was a tad more high-profile, Petrillo said. "He was really proud of being right up in front of the camera. You can see him very clearly," Petrillo said.

One time a friend of John's was in a movie theater on a date watching *School of Rock* when John made his "up in front" appearance. According to Doreen, the friend became excited.

"We were in our kitchen when John got a call on his cell phone from a friend," Doreen recalled. "The guy was screaming. John kept saying, 'What's the matter, what's the matter, what's the matter?' He was at the movie theater on a date. All of a sudden there's John, his face as big as the screen. It's only for like a second, but he goes to his girlfriend, 'That's John.' Being the very animated character that he is, he jumps up, screaming, 'That's my friend John.' Everyone in the theater is telling him to sit down. He sits down, but is trying to convince the girl he's with that he knows the guy on the screen. He calls John, screaming, 'I just seen you, I just seen you.'"

CHAPTER 59

"We Don't Have Answers"

On Saturday, August 12, 2006, Robert Mladinich interviewed the Fishers, Michael and Nancy, and son Michael, twenty-seven, at their home. The Fishers live on a beautiful tree-lined street filled with fashionable upscale homes.

As Mladinich stopped on a street about one block from their house to look over notes just prior to his 2:00 P.M. appointment, he parked in front of a tiny public-works building.

As he looked over his notes, two deer grazed no more than five feet away. He opened his passenger car window to get a better look and they made no attempt to run. Author and deer all gazed at each other without a care in the world.

Mladinich couldn't help but think that Mark came from a place where the deer felt so safe, and where he must have felt equally safe. There was no way this pristine environment could have prepared anyone for the dangers that lurked elsewhere.

The Fishers were gracious hosts. Michael Christopher, Mark's older brother, answered the door. He explained that he had earned his math degree at Montclair, but was currently unemployed.

The author was given a tour of the house, including Mark's room, which had been kept the same as it had been when he was alive. The trophies were still there. The posters of Ken Griffey Jr. and Jimi Hendrix were still on the wall.

Mark's kid sister, Alexis, was now twenty-one years old and was studying communications at Scranton University in Pennsylvania.

The entire family had innate decency and honesty. Despite the fact that the pain of their loss was etched upon their faces, they continued to exude a strong character.

Mark's father said that he had tried getting on with his life, now that Mark was gone, but had not been successful. "I try to enjoy things, but it is hard. It seems like everything you do, you just mechanically go through the motions. I don't have the drives or the dreams that I once had," Michael Fisher said.

"Mark had very strong principles," Mark's dad continued. "He had a lot of friends, boys and girls. Girls loved Mark, mainly because he was such a good listener. He was not a Don Juan, although he could have been.

"Any parent who had kids who played sports wish they had Mark as a son. He wasn't a jock. He didn't pick on anyone unlike him. He was friends with nerds and athletes. He was protective of Alexis. I can't believe a child can be so well-adjusted and have such a good heart. He didn't just do one thing well. He went to college to play football, but when they canceled the program, he didn't want to leave."

Brother Michael Christopher chimed in: "He lived life in a good way. Because there was a four-and-a-half-year age difference, we didn't do a lot of things together when we were young. But as we got older, we started doing things together. If I had errands to run, he'd come along and I liked to have him. Occasionally he'd come to me for advice. More often than not, he'd come to me if something was on his mind, if he had to vent. We are basically a close family, so we would have grown even closer with time. I was looking forward to that."

Nancy Fisher said that her experiences following Mark's murder have left her disillusioned. "I lost all faith in the judicial system," she said. "I always assumed it would work. I was born in another country. The law is good in the book (on paper), but if you have money and power, things move differently.

"I have good memories of all my children, but the only thing that gives me strength is looking forward to the truth. Mark was cheated from such a good life. He had a wonderful future ahead of him. The whole family was affected: cousins and grandparents, aunts and uncles. They hurt as much as we do.

"The worst thing is that we don't have answers. Somebody wanted him dead for no logical reason. We need to know why. Anytime you lose a child to sickness or an accident is terrible. But this is worse because it was done intentionally and we don't know why."

It was clear that the Fishers believed that some of those responsible for their son's death were not prosecuted because they had political connections and were able to pull strings.

On their first encounter with a Brooklyn Homicide DA, Ken Taub, a brusque man by nature, Taub showed them a stack of files and said they were his unsolved homicides, implying that their case was not all that special.

According to Mark's dad: "I told him that the only case I cared about was my case. He was a truly malicious man. He was defensive from the beginning."

Nancy said, "We kept expecting the truth to come out, but it never did."

Nancy's belief is that James DiGiovanni had connections in the Kings County DA's Office and used them to keep his daughter out of trouble. Mark's mom said she was not just shocked that all of those kids were so quiet about what they knew during the long investigation, but also by how "well-coached" they were when they testified at the trial.

As evidence supporting her conspiracy theory, Nancy noted that several network news magazines were all over the case for a time, but then—suddenly and inexplicably— dropped it like a hot potato. More pulling strings, she theorized.

Mark's dad added, "All I know is that my son came there with DiGiovanni and Huggins and he was found dead in front of Huggins's house. So many people familiar with the case have asked us why DiGiovanni and Huggins weren't charged. That's our biggest question.

"I got angry with God. I guess that is normal. But then some decent people spoke with me and told me I can't hold Him accountable."

Nancy added, "I have extremely strong faith and believe that everything happens for a reason. You learn something."

"What have you learned?" the author asked.

"It doesn't matter how much you protect your children. Somebody can come from the back and hurt them," Nancy said.

Asked how he had been dealing with the loss, Mark's

brother said, "Sometimes I'll go to church to help out. And I went on a World Youth Day tour as a chaperone to Paris and Cologne."

Before he left the Fishers' beautiful home, Michael and Nancy told Mladinich about a wonderful gift they had received. A retired NYPD officer, who had subsequently moved to Utica, New York, sent the Fishers a beautiful painting of the Blessed Mother. Although they never met or spoke with him, he said that his son had been killed in Germany and he wanted to show his support.

CHAPTER 60

Scott and Jennifer

Robert Mladinich interviewed Giuca's friends Scott Powers and Jennifer Baker at the Purity Diner on Seventh Avenue in Brooklyn, New York, on August 24, 2006. They were the couple who had been with John Giuca and his brother, Matt, down in Florida when Giuca was arrested there.

Although neither was present on the night of the murder, they said that the John they knew could never be involved in murder, especially if fueled by drugs, booze, testosterone, the desire for street credibility and possibly jealousy.

Jennifer described the first night she met him: "I immediately felt so comfortable around him because he made you feel so comfortable. I'm normally very shy, but he made sure everyone he was involved with was having fun. At one point he came over to me and said, 'Scott's been talking about you for weeks.' He just made me feel part of the group.

"Early on in our relationship (with Scott), I'd bring my girlfriends around," she continued. "John would make sure everyone was smiling and joking. He would tell a joke to ease everyone up. He was a good guy all around."

Scott said that John was the kind of guy "you really loved or really hated." Why hate him? "Envy," Scott said. "Everybody liked him, everybody flocked to him. Jennifer would even say, 'Let's go hang out with John.' He was that kind of guy."

Scott's first strong memory of Giuca came when Scott was about eight, he had been somewhat sheltered and was rarely out of his house. He and John and another friend, named Ian, went to Rocky's Pizzeria on Coney Island Avenue. Scott harmlessly made eye contact with some tough kids. One of them punched him in the face for no reason.

"I'm scared as hell," recalled Scott. "The kid that punched me was about ten years old. I'm like, 'Oh, my God, what should I do?' I was never out of my house. John said, 'He just punched you.' The kid was with two of his brothers. We went outside and all of a sudden they all wanted to fight. John fought all three kids. I'm sitting there and not doing anything. John was only one year older than me, but looked after me like a big brother."

All of those involved in the fight later became friends. One time John saw one of the kids that he'd fought being chased by a Rottweiler on John's street.

"John came out of his house and ran onto a car," said Scott. "He then let the kid come into his house to get away. He had beaten the kid up, now he was showing compassion by letting the kid in his house."

Scott and Jennifer had a very different opinion of Antonio Russo. He was younger and "always bad news." When they were kids, Scott and Antonio had a water-gun fight, which was fun until Antonio hit Scott in the head with the gun.

"I still have the scar," Powers said.

Scott said that years before Mark Fisher's murder, Russo had gone to California for a while, and when he came back, he was a different kid.

"He hit puberty and grew up fast," Scott said. "He thought he was the shit. He was more into getting girls than picking fights. He would talk about it (picking fights), but talk more than really do it."

About the relationship between Giuca and Russo, Scott said, "John looked out for everyone he considered close to him."

Jennifer recalled meeting Russo for the first time. "I remember thinking, 'Who is this kid?'" she said. "There is something really ugly about him. With John, I think it was a feel-sorry relationship. He felt bad for him."

Jennifer knew Albert Huggins long before she met John Giuca. Jennifer and Al had gone to grammar school together, and she didn't have a lot of respect for him.

"He just didn't fit in with John," she said. "He was a doofus."

Scott added, "He was never part of the group. He tried really hard to be cool and to impress John all the time. The only time Albert was allowed to leave his house was to walk his dog."

How did Scott feel about the incriminating testimony Huggins had given at Giuca's trial?

"John is not that stupid," Scott said. "He had no animosity [to Fisher]. Let's say that John is the mastermind. Would he let someone kill somebody in his house? Would he give someone a gun and tell him 'show him what's up' to kill him, if he's a mastermind? The blanket [that Fisher was wrapped in] came from John's house."

Scott and Jennifer had sat in on the trial quite a bit.

Powers said he thought the jury fell asleep during a lot of the testimony. He wished he had had a chance to get on the witness stand and tell the jury about the real John Giuca.

What about the Ghetto Mafia? Scott conceded that it did exist—to a degree.

"But it's not an organization or a crime ring. It's a bunch of friends hanging out," he said. He said every neighborhood had one, then rattled off the names: "South Brooklyn Boys, HPD, Eighteenth Avenue Boys, Ninth Avenue Boys."

The name Ghetto Mafia, Scott said, was supposed to signify that this was a mixed group, with "Ghetto" meaning black kids and "Mafia" meaning white kids.

Scott explained, "The media blew it out of proportion. Nicolazzi found it and dug into it. The only meetings were to make sure that Huggins did not hang out with us and to get away from girlfriends by saying we had meetings to go to."

"When we were little kids, we'd play 'Ditch on Albert,'" said Scott. "When we got older, we found a new way to do it."

The Ghetto Mafia, at its height, had about thirty members. "It's not like people got initiated," said Scott. "Me and John said the initiation was to drink a flaming shot."

If anything, said Scott, the gang made local residents feel safe. "Little old ladies loved us. They loved that we hung out at the back of the apartment building. People in the building liked us there. If they'd come home drunk late at night, we'd hold the door open for them. They didn't have to worry about anything. They knew us since we were kids. We were their own little security system. No one would try to rob them when they'd come stumbling in the building."

One day, while heading to court for the trial, Jennifer

met Doreen, whom she had been somewhat acquainted with. She accompanied Doreen to John's trial and was taking notes when approached by Michael Brick, a *New York Times* reporter.

Jennifer was wearing her "Free John Giuca" T-shirt. Brick sidled up to her and began asking questions. She described him as "nasty" and condescending as he told her that she had spelled Giuca's name wrong—which she hadn't.

Jennifer said she first began to distribute the "Free John Giuca" materials about a week after John's conviction. In retrospect, she wished she had started earlier.

Scott said, "We kept running back and forth to Staples, making copies and handing them out. Everyone we spoke to, we gave a synopsis and asked them to sign the petition. A lot of people wouldn't sign, but a lot did. One time we went on the train with our shirts on. A guy reached into his bag and pulled out the flyer."

Scott and Jennifer had been to visit John in prison. They usually took John's brother, Matt, with them. They would take the bus, seven hours up, seven hours back. The whole experience took nearly a day.

Scott recalled, "We have a real good time, but it's hard to leave. The last time he said, 'I'll see you tomorrow.' He's good-spirited. He's a changed person. He reads the Bible every day. He used to think everyone who read the Bible was crazy."

Scott said he believed that the cops had a personal vendetta against John because "John was going to John Jay College. He was not going there to learn what they do. But as a student, they think that he somehow outsmarted them."

Jennifer said that getting letters from John was a poignant experience. "They are not from a person our age, but from a wise old man," she said.

CHAPTER 61

www.thepamperedprisoner.com

Here's a social phenomenon that befuddles many people: there are women in the world who fall in love and sometimes marry prisoners—often prisoners who are incarcerated for cruel and violent crimes, prisoners who are in for the duration.

These are not prisoners whom they knew and fell in love with on the outside. These are prisoners who committed crimes that caused some degree of notoriety. The women first learned of the men they fell in love with via newspapers or TV.

To serve the needs of these women, a Web site exists, *www.thepamperedprisoner.com*. The site offers prisoners the opportunity to seek affection and understanding along the information superhighway.

John Giuca now lives in Cell 12C08T, in the Upstate Correctional Facility. The prison is in Franklin County, in the town of Malone. It is aptly named. It almost couldn't get any more upstate, being only fifteen miles or so from the Canadian border.

During spring 2006, an ad appeared on the Internet in which John Giuca purportedly said he was lonely and seeking feminine input into his dreary existence. Included with the ad was a photo, his old Screen Actors Guild photo, his eight-by-ten glossy normally used for showbiz purposes.

The ad said: "Hi, my name is John and I was born and raised in Brooklyn, New York. I am now twenty-two years old and the picture of me was taken when I was twenty. So I do look a little different. I have a mustache now."

The ad went on to explain that no one had to worry about being around him, thinking he might be dangerous or anything like that, because he was completely innocent.

The ad promised to fill any prospective girlfriends in on the details of his incarceration after they got to "know each other better." It promised that there would be no secrets.

His life, the ad said, would be an open book to any woman who was willing to give her time and compassion. "I have only been here for sixteen months and it already feels like a lifetime," Giuca wrote. "I am so very lonely."

The ad said that it was a tough adjustment to the nothingness of prison because he'd had a very active social life back in the days when he'd been a free man. His professional life had been of interest as well.

The ad said that he was a card-carrying member of the Screen Actors Guild, the actor's union, and noted that, although he'd had no speaking parts, he had gotten extra work.

"I've worked on many films including *Law and Order* and *School of Rock* with Joe [*sic*] Black . . . and many more.

I was just an extra. But it was a lot of fun," the ad said, getting the name of actor Jack Black wrong.

Then the ad switched subjects—to academics. It said that he'd been a student at John Jay College in Manhattan at the time "this nightmare happened to me." He was only four credits short of getting his associate's degree, he noted.

"I am an avid reader and American history is my favorite subject," the ad said.

The ad said that Giuca wanted the women of the world, at least the ones who read the lonely prisoners Web site, to know that he was not alone in the world, and that he had a sizable support staff.

"My family and lawyers are fighting hard for me and my freedom," the ad said.

The ad described his need for someone to love as "desperate." He was just as anxious, he added, to meet someone willing to love him back. He described himself as a "good hearted and compassionate person."

Then the ad talked about his job. He worked at the prison library, which, he commented, was well-suited to him because of his love for books and thirst for knowledge.

"Please write to me," the ad read in conclusion. "Tell me your likes and dislikes. Your hopes and dreams. Can you shed me some light in all this darkness?"

After that, his "snail mail" address was listed. His birth date (October 8, 1983) was listed, so women could send birthday cards. Then, for all the men out there in cyberspace who were planning on sending mail while pretending they were women, there was the reminder: "Seeking Correspondence With: Women Only."

The ad read, "Expected Date of Release: Appeals pending."

Along with that statement, the Webmaster gave instructions: "You can email John right now, just type your letter and **click here** with John's full name in the subject line.

We will mail your letter for you. Please include your name and mailing address so John can write back. We do not forward photos, attachments or solicitation."

Although the plea for the attention of women only couldn't have been clearer in the ad, a guy can't always get what he wants. Gay men, who no doubt monitor such lonely-prisoner sites, found Giuca's ad and copied his photograph off the site.

That was how John Giuca became the April 26, 2006, "Hottie of the Day" on a popular gay Web site. His photo was shown, and his address at the prison in Malone was listed.

Comments had been added below the photo and the address. That brief text noted that John said he was straight (or "str8" as the author spelled it), but that lonesomeness grew in prison and John might eventually appreciate any attention he received, regardless of gender.

Giuca may have only been "Hottie of the Day" for one day in the spring, but his photo remained posted on the gay Web site for at least several months thereafter, well into the full-blown heat of the summer.

As it turned out, the Internet can be deceiving. John had nothing to do with his "looking for love" advertisement. It had been 100 percent Doreen's idea.

In fact, John had been upset about it when he heard that the ad existed.

"Mom, what are you doing?" he said, according to Doreen.

"I'm trying to find you a girlfriend," Doreen replied—and he got upset.

When it came to the date of Giuca's release, the lonesome optimism of the prisoner's "Love Wanted" ad was not completely deluded. His situation, though bleak, was not hopeless.

His mom had hired him a top-notch appeals lawyer: Lloyd Epstein, of the firm of Epstein and Weil. It was a small firm with offices on Broadway in Downtown Manhattan.

Epstein had a wide range of experience, but he specialized in criminal and commercial litigation in both state and federal courts.

After earning his bachelor's degree at Williams College and his law degree at New York University, he'd practiced criminal law for close to two decades. He had taught criminal law, criminal procedure and trial advocacy at New York Law School, and at the City University of New York Law School, at Queens College.

Epstein had most recently made the papers in 2004 when he successfully had a client's murder conviction overturned. The client was Juan Francisco (pseudonym), a reputed gang member who lived in the troubled Red Hook section of Brooklyn. Francisco was charged with murder in aid of racketeering.

Epstein successfully convinced Judge John Gleeson that his client had been convicted on faulty evidence, that several of the prosecution's witnesses had committed perjury. After Judge Gleeson overturned the murder conviction, charges were dropped and Francisco ended up pleading guilty to giving a false statement when he said he was not at the scene of a murder, a happy compromise for a man who was this close to spending the rest of his life in prison.

"Sometimes," Epstein said at the time, "prosecutors get so invested in their informants—they fall in love with their informants, so to speak—that they fail to objectively see what their informants are all about."

Afterword

During March 2006, Fairfeld University again had to deal with a student who was a victim of violence. This time, thankfully, the results were not as tragic. Tom Foran, a twenty-one-year-old senior, was stabbed at four o'clock in the morning during a party at a beach house at Lantern Point.

Foran, like Mark Fisher, was the kind of student Fairfield was proud of. He'd been scheduled to graduate that May summa cum laude and had applied for valedictorian consideration.

He survived his wound and a suspect was arrested minutes later walking down a dark road. The incident, however, was enough to return a feeling of uneasiness on campus, a reminder that they lived in a safe womb, but that it was a dangerous world out there, in the great unknown—off campus.

Police Officer Dillon Stewart, the first cop to arrive at the scene of Mark Fisher's murder, was shot and killed in the line of duty on November 28, 2005, after stopping a vehicle for a traffic infraction. The gunman opened fire without warning. Stewart pursued the gunman until he abandoned his auto. The gunman was arrested for Stewart's murder, as well as the attempted murder of an off-duty officer nine days earlier. Stewart was posthumously promoted to detective.

Phil Slocum was the guy Albert Huggins told John Giuca to call soon after the young men realized they might be in big trouble. Slocum was a smart choice. He was a defense attorney, a veteran of big cases and—perhaps most important of all—a friend of the Huggins family.

Apparently, political aspirations were not an unknown quantity among the Hugginses and their friends. Albert's mother had twice run for political office, unsuccessfully, and during the 2006 primaries in Brooklyn, Slocum officially joined the ranks of politicians when his name appeared on the ballot.

On his online campaign site, Slocum said he was the perfect man for the Second Judicial District, covering Brooklyn and Staten Island, because he was a lifelong resident of Brooklyn, married, a father and a grandfather, active with school and athletic groups, a former assistant district attorney and, as a defense attorney, the defender of record in court in fifty Class-A felony cases. He'd gotten his B.S. at Fordham, and his J.D. in 1982.

His campaign for judge was unsuccessul. He garnered only 12½ percent of the vote and finished fifth in a six-person primary race.

Thomas Hassan and James Petrillo, the two friends of John Giuca's who were charged with intimidating a witness in connection with the murder of Mark Fisher, went to trial. Hassan was defended by William V. Ferro, of the firm Ferro, Kuba, Mangano, Sklyar, Gacovino & Lake, P.C., which have offices in Manhattan and on Long Island. The firm's take on the case, which they adapted into a self-promotion on their Web site (*www.ferrokuba.com*), went like this: "A Brooklyn jury saw through the bells and whistles of the District Attorney's case and found FKMS client Tommy H. not guilty of intimidating a witness. Our client was arrested and charged almost one year ago with intimidating a witness and other crimes stemming from the investigation into the highly publicized Mark Fisher murder. The DA obtained a silent indictment and the case proceeded to trial in Brooklyn Supreme Court before Judge Alan Marrus. The DA charged that a life threatening statement was allegedly made by our client and co-defendant James P. to Tommy's girlfriend. The DA called four New York City detectives as well as other civilian witnesses to establish that the defendants were part of a street gang called the 'Ghetto Mafia.' FKMS partner, William V. Ferro, was able to cross examine the prosecution's key witness in a way which made the claims of a threat somewhat unbelievable and showed that the Ghetto Mafia was nothing more than a group of friends. While the jury saw the Sopranos episode in which Adriana was killed for cooperating with the FBI, Mr. Ferro argued to the jury the difference between the fictional TV show from the reality of this trial. The defendants faced seven years incarceration if convicted. The jury agreed with Mr. Ferro's position and returned a verdict of not guilty."

In 2006, Scott Powers was a liberal arts major at Kingsborough Community College, with hopes of becoming a firefighter, as well as an entrepreneur.

* * *

On March 11, 2006, the same week that John Giuca was transferred to the state prison system, the *New York Times* reported that supporters of John Giuca had been quietly attending unrelated trials in Brooklyn that were being prosecuted by those who got Giuca convicted. Starting in February, recognizable faces from the Giuca case began to appear in the spectator section of courtrooms in cases that were being prosecuted by Anna-Sigga Nicolazzi.

Because of the sightings, Nicolazzi was being escorted around the courthouse by a female bodyguard wearing a bulletproof vest and carrying a walkie-talkie labeled "Kings County DA."

A courthouse employee, who refused to be named, said, "I don't know where this is going with this group, but you could have a potential stalking situation. You have to know that this is not an ordinary group. It's a whole neighborhood who seems to have nothing better to do than come sit in court. It's a little frightening."

Giuca supporters first started popping up in the vicinity of Nicolazzi in February at a trial in which the ADA was prosecuting two men in the rape of a twenty-one-year-old woman. It was the second time that the men had been prosecuted.

The first trial had ended in a mistrial after the defendants stabbed a lawyer and tried to grab a court officer's gun. The second trial, understandably, was being held in the defendants' absence.

In the courtroom on the first day of the second trial were a couple of faces that Nicolazzi recognized. One was John Giuca's mother, Doreen Federicci, and the other was Jennifer Baker, one of the supporters in the "Free

John Giuca" T-shirts who had handed out pamphlets outside the courtroom following Giuca and Russo's sentencing. There were others.

Baker, who was also the author of the "Free John Giuca" petition that was available for the signing on the Internet, identified herself as a reporter from a weekly newspaper. She was telling the truth, too. Jennifer was studying journalism at the City University of New York.

Jennifer did not envision herself as particularly menacing and neither did Doreen. They both thought that Nicolazzi was being overly dramatic about their visit to the courthouse.

"She's a tough woman who does her job," Baker said of Nicolazzi. "She's not the type to be afraid—[and] of me, of all people. She had a bodyguard who was littler than me."

Jennifer said she was involved in a college project unrelated to this case. She was covering another murder trial, where two defendants raped, tortured and killed a Hunter College student.

When told about Baker's attendance at the Brooklyn courtroom, Giuca's lawyer, Sam Gregory, said, as far as he knew, it was not a part of any organized effort.

"Maybe Ms. Baker is planning to go to law school or something," he opined.

Outside the courtroom Giuca's mother refused to comment on why she was there. She did, however, repeat her message: "My son is innocent, and if it takes fifteen years, he is going to walk out of prison."

Trish McNeill, the redheaded prosecutor, never saw a break in the action just because John Giuca and Antonio Russo were behind bars. As of the spring of 2006, she was traveling back and forth to Florida, where she was assisting in the prosecution of a federal RICO case involving the Cuban Mafia. That case dated back to the 1980s.

Josh Hanshaft, who was on the investigative team that busted the Mark Fisher murder case, but did not participate in the courtroom prosecution of Giuca and Russo, became the lead investigator in the "Brooklyn Bones" case against funeral parlor owners.

"I am living and breathing that case," he said during the spring of 2006.

John Giuca's half brother, Matt Federicci, was a senior in high school during spring 2006 and was planning to attend college in the fall. Matthew had had some social difficulties following John's arrest and incarceration, said Giuca's attorney, Sam Gregory, but, hopefully, the worst was behind him.

"He took this real hard. It had a tremendous impact on him. He's struggled emotionally, but doing better now. Hopefully, he'll come [back] all the way," Gregory said.

According to Doreen, Matt was affected most deeply when John was arrested. Plans for Matthew to go to college after graduating from prep school had to be temporarily scrapped.

"It affected him really bad," said Doreen. "John and Matt are opposite. John will talk like crazy. Some people say he's a real mama's boy. Matt keeps everything bottled up.

"Matt became a wanderer. He was devastated. I don't think he realized the seriousness of it and thought John would walk out the door. He thought the truth would set you free."

* * *

Doreen Federicci said that her faith in the justice system had been cracked by John's experiences. She had once seen justice as an inevitable thing, but now she saw it as haphazard.

She had believed that there were those who dedicated every waking moment to making sure that the guilty were punished, and—even more important—that the innocent remain free to pursue happiness.

It was a dream, now she was awake. She now believed that the justice system was filled with tired and apathetic men and women who practically yawned as they figuratively flipped a coin.

What can a mere citizen, a *mother*, do when a butcher of justice peeks from beneath his blindfold and lays a heavy thumb on the scales?

"I see the whole justice system differently now. No one really cares," Doreen said.

Doreen believed that the jury might have been irreparably prejudiced against her son when the judge allowed them to hear about John's previous arrest for firing a gun following a drug deal gone awry in the Greenwood Heights section of Brooklyn.

"Prospective jurors hear this and think this kid is nothing but trouble," she said. "The media convicted John. They damaged him beyond repair. They kept throwing that out. My son was set up.

"How do you fight when they have unlimited resources? If acting in concert brings you twenty-five years, John should do a year for maybe possession. How much time do you get for interfering with an investigation?

"The detectives know it, but John can't prove it because he wouldn't *fucking* talk. John didn't have the advantage. Even if he walks out the door, he's ruined, he's shell-shocked."

If she had to be critical of Sam Gregory's perform-ance while defending her son, it would be that the lawyer skimmed too quickly over John's behavior during the hours after the murder.

John had behaved like an innocent person. He had been confused about what had happened. He'd thought that Meri and Mark had left the party together, and when he heard that Mark had been shot, he was worried about Meredith's whereabouts.

It was Al Huggins who had testified that John was preoc-cupied with Meri during the hours following the murder.

The prosecution, Doreen believed, made it seem like John was concerned about Meri's whereabouts because he wanted to get to her and tell her that she should shut up about what she had seen and heard the night before.

But Doreen knew that was bullshit. John was worried about Meri's whereabouts because he thought that she might be lying in a street somewhere just like the foot-ball player with whom she came to Brooklyn.

This was glossed over in the courtroom, she would complain. "Why didn't Gregory bring out statements by Albert Huggins that he was *worried* about her? He didn't want to find her to shut her up," Doreen said.

"No matter what part of the story people want to be-lieve, I don't see anything that deserves him to be away for twenty-five years," Petrillo interjected.

Asked about Giuca's earlier shooting arrest, Petrillo said he believed that it complicated John's later situation greatly. "They pushed him into such a corner. He was ag-onizing over that, wondering, 'If I plead guilty, when I go before the board twenty-five years from now, they're going to say look at this, he has a history.'"

Doreen said she was aware that amateur psychologists would look to her and her husband for causing factors to what they believed to be the crux of John Giuca's personality. Go ahead and look, she said.

"Was John spanked as a child? Was he neglected?" Doreen said, her eyes widening. "He was *not* spanked as a child. I believed in talking to him and having him reason."

Police, Doreen complained, had used high-tech detective techniques to gather evidence against her son, but their logic wasn't always that high-tech, and they made unwarranted assumptions.

Take, for example, the cell phone call. Police had discovered that Matthew called John on the morning of the murder and this was evidence that John had been out of the house when Mark Fisher was killed.

But it was an erroneous assumption, Doreen pointed out. Just because John called Matthew on his cell phone did not mean that they weren't both inside the house at the time. It was a big house.

"They (police) held Matthew over John's head because of one phone call they made to each other. I don't know how big your house is, but we call each other all the time to come down to dinner. What about this phone call [did they] focus on. They assumed John is out of the house. He was so worried about Matthew," Doreen said.

The jury, Doreen said, had been most prejudiced of all by the testimony regarding John being the leader of a gang and ordering neophytes to "get a body" in order to become a full-fledged member.

Could there be any bigger, steamier pile of bullshit than that? Doreen wondered.

"The gang initiation was all you ever heard about," she said. "They want to sell papers. Bullshit! They know how the public feels about that. They'll say, 'Put this guy away for the rest of his life.' There was so much gang stuff, but, in reality, nowhere near what they were saying. Did it consist of twenty people or five people? What did you have to do to get into this gang?"

John Giuca was invited to participate in the preparation of this book, but, in a letter postmarked July 28, 2006, from the Upstate Correctional Facility, Giuca politely declined the invitation.

He wrote that he was thankful but "respectfully" declined, on his lawyer's advice.

His innocence, he claimed, was a fact, and that he lost all faith in the justice system on the day he was convicted.

"Apparently the courtroom is a stage where the actors who put on the best show are victorious," he wrote.

Giuca concluded his letter by quoting an unnamed Supreme Court justice who once said, "We set our sights on the embarrassing target of mediocrity. I guess that means about halfway. And that raises a question. Are we willing to put up with halfway justice? To my way of thinking, one-half justice must mean one-half injustice, and one-half injustice is no justice at all."

Just as revealing as the contents of the letter was how it was written, in carefully formed printing, all upper case, many of the letters embellished with flairing tails and serifs. Giuca was clearly a fellow with a lot of time on his hands.

Those who loved Mark Fisher still feel haunted and angry at the savage seduction that ended his life. As is true with many tragedies, a "perfect storm" of happenstance had to occur in order for the crime to take place.

If Mark's friend Chris had not asked him to go into the city with him that Saturday night, Fisher would be alive today. If the college kids had not run into their friend from school Angel DiGiovanni, who was, in turn, friends with Al Huggins, John Giuca's childhood friend, and Meri Flannigan, a girl whom Fisher took an instant liking to, Mark would never have crossed the East River into Brooklyn that night.

If John Giuca's ID had been accepted at the downtown bar, or at Model T's, he wouldn't have been outside on the street, where he would run into Fisher, Huggins and the two young women.

All of this bad luck, and yet it was ill fate dressed up in seductive clothing, a disguise so complete that Fisher never realized he was in danger. Even when he was warned that there might be trouble, it never occurred to him that the trouble was meant for him. He thought only in terms of winning.

Fisher thought he was getting lucky—right up until the moment he realized his luck had run out.

ABOUT THE AUTHORS

Robert Mladinich is the author of *From the Mouth of the Monster: The Joel Rifkin Story* (Pocket Books). He is a retired New York Police Department second-grade detective who has investigated numerous homicides, and was named NYPD "Cop of the Year" in 1985 for his work as a patrol officer in the South Bronx.

Michael Benson is the author or co-author of forty-one books, including the Pinnacle true-crime book *Betrayal in Blood*. He's also written *Who's Who in the JFK Assassination* (Citadel) and *Complete Idiot's Guides to NASA, National Security, the CIA, Submarines, and Modern China*. Other works include biographies of Ronald Reagan, Bill Clinton and William Howard Taft. Originally from Rochester, New York, he is a graduate of Hofstra University.

Together, the authors wrote *Lethal Embrace* (Pinnacle, 2007).

MORE MUST-READ TRUE CRIME
FROM PINNACLE